North U.
PERFORMANCE
RACING
TRIM

BILL GLADSTONE

North U.
Performance Racing Trim
fourth edition.

Bill Gladstone

© 1983 by Bill Gladstone

Published in 2000 by
North U Performance Racing Seminars
in Evanston IL.

ISBN 0-9675890-1-0

Additional copies available through:
North Sails
Performance Racing Seminars
1114 Madison St
Evanston IL 60202-2125 USA

Printing History
As *Performance Racing Technique*

First Edition	1983
Second Ed. 1st printing	1984
Second Ed. 2nd printing	1985
Second Ed. 3rd printing	1986
Second Ed. 4th printing	1987
Third Ed. 1st printing	1987
Third Ed. 2nd printing	1989
Third Ed. 3rd printing	1990
Third Ed. 4th printing	1991
Third Ed. 5th printing	1993
Third Ed. 6th printing	1994
Fourth Ed. 1st printing	1996
Fourth Ed. 2nd printing	1998

Performance Racing Trim

Contents

PART I - INTRODUCTION

CHAPTER 1 - BOAT SPEED, BOAT HANDLING AND THE RACING PYRAMID 1
1.1 Why Do We Race Sailboats? 2
1.2 The Pyramid 2
1.3 Boat Speed and Boat Handling 4
1.4 Performance Analysis 4
1.5 Using this Book 6

CHAPTER 2 - INTRODUCTION TO BOAT HANDLING 7
2.1 Introduction 8
2.2 Crew Organization Principles 8
2.3 Practice 10
2.4 Finding & Training Crew 11
2.5 Don't Kill the Messenger 12
2.6 Can We Talk? 13

CHAPTER 3 - INTRODUCTION TO TRIM: CONCEPTS AND DEFINITIONS 15
3.1 Introduction 16
3.2 Theory of Lift 17
3.3 Tuning Shape to Conditions 22
3.4 Performance Goals 27
3.5 Conclusion 28

PART II - UPWIND PERFORMANCE

CHAPTER 4 - UPWIND BOAT HANDLING 29
4.1 Introduction 30
4.2 Tacking 30
4.3 More Upwind Boat Handling 34
4.4 Conclusion 36

CHAPTER 5 - GENOA TRIM & CONTROLS 37
5.1 Introduction 38
5.2 The Genoa Trimmer 39
5.3 Genoa Power 40
5.4 Sail Selection 42
5.5 Genoa Controls 44
5.6 Jib Reaches 52
5.7 Conclusion 53

CHAPTER 6 - MAINSAIL TRIM & CONTROLS 55
6.1 Introduction 56
6.2 The Mainsail Trimmer 57
6.3 Mainsail Power 58
6.4 Mainsail Controls 60
SIDEBAR - Vang Sheeting 65
6.5 Reaching and Running Trim 66
6.6 Conclusion 66
Addendum: Fully Battened Mains 67

CHAPTER 7 - UPWIND HELMSMANSHIP 69
7.1 Introduction 70
7.2 Garbage In… 70
7.3 Steering Upwind 72
7.4 Calling Trim from the Helm 74
7.5 Driving at Starts 76
7.6 Upwind Helmsmanship - Conclusion 78

CHAPTER 8 - UPWIND TRIM SOLUTIONS 79
8.1 Introduction 80
8.2 Total Power Trim 80
8.3 Moderate Air Trim 82
8.4 Light Air Sailing 84
8.5 Heavy Air Sailing 85
8.6 Trim and Tactics 86
8.7 Trim Solutions 88
8.8 So Many Choices… 94

Continued…

Performance Racing Trim

Contents (cont.)

PART III - DOWNWIND PERFORMANCE

CHAPTER 9 - DOWNWIND BOAT HANDLING 95
9.1 Introduction 96
9.2 Spinnaker Sets 97
9.3 Spinnaker Jibes 104
9.4 Spinnaker Take Downs 116
9.5 Spinnaker Peels 122
9.6 The Three Halyard System 126

CHAPTER 10 - ASYMMETRICAL SPINNAKER HANDLING 129
10.1 Introduction 130
10.2 Asymmetrical Handling 130
10.3 Asymmetrical Spinnaker Sets 131
10.4 Asymmetrical Spinnaker Jibes 132
10.5 Asymmetrical Takedowns 134
10.6 Conventional Boats 136
10.7 Conclusion 136

CHAPTER 11 - SPINNAKER TRIM 139
11.1 Introduction 140
11.2 Initial Trim 140
11.3 Reaching Trim 141
11.4 More Reaching Trim 146
11.5 Running Trim 148
11.6 Conclusion 153

CHAPTER 12 - ASYMMETRICAL SPINNAKER TRIM 155
12.1 Reaching 156
12.2 Broad Reaching 158

CHAPTER 13 - DRIVING DOWNWIND 161
13.1 Introduction 162
13.2 Steering on Reaches 162
13.3 Driving on Runs 164
13.4 Not Steering Downwind 166
13.5 Jibes and Roundings 168
13.6 Conclusion 168

PART IV - SPECIAL TOPICS

CHAPTER 14 - BOAT PREPARATION 169
14.1 Introduction 170
14.2 Bottom Preparation 170
14.3 Below Deck 172
14.4 On Deck 172
14.5 Conclusion 172

CHAPTER 15 - RIG TUNING.. 175
15.1 Introduction 176
15.2 Tuning Masthead Rigs 176
15.3 Tuning Fractional Rigs 180
15.4 Conclusion 181

CHAPTER 16 - PERFORMANCE INSTRUMENTS...................... 183
16.1 Introduction 184
16.2 The New Information 184
16.3 Performance Predictions 185
16.4 Sample VPP's 186
16.5 Target Boat Speeds 188
16.6 Upwind Targets 188
16.7 Downwind Targets 191
16.8 Racing with Level 1 Instruments 192
16.9 Instruments and Tactics 193
16.10 Conclusion 193

CHAPTER 17 - CONCLUSION 195
17.1 Climb the Pyramid 196
17.2 A Tactical Wizard 196
17.3 About this Book 196
17.4 Thanks 196
Order Form 198

CHAPTER 1 - BOAT SPEED, BOAT HANDLING AND THE RACING PYRAMID

1.1 WHY DO WE RACE SAILBOATS?
1.2 THE RACING PYRAMID
1.3 BOAT SPEED AND BOAT HANDLING
1.4 PERFORMANCE ANALYSIS
1.5 USING THIS BOOK

Tactics

Boat Speed

Boat Handling

Chapter 1 - Boat Speed, Boat Handling and the Racing Pyramid

1.1 Why Do We Race Sailboats?

Sailboat racing requires a broad mix of skills: We need sailing and boat handling skills; an understanding of wind and weather; and knowledge of tactics, strategy, and rules. We also need specialized sail trimming technique; organizational skills to manage crew; and analytical skills to grapple with information. We need to be able to set goals and establish priorities, concentrate amidst chaos, ignore discomfort, and learn from our mistakes.

None of us can master all the skills. Part of the enduring appeal of racing is the breadth of the challenge it presents. Not only can we never master all the skills; we are challenged in new ways every race, for no two races present the same mix of challenges.

Sailing's appeal goes beyond these challenges. We enjoy racing for the chance to be out on the water, for the thrill of working with the wind, for the challenge of competition, and for the camaraderie it brings.

1.2 The Pyramid

The building blocks of successful racing can be diagrammed in a hierarchical pyramid. *Tactics* lie at the top of the racing pyramid. Beneath tactics lie *Boat Speed* and *Boat Handling*. In order to race successfully you must work your way up the pyramid. To win races your boat handling must be second nature, and you boat speed second to none. Fig. 1.

Boat speed and boat handling are distinguished from tactics in several ways. For one, boat speed and boat handling are entirely within your control, while tactics involves factors of wind, current, and competitors which are decidedly beyond our control. Boat speed and boat handling, like a strong defense in basketball, will make you competitive everyday. Tactics, like a hot shooting touch, is great when you've got it - but is not something you can count on day in and day out.

Boat speed and boat handling are distinguished from tactics in another way: Tactically there are opportunities for enormous gains and losses, particularly in shifty wind conditions. The gains and losses from boat speed and boat handling accrue much more subtly. Sure, you can lose plenty if you drop your spinnaker in the water and wrap it around your keel, but more commonly the gains are a few feet here, a boat length there. But they add up, and they are the margin of victory.

Fig. 1 - The Racing Pyramid

Boat Handling and Boat Speed form the base of our racing pyramid. You will win races when your Boat Handling is second nature, and your Boat Speed second to none.

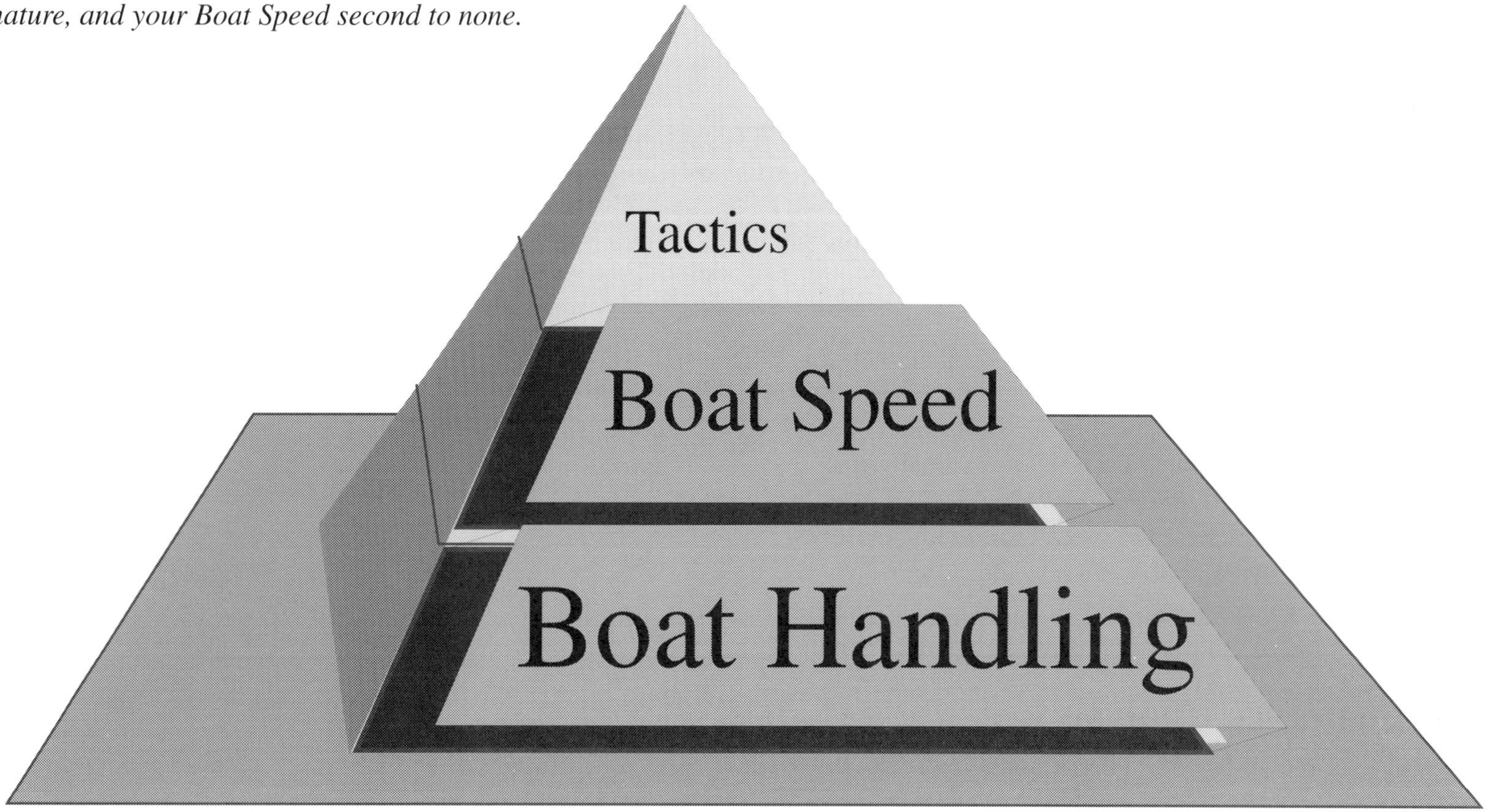

Tactics

Boat Speed

Boat Handling

1.3 Boat Speed and Boat Handling

In this book we will explore boat handling and boat speed. If you believe you need help with tactics you may be in for a surprise. When your boat handling is second nature, and your boat speed second to none, you may suddenly find you are a tactical wizard. If you'd still like to know more about tactics refer to the companion volume, *Performance Racing Tactics*.

Good boat handling is a prerequisite to successful racing. You must *sail* well before you can *race* well. Fundamental to good boat handling is good, regular crew. We'll explore how to find, organize, and train crew. We'll also look into specific techniques for boat handling upwind and down, including spinnaker work for conventional and asymmetrical spinnakers. Fig. 2.

Good boat speed is also essential to successful racing. We will look at trim theory, and study each sail individually, and then as an integrated piece of the performance puzzle. Fig. 3.

As we study sail trim and boat speed issues more closely we will see that the difference between fast and slow is just 1 to 2%. We'll find that the cumulative impact of every nuance of trim adds up to the difference between winning and losing.

1.4 Performance Analysis

So, how are your skills? The *Performance Analysis* presented here is intended to help you look at your own racing skills and focus on areas of strength and weakness. Fig. 4.

You should think not only about your own skills but the overall skills on the boat you race. If you are a tactical king you need to team up with a boat speed druid and a boat handling wizard. Of course, if you race single handed you'll need to be all these things!

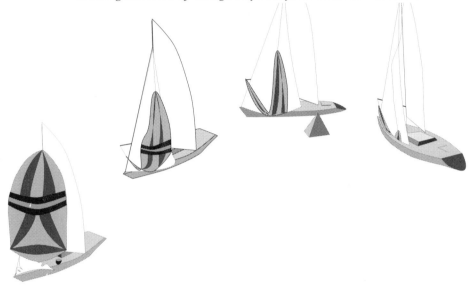

Fig. 2 - Consistent performance requires that you master the things you can control - boat handling and boat speed; while making the best of things beyond your control - tactics.

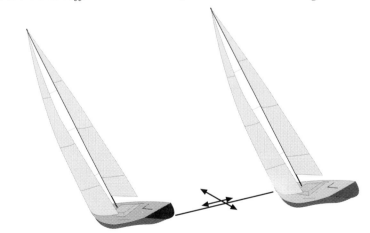

Fig. 3 - The difference between good and great boat speed is just 1 or 2%. The difference is subtle, but critical to racing success.

Fig. 4 - Performance Analysis

Which are your strengths? Where are your weaknesses?.. **Strength Weakness**

TACTICS

Tactics Section:
Upwind strategy, tactics, and rules. .... _____ _____
Downwind strategy, tactics, and rules. .... _____ _____
Starting strategy, tactics, and rules. .... _____ _____
Round the buoys and port to port / distance racing. .... _____ _____

BOAT SPEED

Boat Speed Section:
Upwind in light, moderate, and heavy winds. .... _____ _____
Helming, mainsail trim, headsail trim. .... _____ _____
Reaching in light, moderate, and heavy winds. .... _____ _____
Helming, mainsail trim, headsail trim. .... _____ _____
Running in light, moderate, and heavy winds. .... _____ _____
Helming, mainsail trim, headsail trim. .... _____ _____

BOAT HANDLING

Boat Handling Section:
Do you have a full, regular crew? .... _____ _____
Upwind: Tacks, reefs, and sail changes. .... _____ _____
Downwind: Spinnaker sets, jibe sets, jibes, ... _____ _____
Take downs, floater takedowns, and peels. .... _____ _____
Consider each maneuver from each position on the boat. .... _____ _____
Can you work the cockpit, pit, mast, or bow for all evolutions? .... _____ _____

PREPARATION

Last years fleet position: .... _____
Goal for next season: .... _____

Equipment:
The hidden foundation of the pyramid is preparation. Your boat and equipment must be in competitive condition. Yes, every little bit does matter. The difference between winning and mid-fleet is the sum of many little things.

Boat: Hull condition, keel and rudder shape.
  Weight distribution below decks.
Equip: Rigging, hardware condition and suitability.
  Instrumentation - working, calibrated, integrated?
Sails: Is your inventory complete, and in excellent condition?

1.5 Using this Book

Performance Racing Trim is the most complete book on racing sail trim, boat speed, and boat handling. As such, the book covers a broad spectrum of topics, some of which you will find of more immediate interest than others. While the material in later sections builds on earlier chapters, each chapter is written to stand alone, and can be read independently.

If you are looking for an answer to a particular question, you can skim quickly by studying the illustrations and reading the captions. When you hit upon an area of particular interest, dig into the text for more details. You can also use this skimming technique for a quick review as needed.

The ideas presented here are by no means the final word on racing technique. They are a starting point. Use the information here as a foundation. Build on it to further your own racing success.

If you are looking for an answer to a particular question, or just want to skim the book, you can read the captions. When you find an area of particular interest, you can dive into the text for details.

CHAPTER 2 - INTRODUCTION TO BOAT HANDLING

2.1 INTRODUCTION

2.2 CREW ORGANIZATION PRINCIPLES

2.3 PRACTICE

2.4 FINDING & TRAINING CREW

2.5 DON'T KILL THE MESSENGER

2.6 CAN WE TALK?

Tactics

Boat Speed

Boat Handling

CHAPTER 2 - INTRODUCTION TO BOAT HANDLING

2.1 Introduction

If you want to drive the boat, trim the sails, watch the instruments, read the compass, track the fleet, and call tactics, then you should race single-handed. A skipper who fails to make good use of his crew through careful division of responsibilities is handicapping himself, and will not succeed against well balanced teams.

This chapter will explore Crew Organization and Boat Handling. We'll start by defining broad areas of responsibility on a boat. We also will explore a set of principles to help guide you and your team, and then explore specific training methods. Finally, we will delve into the mystery of where to find good crew.

Subsequent chapters will look at specific upwind and downwind boat handling techniques. We assume here that your boat is properly laid out and equipped. In fact, the equipping and preparation of your boat is the hidden foundation of your racing pyramid. It is covered in detail in Chapter 14 of this book.

2.2 Crew Organization Principles

Crew assignments should be based on the number, skill, experience and interest of your crew. Each crew position should have clearly defined responsibilities during each maneuver. The maneuvers should be executed the same way each time.

Your crew must be organized so each block of the pyramid gets the attention required. A crew boss is needed to orchestrate boat handling. Sail trimmers and a driver are needed to focus on boat speed, and a tactician is needed to manage the course. As soon as you have more than one person on the boat it is time to divide up the chores. On championship two person boats the driver drives and the crew does tactics. As the crew number increases the responsibilities should be further divided. On a three person crew the forward crew and driver focus on trim, while the middle crew handles tactics.

Boat Handling Principles

As you train and organize your crew it will help to have general principles to guide you: Fig. 1.

Divide and Conquer

Perhaps the most powerful principle is *Divide and Conquer*. During each boat handling evolution divide the crew into two teams: One team should sail the boat with what you've got while the other team takes care of the evolution. No one should serve on both teams.

Define crew positions.

Each crew position has a specific responsibility during each evolution or maneuver. You need to figure out the correct number of crew, define each position, and then sail with a full complement of crew each time you race. Once positions are defined then you can plug new people into a specific position with clearly defined responsibilities. It helps to write out and diagram your standard maneuvers. This will help during routine evolutions, and during the inevitable ad-lib.

Create crew pairs

A second guideline which is particularly useful as you bring aboard new crew is *crew pairs*. Ideally, you would have the same people in the same position for every race *[yea, right - if pigs could fly]*. Since you can't expect to have all the same people all the time, you want to have a nucleus you can count on. New (or less experienced) crew should be paired with a regular crew member. For example, a new mast crew can be paired with an experienced foredeck, an experienced trimmer can watch over a new grinder or trimmer.

Do your job

One final principle is *Do Your Job*. If one person is having trouble completing a task that can create a problem. When the next person tries to help out, and leaves part of his job undone, the problem grows. Pretty soon the entire crew is one half position out of place - each trying to help another - and you have a huge mess.

Fig. 1. - Several principles should guide you in crew organization:
First, for each manuever the crew should be divided into two teams - one to sail fast with the sails you've got, the other to get sails up and down...
Second, each boat handling evolution - tacks, jibes, sail changes - should be broken down into a step by step procedure. Each crew member should have specific responsibilities during each maneuver.
At a spinnaker set, for example, the driver and trimmers should sail fast with the main and jib, while other crew manage the hoist.

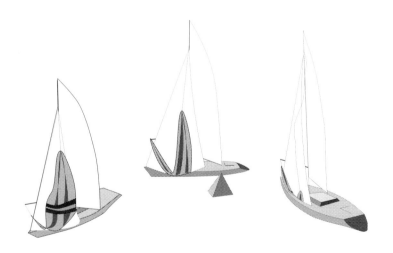

2.3 Practice

The key to developing good crew work is practice. It is simply impossible to train crew during a race. There is not enough time teach and learn, and there is too much to do. You must practice to win. It is that simple.

Practice Drills

As you plan your maneuvers keep the *Divide and Conquer* principle in mind. Always have part of the crew focused on racing fast with what you've got, while the balance of the crew attend to the boat handling maneuver. Try a simple walk through with no sails to figure out the rough details and positioning. Then, go out on the water and go through maneuvers one at a time. Tacks, jibes, sets, douses, reefs, sail changes, plus straight line trim and speed. Detail each person's responsibility during each maneuver. Once you can run through each evolution smoothly in open water try it around a closed course of buoys to add the element of timing. Fig. 2.

Another excellent drill is to perform maneuvers in total silence. A single word from the helmsman (or crew boss) is all that is needed to initiate the maneuver. In silence you learn to watch and work with your crew mates. Learning to work quietly keeps the airwaves open for remarks to deal with the unexpected.

Another effective practice tool is rotating crew positions. If the pit and foredeck, for example, switch places, each will understand better what is going on and anticipate the other's needs during a race. Similarly, trimmers and drivers can trade places and better understand how they impact each other.

Find a Tuning Partner

When your crew work is smooth, find another boat to practice with. Sail parallel courses to work on boat speed. Use

Fig. 2. (below)- Practice each maneuver, one at a time, in open water; and then around a fixed set of buoys.

Fig. 3 (at right) - To really learn trim you need to find another (well sailed) boat to practice and tune with. A training partner also adds competitive fervor to boat handling drills.

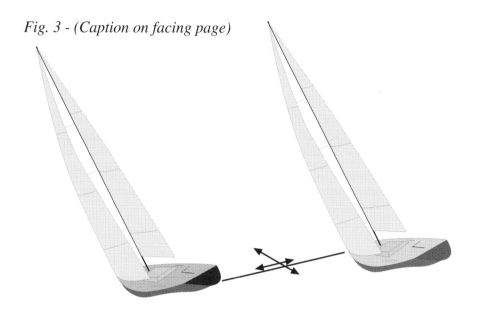

Fig. 3 - (Caption on facing page)

cat and mouse drills to improve boat handling. Try short match races to add competitive fervor. When you are confident of your boat handling and speed then you are ready to race. Fig. 3.

The difficulty of boat handling increases with the wind. Keep practicing until you are confident in all conditions. Try to refine your techniques to reduce crew movement. Pay attention to weight placement all the time. Figure out ways to keep weight properly placed as much as possible.

Your crew organization and crew assignments are dictated in part by your boat's layout. If you find one crew member is over burdened during a particular maneuver look into reorganizing the crew - and perhaps changing your layout, to redistribute the load.

2.4 Finding & Training Crew

Q. Where do you find good crew?
A. Good crew are not found, they are made.

Find eager inexperienced crew and train them. There are plenty of people out there who would love to be involved. Put up notices at the local sailing school, yacht club, and college sailing programs. Find people whose company you enjoy and train them carefully, with patience and understanding; in practice sessions, not on the race course; with big ears and a small voice.

A crew you train will be loyal and trustworthy. S/he will not run off when the next hot new "fast ride" comes along. Plus, you will be able to train your crew to your standards.

Women are among the best crew, and they are often overlooked. While some women may not have the raw muscle bulk of men they overcome this through more careful attention to detail and technique. Note also that some of the very fastest helms*men* are women.

Q. I've trained 'em. Now, how do I keep 'em?

A. As each crew member masters the responsibilities of a particular position new responsibilities must be added. One way to add responsibilities for your crew (and reduce your burden) is to turn over part of the care of the boat, or crew finding, or regatta planning, to your crew.

Another way to keep crew involved is to rotate crew positions for some low key events. Get off the helm for the beer can races; put the pit crew on the bow; see what the crew want to try. This will give the crew the chance to learn new skills, and the better understanding of the whole boat will also improve crew performance when they go back to first string positions for major events.

If your crew are stuck in a rut they will go elsewhere to seek new challenges. You also have to keep your boat, sails, and equipment competitive. If your crew feel the boat is holding them back they will look for a new ride. You may have to seek new challenges by seeking out tougher competition. Eventually, after you have mastered your present boat and retired all the trophies in your fleet, you will have to get a more sophisticated boat.

Another way to keep crew is to win. Aye - there's the rub.

2.5 Don't Kill the Messenger

No one likes to receive bad news, and no one likes to deliver it. Legend has it that in Medieval times if a messenger delivered bad news he was put to death.

On the race course bad news can be the most important information you receive. Bad news is needed promptly because it often requires action. Good news can more easily wait. When things are going well there is no urgency for change. Yet most crew members are eager to deliver good news, while bad news is often slow to get through.

How often have you sailed a windward leg with reports that all was well only to arrive at the windward mark in the middle of the fleet? The bad news - "We are slow" or "We're going the wrong way" - must get through, and the sooner the better, so you still have time to do something about it.

Of course, no one likes to be a "nay sayer," so how can you get your crew to give you the bad news you so desperately need?

The goal is quality information without distracting chatter. You can find out what is going on without looking by asking your crew for reports. Ask specific questions until the crew understand what kind of information you are after.

You need to create an atmosphere where you view your performance objectively and work to solve problems as a team.

Without accurate information you have no basis for evaluating your performance and responding appropriately. Of course there is a downside - the more information you have the greater the chance for truth to get in the way of opinion and wishful thinking.

Remember. Also, that a crew member's report of something you already know is not necessarily chatter. A snap response of "I know" will discourage further reports. A simple "Thank you" will do. The report has, after all, confirmed something (you thought) you knew. The goal is not to claim credit for being the first to know. The idea is to circulate any important information.

It's a Write Off

The same principles apply to your business. If you want to be able to continue to afford to race sailboats then you need to confront problems in your business head-on. If you ignore problems, pretend they don't exist, or discourage your staff from openly dealing with troubles then your business will soon be in trouble. There; now this is a management training text - you can write off the cost as a business expense.

And while we are on the subject, you can also apply the pyramid to your business. The base of your business pyramid is product (or service). If the thing you are selling is not fundamentally sound then success is difficult. Next are your production, distribution, and sales efforts. These bring your product to market. We all know that a great product is not enough.

Finally there are tactical business issues for dealing with things you cannot control - like behavior of competitors, and other outside forces.

Structure your business and focus your effo… [Sorry - got a little carried away with this digression. If you'd like to know more about our business services, and what we can do for your business, give us a call, or drop us a line.]

2.6 Can We Talk?

Driver to Trimmer: "Give me a little jib sheet."
Foredeck to Pit: "Give me a little halyard."
Sheet trimmer to guy trimmer: "Give me a little guy."

Effective communications requires a common language. You can improve communications on your boat by agreeing on consistent terminology and avoiding ambiguous or non specific instructions. It doesn't really matter what words you use as long as everybody is using them in the same way.

Here's a catalog of terms I like to use:

For sail trim, including sheets, guys, and other running controls, like vang, cunningham, outhaul, backstay, runners, use *Trim* and *Ease*, and use specific amounts. Instead of *Give me a little jib* try *Trim the jib two inches*. If you aren't sure how much you need make your request with a specific reference so the trimmer will know the order of magnitude: *Trim about two inches* will give the trimmer a better idea of what you want.

By using *trim* and *ease* for sails we can save *in* and *out* for weight. People move *in* and *out*, with sails you *trim* and *ease*.

Halyards can be tricky for a couple of reasons. One is that there are times to hoist or drop, and times to take up or ease down a little. You need to make clear which is which. Problems are compounded by difficulties hearing requests from the bow as the foredeck crew bounce around. Hand signals to reinforce words can minimize misunderstandings. Here are some ideas:

Take up - Take up slack (and one finger up).

Hoist - All the way up (and thumbs up).

Slack or *Ease* - Ease down a little (and one finger down)

Lower - Ease down all the way (and one thumb down).

Drop - Let halyard run (and two thumbs down).

Hold - Hold it there or stop (gets a fist).

Fig. 4 - To get what you want you have to know how to ask for it. Use specific terms.

Trim *and* Ease *apply to sheets and other sail controls.* In *and* Out *apply to crew weight, which also moves* fore *and* aft. *With halyards, you often* ease down *or* take up *slack before you* hoist *all the way. Sometimes you* ease *a* halyard, *sometimes you* drop *it.*

Did you mean ease, not drop?

The other area of confusion is in amounts. How much is *a little trim* or *a little halyard*? Guess at specific amounts. With new or less experienced crew "a little" can go a long way. Try, "Take up the jib halyard three inches" instead of "Give me a little jib halyard," which might get you six inches and a ruined sail. Sometimes you ease a halyard to make sure it isn't jammed before you drop it. Fig. 4

Specific directions will get you the desired results. Otherwise you may end up exchanging words and gestures not repeatable in this family oriented text…

CHAPTER 3 -
INTRODUCTION TO TRIM:
CONCEPTS AND DEFINITIONS

3.1 INTRODUCTION

3.2 THEORY OF LIFT

3.3 TUNING SHAPE TO CONDITIONS

3.4 PERFORMANCE GOALS

3.5 CONCLUSION

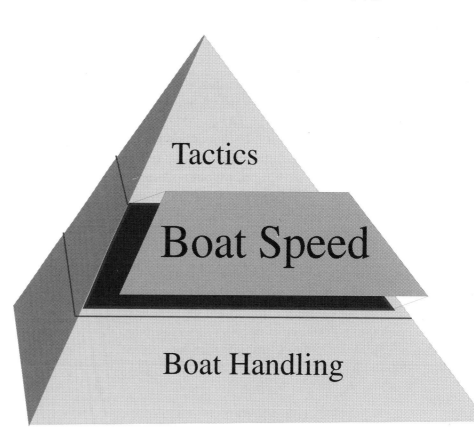

CHAPTER 3 - TRIM CONCEPTS AND DEFINITIONS

3.1 Introduction

What makes a boat go? Downwind, at least, it would appear to be pretty straight forward; but sailing upwind is quite another matter. While perhaps not a miracle, efficient upwind performance- *working against the force that drives you* - is certainly a marvel of modern design. The forces at work are complex, and they are not entirely understood - at least not by me.

In this chapter we will take a look at the theory of upwind sailing and attempt to create a theoretical framework to guide us in trim. We'll start with some definitions to establish a common language. We will also look at a variety of performance factors and see how they fit into our theory.

Sailboats are sometimes described as airplanes with one wing in the air and the other wing in the water. This is of course a lie. Wings provide the lift for planes, but not the thrust. Yet sails, like wings, are lifting foils. They are shaped to maximize lift and minimize drag for the expected conditions. Like adjusting flaps on a wing, sail shape can be fine tuned to suit particular conditions.

Basic sail shape is described in terms of the amount and position of depth or *draft*. A sail could be described as having a draft of 10% at 40% for example. This would mean that the draft at the deepest point would be one tenth (10%) the *chord length* or distance from the luff to leech; and that the deepest point is located 4/10 (40%) from the luff to the leech. Fig. 1.

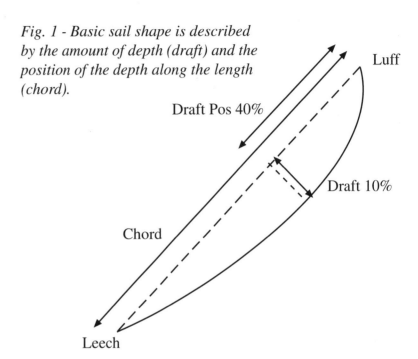

Fig. 1 - Basic sail shape is described by the amount of depth (draft) and the position of the depth along the length (chord).

Luff

Draft Pos 40%

Draft 10%

Chord

Leech

In addition to basic concepts of draft amount and position, sail shape can be further described in several ways. Smoothness of shape, horizontal shape distribution and exit shape, vertical shape distribution, angle of attack, and twist. The overall dimensions of a sail can be described as the ratio of height to width, or *aspect ratio*. In a moment we will take a closer look at each of these concepts, and how variations in sail shape effect performance; but first it is time to discuss the theory of lift (and other lies).

3.2 Theory of Lift

While the existence of lift and related forces are generally recognized (planes fly and boats sail) the theory of how lift is generated remains a point of contention. The old *slot affect* and *venturi* models have been debunked,, and replaced with *Circulation Theory* , which center on satisfying the *Kuta Condition* and so forth. Without getting into deep theory - which I don't grasp well enough to write about - let's take a look at what we know about sail shape, lift, and performance. We'll start with flow:

Flow

Air flows around a sail (or wing). The air flowing around the outside travels further, *and faster*, than the air inside. Wait right there: Why must it flow faster just because if flows further?

Why Faster Flow Around the Outside?

Imagine if the air flowing around the outside did not flow faster than that on the inside. As the inside air reached the leech the outside air would not be there yet. A vacuum would form on the outside of the leech. The air on top is then drawn in to fill the vacuum, which accelerates its progress - *it flows faster* to fill the vacuum. Fig. 2ab.

Stall

Incidentally, accelerating the air around the outside is not the only way to fill the vacuum. Air from the inside can double back around the trailing edge to fill void. This happens when the flow around the outside separates from the sail before it reaches the leech. When this happens the sail, (or wing) is *stalled*. (We see this on mainsails when the leech telltales disappear behind the leech.) Fig. 3.

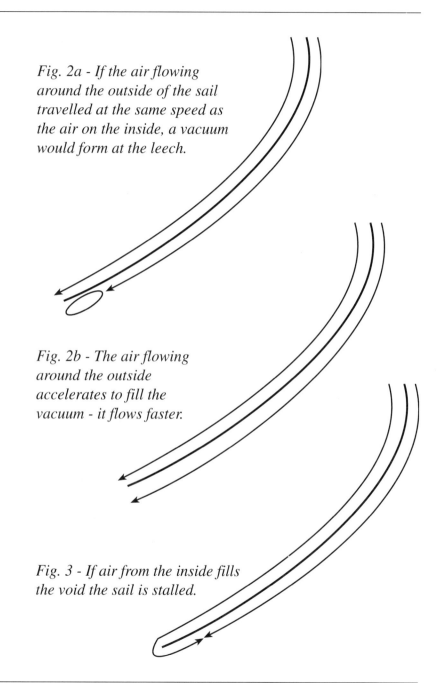

Fig. 2a - If the air flowing around the outside of the sail travelled at the same speed as the air on the inside, a vacuum would form at the leech.

Fig. 2b - The air flowing around the outside accelerates to fill the vacuum - it flows faster.

Fig. 3 - If air from the inside fills the void the sail is stalled.

How Much Further?

So the air does flow faster around the outside because it flows farther - but sails aren't very thick. It doesn't seem far enough farther to make a difference.

In fact the air flowing on the inside of the sail does not follow the exact contour of the sail. The high pressure on the inside creates a cushion, or boundary layer, that the air flows over. In effect, the air cuts the corner - taking a much shorter route. On the outside of the sail there is also a thin boundary layer. The low pressure on the outside pulls the flow to the sail, keeping it attached. Fig. 4.

Forces of Lift

The faster moving air exerts less pressure on the sail than the slower moving air. (*Bernoulli's Principle* states that a fast moving fluid exerts less pressure than a slow moving fluid). The relatively low pressure on the outside of the sail creates lift perpendicular to the chord of the sail. Fig. 5.

When we put these sail lift forces on a boat we find a large, unwanted, heeling force; and a relatively small forward force. One goal of trim is to improve this mix. Fig. 6.

Main, Jib and Upwash

The combined effect and interaction of the main and jib is a dangerous theoretical frontier. What is known is that the two sails work together to create a combined lifting force greater than the sum either could create alone.

We also know that as the air approaches the sails it is slowed and bent. Since this slowing and bending of the air occurs upstream of the sails it is called *upwash*. As a consequence of upwash the jib sails in a relative lift and the main in a relative header. This is manifest in the way we trim,

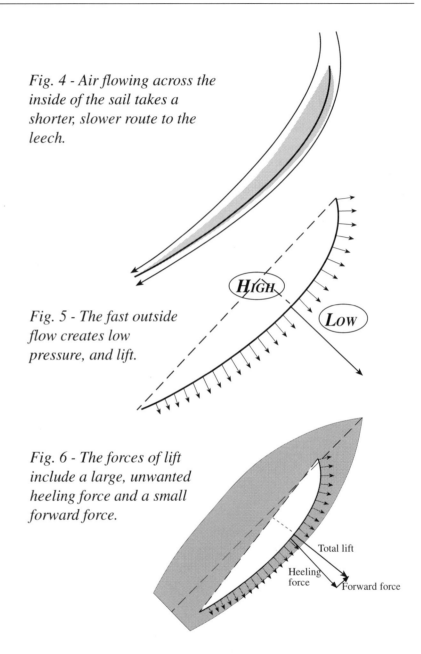

Fig. 4 - Air flowing across the inside of the sail takes a shorter, slower route to the leech.

Fig. 5 - The fast outside flow creates low pressure, and lift.

Fig. 6 - The forces of lift include a large, unwanted heeling force and a small forward force.

Fig. 7a - Air approaching the sail plan splits, putting the jib in a relative lift, and the main in a relative header.
Fig. 7b - Think of the sails as elements of a single foil.
Fig. 8 - The total force from the sails can be broken down into a large heeling force and a small forward force.

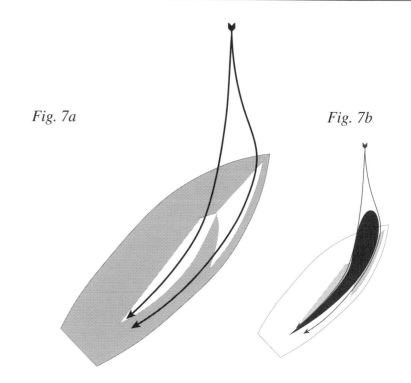

Fig. 7a   Fig. 7b

since the main is often trimmed to center line while the jib is trimmed ten degrees off center (more or less). This lift makes the jib more efficient; that is, its lifting force is rotated further forward, creating more forward force and less heeling force. While the main sails in a relative header it benefits in that the jib helps shape the flow of air around the main. Thus, although it is trimmed to the center line, air flows all the way to the main leech. Fig. 7.

The Slot

Not all the air flows outside the jib or inside the main. Some flows through the slot, but not as much as you might imagine. Upwash steers air around the slot. The air which does flow through the slot is slowed as it approaches. It accelerates through the slot and is bent to flow onto the back of the main.

Add it Up

You can even view the main and jib as inside and outside sections of a single foil. The full shape of the foil is filled out by a pressure bubble around which the upwash flows.

No matter how you look at it, when you take the main and jib together we find a combined force which is predominantly heeling force, with a very small forward force. Fig. 8.

Fig. 8

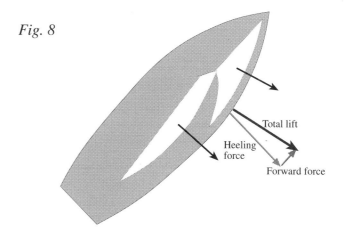

Total lift

Heeling force

Forward force

Keel Lift

Were it not for the boats underbody, particularly the keel (or other foil), the side force would be dominant; and we would not be able to sail upwind. Fortunately, the keel generates lift which nearly offsets the side force of the sails and allows us to sail to weather (with only a few degrees of leeway). Fig. 9.

"But wait a minute, how can the keel generate lift when it is symmetrical?" I hear you ask.

"Ever see a plane fly upside-down?" I reply cleverly. Fig. 10.

The issue here is *angle of attack*. While the keel is symmetrical the water does not hit it straight on; due to leeway the water hits the keel from a few degrees to leeward and does not *see* a symmetrical shape. It sees a foil with a long and a short side; and lift is generated perpendicular to the angle of attack. Fig. 11.

Speed First

In order for the keel to generate lift it must first be moving through the water. You need speed first, before you try to point. Look again at the forces on the boat: Only the keel takes you upwind. The sails push you downwind. The keel will take you upwind when you are moving fast. *Speed First.*

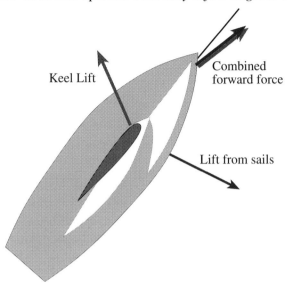

Fig. 9 - The combined lifting forces of the sails and keel allow us to sail upwind with only a few degrees of leeway.

Keel Lift

Combined forward force

Lift from sails

Fig. 10 - Although the keel is symmetrical, the forces on the keel are not symmetrical. It generates lift due to angle of attack. The same principle allows a plane to fly upside down.

The Combined Force of Keel and Sails

The combined forces of the keel and sails drive us forward. Note that only a very small fraction of the forces generated are actually translated into forward force. Most of our trimming and fine tuning effort is directed at improving this mix of useful and useless forces. Even a slight improvement in the mix can make a big difference in performance. Every little bit counts *alot*. Fig. 11.

This small forward force must then fight a tremendous amount of friction (drag) to push the boat through the water. Here again, a very small reduction in friction through better bottom preparation and refined keel shape can result in a significant gain in speed.

Theoretical Conclusion

Most races are won or lost by minutes, or even seconds, over many miles and hours. The margin of victory is the sum of many small things. Every detail is important. Everything shows up in the results.

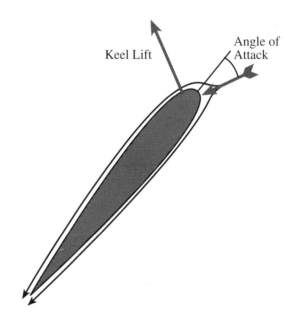

Fig. 11 - Keel Lift. The keel generates lift perpendicular to the angle of attack of the water. The angle of attack is created by leeway.

Keel Lift

Angle of Attack

3.3 Tuning Shape to Conditions

The sailmaker's goals in designing and building a sail are two; first, to create a fast shape, and second, to create a shape which can be fine tuned to perform well in a variety of conditions.

As sail trimmers our goals parallel those of the sailmaker; first to achieve the designed shape, and then to fine tune to conditions. We must consider each element of sail shape in striving toward these goals.

Draft

The depth, or amount of draft, in a sail controls the power, acceleration, and drag of the sail. More depth creates more power and acceleration; while a flatter sail has less drag and a narrower angle of attack for closer pointing. A deep sail is best to punch through waves and chop, and after tacking. A flat sail will be faster in smooth water. In overpowering conditions a flat sail is also best. Fig. 12.

Airliners create a deep shape with the flaps down for extra lift at low speeds during takeoff and landing; but pull the flaps in for a flatter shape and less drag for high speed cruising.

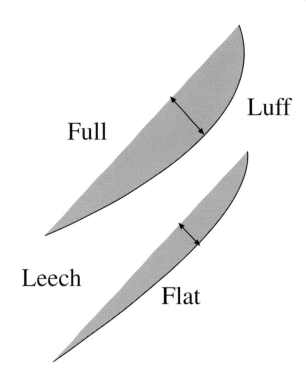

Fig. 12 - DRAFT. Depth equals power.
A deep or "full" shape is best for power and acceleration. A flat shape is faster in smooth water because it creates less drag. A flat sail is also best when overpowered in heavy air.

Draft Position

Generally, the goal is to maintain the designed draft position (about 40%-45% in mains, 30-40% in jibs) to keep a smooth, even shape. A draft forward sail will be more forgiving steering in waves, and will create less drag; a draft aft sail will be better for pointing, but is a higher drag shape. Fig. 13.

Horizontal Shape

There is more to sail shape then depth and position of draft. Horizontal Shape describes the shape from luff to leech. Most sails are designed with a fair, even curve to promote attached flow. Large overlap genoas are cut flatter in the aft sections where they overlap the main to allow for close sheeting without interfering with the main. Main sails are shaped evenly from luff to leech. Spinnakers are shaped round at the edges and flatter across the middle. Some sails have a kinked shape, though not by design. Fig. 14.

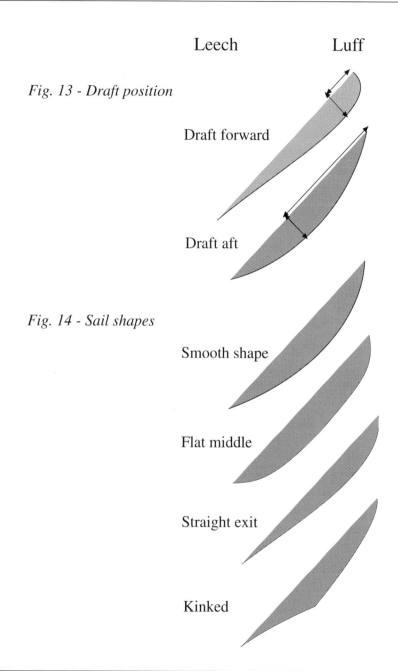

Leech   Luff

Fig. 13 - Draft position

Draft forward

Draft aft

Fig. 14 - Sail shapes

Smooth shape

Flat middle

Straight exit

Kinked

Fig. 13 - Sail shapes are described by draft position. Draft forward shapes are more forgiving; draft aft shapes point higher but create more drag.

Fig. 14 - In addition to the amount and position of draft, sail shapes can vary in other ways. Some examples are shown here.

Vertical Shape Distribution

Sail shape varies vertically as well as horizontally. Different wind characteristics and sail dimensions necessitate a slightly deeper shape aloft than alow. This fact is counter to the intuitive response, which suggests more shape down low for less heeling moment. We want more shape aloft for three reasons: Fig. 15.

• There is stronger wind up high. More draft aloft helps pull extra power from this fresh breeze.

• The short chord length necessitates a more powerful shape, to get all the available power over the short distance. The short chord length has a better lift/drag ratio, so the extra shape gives extra power but does not create excessive drag.

• A deeper shape aloft keeps air from escaping up the sail in a path perpendicular to the leech. The air is forced into a more nearly horizontal path. The air stays on the sail longer for extra power, and there is less tip vortex as well.

In heavy air heeling moment does become a factor, and a flatter shape up high is desirable. In fact, much of our sail shaping effort is devoted to flattening (and spilling) the upper part of our sails as the wind speed builds.

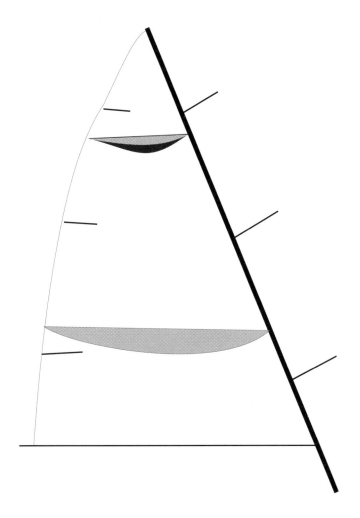

Fig. 15 - In light and moderate winds sails are trimmed to be deeper aloft than alow. In heavy air the top of the sail is flattened to reduce heeling forces.

Twist

Twist is the relative trim of the sail high and low. A sail has lots of twist when the upper part of the sail is open. The opposite is a closed leech, with little twist. Fig. 16.

The stronger winds aloft necessitate some twist. The stronger wind up high creates a more open apparent wind angle aloft. The upper part of the sail is twisted out relative to the lower part of the sail to match the more open apparent wind angle. The sailmaker designs twist into the sail.

Twist can be fine tuned to match sail shape to the prevailing wind and sea conditions, and to match our performance goals.

Fine tuning twist is one the most powerful trim adjustments we can make. We'll offer a few generalizations here; details will be covered in upcoming upwind trim chapters.

We increase twist by easing the sheets, and reduce twist by trimming. Generally, less twist will provide better pointing, more twist is preferred for speed and acceleration. For example, coming out of a tack sails are trimmed with extra twist, with final trim coming only as the boat accelerates to full speed.

In overpowering conditions power can be reduced by easing the sheets and increasing twist - spilling the top of the sail, or by flattening the sail shape. Either way, you reduce power. Which is preferred? Generally, in wavy conditions it is preferred to use twist to control power. In smooth water conditions reducing power through flatter sail shapes is preferred. One of the challenges of trimming is achieving the correct total power, and achieving the correct mix of power - the correct mix of shape and twist.

One final generalization: The shape and twist of the main and jib should be matched.

Fig. 16 - Twist is the difference in trim of the sail high and low. Sails are designed with some twist to match differences in wind high and low. We fine tune twist to match sailing conditions and performance goals.
Boat A has closed leeches, with little twist.
Boat B has open leeches, or lots of twist.

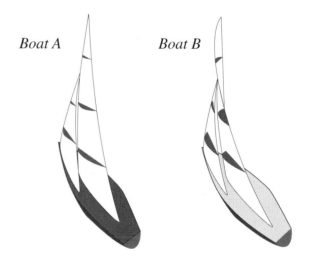

Boat A   *Boat B*

Mains and Genoas

Designed shapes in genoas and mainsails have a number of differences, some of which have already been mentioned.

Genoas are generally deeper than mainsails, and more difficult to adjust. When one genoa is overpowered we change to another. Large overlap genoas are designed with a flat or "straight" shape aft. This exit shape allows closer sheeting without clogging the slot or interfering with the main, and it also reduces drag. Consequently most of the shape in genoas is built in the forward section, and our trim efforts are concentrated in tuning this forward shape.

Mainsails, on the other hand, carry shape throughout. The turbulence from the mast reduces efficiency in the forward part of the sail, so we focus on the leech to trim for speed, pointing, helm balance, and heel.

Aspect Ratio.

Experience has confirmed the theoretical notion that tall sails with short chord length (high aspect ratio) are more efficient than low, wide (low aspect) sails. High aspect sails (and keels) create more lift with less drag. This efficiency is particularly strong when main and jib are considered together. Adding overlap offers diminishing returns. A 150% genoa, even with all its extra area, is not much faster than a 110% sail. Fig. 17.

Development of higher, narrower sails is limited by sail material strength, rig engineering constraints, rules, and righting moment (heeling forces).

In fact, new sail materials and rig designs have brought us to new heights in high aspect design. #3 genoas are now built to hold shape and withstand tremendous leech loads. The efficiency of various sail mixes will be discussed in more detail as we cover trim technique.

Fig. 17 - A tall narrow (high aspect) sail (or keel) is more efficient than a low aspect sail. A high aspect sail will be closer pointing, while the low aspect sail is more powerful. We are limited by materials and heeling forces in the design of rigs, and water depth in the design of keels.

Keels

While we can't trim 'em (thank goodness - racing is complicated enough) the shape and condition of your keel is as important to your upwind performance as the shape and condition of your sails. See Chapter 14 - Boat Preparation for more on keels and keel shapes.

3.4 Performance Goals

So much for a theoretical framework. In practical terms, what sort of performance framework will lead us to competitive upwind performance? We need performance goals.

For upwind racing the goal is to achieve the optimum mix of boat speed and pointing. The figure shows a performance curve. The high point on the curve shows the best mix of speed and pointing. The boat sailing there is achieving optimum VMG - Velocity Made Good. Fig. 18.

Measuring Performance

How do you know if you're at the right spot on the curve? Sometimes it is hard to tell.

The best and truest measure of performance is racing in a strict one design. If you are higher and or faster than the boats around you then you are on the high point of the curve.

You can also measure performance against other boats of different design, although differences are hard to attribute: *Are we beating him because our boat is faster, by design, than his, in these conditions; or are we outsailing him?*

Judging performance independent of benchmarks is tricky. Without other boats around we tend to sail a little low and a little fast. Interestingly, we tend to sail a little too high and slow when other boats are around.

You can also measure performance with instruments. If you change trim and improve pointing with no loss of speed, or increase speed with no loss of pointing, then you are doing better. Harder to judge is a change which trades in some of one (speed/pointing) for the other. Without other boats to measure against it can be difficult to tell.

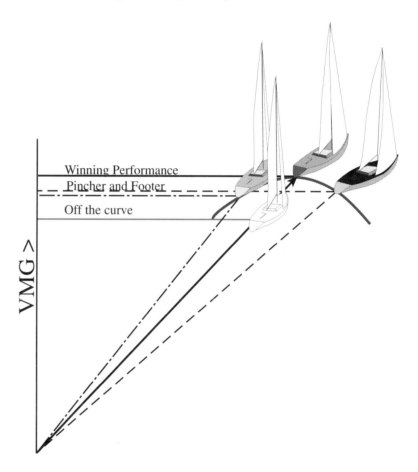

Fig. 18 - The goal of upwind performance is to optimize the mix of boat speed and pointing to maximize VMG.

Winning Performance
Pincher and Footer
Off the curve

VMG >

With integrated instruments and performance predictions you can race against yourself. Sophisticated computer and instrument packages will show you your performance against predicted performance. The best packages will record real world performance and add it to the stored data. You then compete against yourself, trying to improve upon past performance in similar conditions. The power of these systems is daunting, and is covered in some detail in Chapter 16 - Performance Instruments.

Trim and Performance

As we study the details and techniques for upwind trim we will consider three positions relative to the optimum: Low and fast, high and slow, and below the curve.

Generally, if you are on the curve, but at the wrong spot, subtle changes in trim will get you where you want to be.

On the other hand, if you are simply off the pace then a fresh approach may be needed. With so many factors involved in upwind performance it can be difficult to know were to begin. We will provide a framework to help you work through the variables. Fig. 19.

Performance Conclusion

The next *section* will explore the variables in upwind sail trim and relate changes in trim to changes in sailing conditions. The next *chapter* will start our exploration of the details of upwind trim technique.

3.5 Conclusion

We now have a basic understanding of sail shapes and the terms used to describe those shapes. This concludes the introductory section of the book. The next section - Chapters 4 through 8 - cover Upwind Performance.

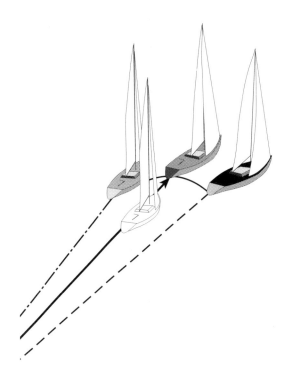

Fig. 19 - The trimmers and driver work as a team to optimize performance. If you are on the curve, but a little high or low, then subtle changes in trim can set things right. If you are off the curve then more dramatic changes are called for.

CHAPTER 4 - UPWIND BOAT HANDLING

4.1 INTRODUCTION

4.2 TACKING

4.3 MORE UPWIND BOAT HANDLING

4.4 CONCLUSION

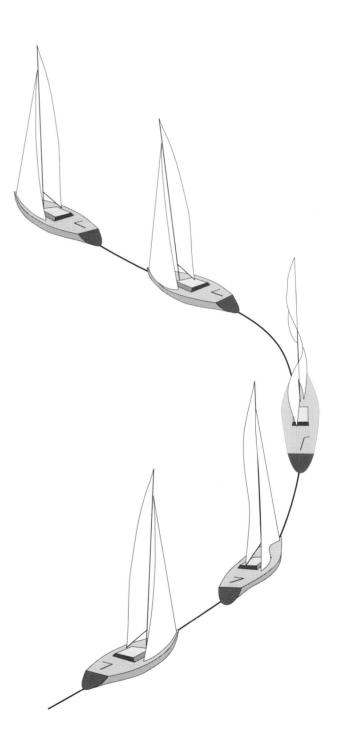

CHAPTER 4 - UPWIND BOAT HANDLING

4.1 Introduction

It would be easy to dismiss this topic as easy and insignificant. Everybody can tack. What more is there? For starters, there are tacks. There are good tacks and bad tacks. Tacks in smooth water and chop. Roll tacks, slam tacks, and fake tacks.

There are other upwind boat handling issues as well. Reefs and genoa changes are rarely made during a leg, but there will be occasions each season when they are needed, and can win you a race. There are also good and bad ducking techniques, and there are ways the crew on the rail can help performance in subtle, but significant ways.

Don't forget: The difference between fast and slow, between the lead and the pack, is just a couple of boat lengths per mile.

4.2 Tacking

The difference between a good tack and a poor one can be measured in boat lengths. In a race where you tack ten times good tacks can provide the margin of victory. And in a close duel superior tacks will allow you to break free from, or keep control of, a rival. There are a number of elements which make up a good tack. Fig. 1.

Tactician

First, if you have some flexibility in timing your tack, look ahead for a smooth spot to tack in. Avoid waves, chop, and wakes coming out of the tack. Also, make sure you will be in clear air coming out of the tack - don't tack into bad air.

Driver

The courtesy of a preparatory hail, *"Ready about,"* increases the likelihood of a good tack on *"Hard-a-Lee."*

A proper tack starts with a slow, smooth turn. Many drivers turn too fast. Some wind up by bearing off before they turn, which is also wrong. A slow smooth turn will preserve momentum and allow the boat to coast upwind. As the boat comes head to wind and speed is lost, turn more quickly to finish the tack.

In waves a faster turn is called for, as momentum will be lost more rapidly. Start the turn on the face of one wave and turn quickly as the bow pops free over the crest. Try to get the bow around so the next wave pushes the bow down on the new tack, not back to the old tack. In a short chop it may not be possible to get around fast enough. Fig. 2 (next page).

During the turn the helmsman must change sides and settle into position to work the boat up to speed. Come out of

Fig. 1 - Tacking
You should always be ready to tack. The winch should be pre-loaded with a full set of wraps. The working sheet should be flaked and ready to release.
Start with a smooth easy turn. Let the boat coast upwind. Release when the sail luffs half way across the deck. By grinding full speed throughout the tack over-rides can be avoided and there will be no need to pause to add wraps. Call speeds coming out of the tack. Gradually trim the sail home as full speed returns.

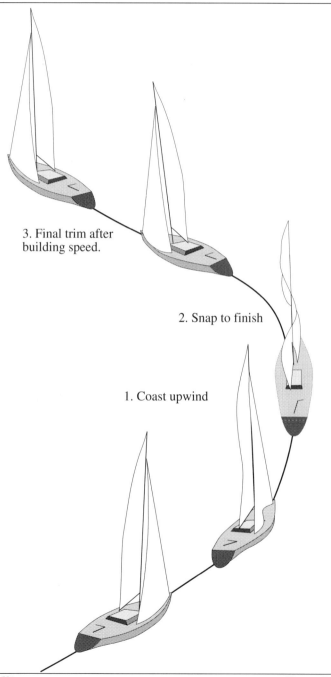

3. Final trim after building speed.

2. Snap to finish

1. Coast upwind

the tack a few degrees low of course and squeeze up as speed builds. Getting up to full speed is your priority coming out of the tack. Don't let anything distract you from your mission.

Crew Movement

You should always be ready to tack. The lazy jib sheet should be loaded on the winch and the working jib sheet flaked at the completion of the previous tack. At *"Ready about"* the trimmer should make sure he is prepared to release and the tailer should check the new winch, take up slack on the lazy sheet, and put the winch handle in place. No one else should move. You slow the boat if you get off the rail at *"Ready about"* and you telegraph your moves, letting your rivals know you are about to tack.

At *"Hard-a-Lee"* sit tight. The grinder should move into position as the boat stands up. There is nothing to grind until after the release anyway. The longer you hike the faster the boat will be going into the tack.

The Release

The release should not start until the genoa is backed half way across the foredeck. Then ease out one arm length before spinning the remaining wraps off the winch. The sheet should be flaked in advance. Make sure it runs.

Roll Tack

Every boat can *Roll Tack*, not just dinghies. In light and moderate winds a roll tack uses crew weight to help steer the boat and tack the sails. Here's how: First, heel the boat to leeward to generate weather helm and start the boat turning up into the wind. Next, as the boat passes through irons roll weight to the old windward / new leeward side. This will push the boat through the second half of the turn, and throw the sails across the boat. Finally, as the sails come over, the crew move up to the new windward side. This hikes the boat flat, and helps accelerate the flow of air across the sails, and thus helps the boat accelerate out of the tack.

Tail and Grind

The genoa should be trimmed hard from the moment it is released. The tailer should pull in long even strokes across his body. The grinder should grind full speed right from the start, even when there is no load. It is sometimes helpful to have another crew member help the sail around the rigging and drag the clew aft.

With the grinder spinning the winch full speed he can help the tailer bring the sail through the tough spots. By keeping the winch drum spinning he also prevents over-rides. This allows all the necessary wraps to be laid on the winch from the start of the tack. By laying all the wraps on in advance you don't have to stop to add wraps during the critical moments when the sail loads up.

Trim out of the Tack

Trim for extra power and better acceleration out of the tack. Pull the jib leads forward a few inches and trim three to six inches short of full trim initially. Grind to final trim as speed builds. If you want to adjust controls, such as the backstay, for acceleration out of the tack, do not wait until the turn is completed to make the adjustment. Do it just before you tack, or as you tack, so you can concentrate on building speed out of the tack.

Once the sail is nearly trimmed the grinder can move to the rail and the tailer can trim the last few inches as the boat accelerates. The trimmer should call out boatspeeds so the helmsman knows when the boat is approaching full speed.

Hike

If time allows, hike first. Don't set the pole, or clear halyards, or do housekeeping immediately after you tack. Hike out, settle the boat, and let the driver concentrate. Wait until you are up to full speed before you start moving around. This holds true in light air as well. Even when hiking weight is not needed, movement robs speed and disrupts concentration.

More Tacking Ideas

Tactically there will be times when you will not be able to execute the desired glide in and quick finish described here. When tacking in traffic you may need to execute a *slam tack*, where you slam the boat into a small opening. There will also be times - at starts for example - where an exaggerated coast in irons is called for to reach the desired location coming out of the tack.

Here's another idea: Tack through a wind shadow. If you are about to tack and there is a boat passing on the opposite tack downwind, tack through his wind shadow. There will be

Fig. 2 - Tacking in waves requires a faster turn than a smooth water tack. Start your turn in the trough of a wave so the bow will pop free at the crest. Try to push the bow around quickly enough so that the next wave pushes your bow toward the new tack, not back to the old one.

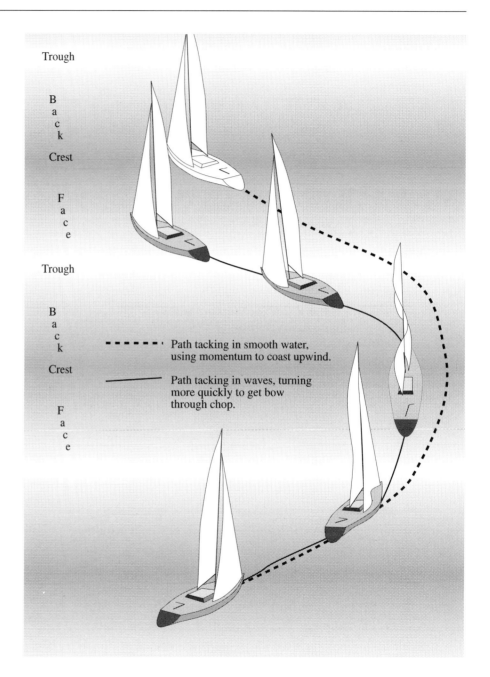

Trough

Back

Crest

Face

Trough

Back

Crest

Face

- - - - - Path tacking in smooth water, using momentum to coast upwind.

———— Path tacking in waves, turning more quickly to get bow through chop.

less drag and windage in reduced air of wind shadow. You may as well be tacking as you can't sail well in the shadow.

One more thing: Tactically, you should add a fake tack to your repertoire. Signal your crew with some clever code, like, "Ready about Wally?" to which they reply "Ready Beave." Put the helm down and turn to the point of the jib release. If your opponent falls for it, you can pull back. If your opponent doesn't tack, you can finish the turn as a normal tack. Hail either "*tack*" or "*no*" to signal your decision.

Fig. 3a - A proper duck involves a smooth turn, with sails eased to build speed. You gotta look ahead. You want to avoid the "crash tack" (3b), "Oh my god!" duck (3c) and the "ease the main, EASE THE MAIN" insurance incident report (3d).

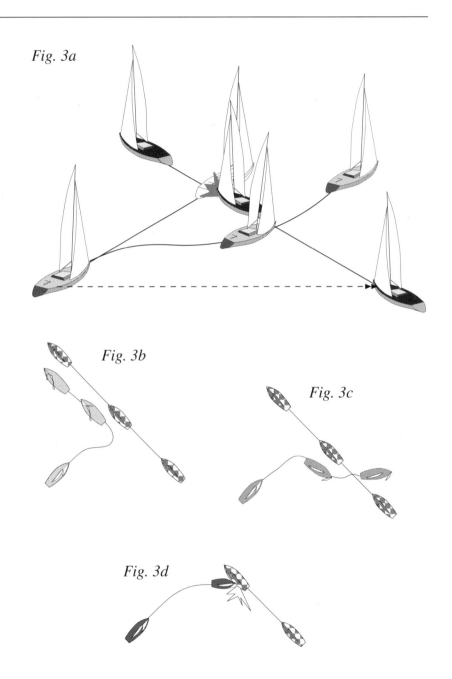

Fig. 3a

Fig. 3b

Fig. 3c

Fig. 3d

4.3 More Upwind Boat Handling

Straight Line Sailing

There are plenty of useful things for crew on the rail to do on a windward leg, aside from talking about their hangovers. Here are a few:

Find the windward mark (and the next mark).

Look ahead for changes in conditions.

Observe earlier fleets on the next leg (and plan strategy).

Plan ahead for the rounding - Bear away or jibe set?

Call immediate wind and waves.

Keep track of other boats.

Move to maintain proper heel.

These chores are, of course, in addition to badgering the driver to stop pinching.

Ducking

A proper duck is important to a successful reversal, as described in *Performance Racing Tactics*. To duck the sails must be eased as the helmsman bears off, and the sails retrimmed as the boat comes back on the wind. With a coordinated effort the loss from ducking a starboard tack boat can be minimized. The first trick, of course, is to look ahead so you see the other boat coming. The second trick is to keep greed from clouding your judgement about whether you can cross or not. You can cross only if the bearing from your stern to the starboard boat's bow is increasing. The figure shows several ducking variations - only one of which is recommended technique. Fig. 3abcd.

Reefing

It is rare to take a reef during a round the buoys race. Usually we just flog the full main and hang on until the end of the leg. Once or twice a season a squall will roll across the course, and an immediate reef will be in order. If you can reef efficiently, you win. Those who are not practiced and prepared lose. And they beat the crap out of their sails as well…

Taking a slab reef in the main should take less than 60 seconds. Here's how to do it:

Release the boom vang.
Lower the halyard to a preset mark.
Pull down the luff of the sail and secure the reef tack.
Grind the halyard to full tension.
With the sheet eased grind the reef line in.
Trim the main and reset the vang.

The key is to be organized for each step before you start. And divide the jobs. Keep as many crew as possible on the rail. All lines should be tailed from the rail, for example.

The genoa should be eased two inches and the helmsman should drive off slightly to keep power and speed while the reef is set; but be careful not to drive off too far as the rig is unbalanced while the main luffs.

If you tie in the reef, use brightly colored sail ties so you will not forget to take them out before shaking the reef. The reef points are only used for tieing up the loose sail - they are not strong enough to carry load.

Genoa Change

A genoa change is a major distraction, and should only be undertaken when absolutely necessary. Often, in a building breeze, it is possible to hang on with what you've got, rather than change down. In a squall change down for the sake of performance and for the life of your sail. In a dieing breeze it is more critical to change up to the appropriate sail.

There are three variations on genoa changes with a twin grooved headstay. The inside set, where the new sail is hoisted inside and the old sail dropped outside; the outside set, where the new sail goes up in the free groove outside the old one; and the tack set, where the new sail is hoisted inside, the boat is tacked, and the old sail is dropped inside.

Unless tactical considerations dictate otherwise the tack set is easiest and fastest, as the crew never has to work on the outside. Outside hoists and outside drops are difficult, as it is hard to get the outside sail under the foot of the inside one. Freeing the tack of the inside sail will create a gap under the sail, allowing the outside sail to pass more easily.

It is best to start the race with the genoa in the port groove so an inside set can be done on starboard tack, minimizing the chances of having to tack suddenly. One exception is a skewed beat heavily weighted to port tack.

Bring the new sail to the windward shrouds and prep it. Find the tack, check that the luff is straight, and attach the new halyard. Do all this before going forward to the bow. The new genoa lead should be set to a pre-marked position and a new sheet led. For a tack set simply use the lazy sheet from the old sail. The old halyard should be flaked so the old sail can come down as soon as the new sail is up.

When everyone is ready take the new sail forward and put the head in the luff groove. Start the hoist, and hook up the tack as the sail goes up. Don't overhoist if the tack is not secure as you near full hoist. Once the new sail is up [tack if you are doing a tack change and] drop the old sail.

Once down the old sail should be pulled aft along the weather rail and flaked. Before devoting crew attention to this house keeping chore first make sure you are properly trimmed and up to speed with the new sail. Then take care of the old one. At a minimum flake the luff and secure it with a sail tie so the sail is immediately available if needed. If the sail can be flaked and turtled so much the better. A fast genoa change will cost several boat lengths. A bad one...

Incidentally, all sails should be stowed systematically so they can be found immediately as needed. Before the race put them in position where the weight will be least harmful - usually on the cabin sole. Once in place you cannot rearrange them during the race. They absolutely must not be left in the bow. Weight in the bow is a speed robber. Get your sails (and everything else) out of the bow.

A Few Words on Flaking

We'll take a moment here to rant about flaking genoas properly so they hoist easily. Simply put, the luff must be flaked straight. Since the luff is longer than the leech folds in the luff will need to be wider than those in the leech. Initially, to get the luff straight, take two or three full folds in the luff with small folds in the leech. The luff flaker leads, the leech flaker follows. The luff flaker should keep moving, taking wide folds which stack one on top of the other. It doesn't matter if the leech flaker falls several folds behind.

Note: If you are a foredeck crew inspect to make sure sails are flaked to your satisfaction. Or suffer the consequences...

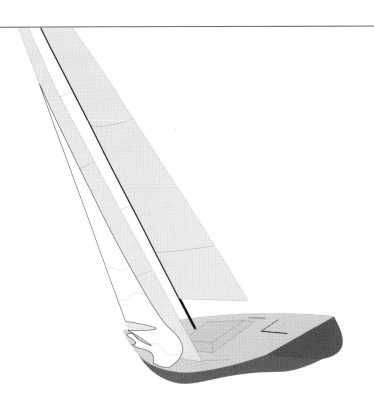

Fig. 4 - Snafus - such as a jammed luff tape during a genoa change - can ruin a race.

4.4 Conclusion

It is true: There aren't very many races where skippers cite superior upwind boat handling as the reason for their victory. But snafus - such as winch overrides, tangled sheets, jammed jib luffs, and the like - can snatch defeat from the jaws of victory. Fig. 4.

Upwind boat handling is just one small block in the pyramid of power. Don't stumble over it.

CHAPTER 5 - GENOA TRIM & CONTROLS

5.1 INTRODUCTION

5.2 THE GENOA TRIMMER

5.3 GENOA POWER

5.4 SAIL SELECTION

5.5 SAIL CONTROLS

5.6 REACHING TRIM

5.7 CONCLUSION

CHAPTER 5 -
GENOA TRIM AND CONTROLS

5.1 Introduction

Genoa trim is a never ending process; the genoa sheet and other controls require constant attention to maintain optimum shape and performance. Every fluctuation in conditions requires a corresponding change in trim. Don't expect huge leaps in speed. Work for a boat length here, and a few feet there. Great trim is the sum of many small adjustments. It adds up.

This chapter will start with a look at the role of the jib trimmer in upwind performance. From there we will consider the sources of genoa power and proper sail selection. Next, we will look at each genoa control. We will start from the initial set of each control, and then move on to refined sail trim, matching genoa shape to sailing conditions. Fig. 1.

In subsequent chapters we will explore mainsail trim and helming. Later, in Chapter 8, we will also explore upwind performance problems and suggest methods for resolving them.

Fig. 1 - Genoa trim is a never ending process of trim and fine tuning to match sail shape to the prevailing conditions and performance goals.

5.2 The Genoa Trimmer

The genoa trimmer guides the boat upwind. Through sail trim, and through communications with the driver, the genoa trimmer guides the boat to the optimum balance of speed and pointing.

The genoa trimmer monitors performance moment to moment, using one or all of the following:
- Comparison to other boats.
- A target boat speed standard.
- Immediate past performance (i.e.: How are we doing now compared with a moment ago?).
- The boats feel. A good trimmer will be able to feel a loss of power before it shows up as a loss of speed.

Based on current performance the trimmer directs adjustments to improve (or maintain) performance. Changes include adjustments in genoa trim, changes in mainsail trim, and changes in driving style. It is critical for the trimmer to communicate the current state of performance, to suggest the means to improve, and then to report on progress as adjustments take hold. As we explore genoa trim further we will look at the specific adjustments which might be called for in a variety of conditions.

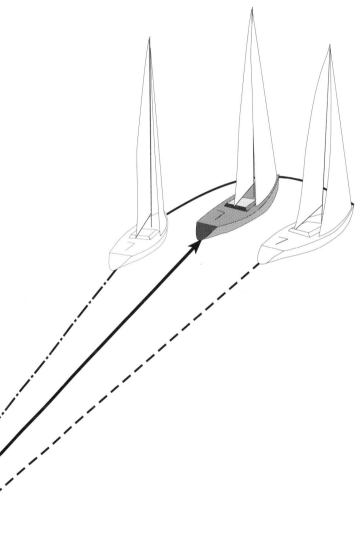

Fig. 2 - The Genoa Trimmer guides the boat upwind. After analyzing performance the trimmer makes adjustments to more closely match performance to objectives.

5.3 Genoa Power

There are three sources of sail power: Angle of attack, shape, and twist.

Angle of Attack

The genoa derives power first through angle of attack. Trim the sail in, and you add power. Let the sail out and you reduce power. Heading up also reduces angle of attack and power. Fig 3.

Angle of attack is increased by trimming the sheet or by falling off.

Shape

Deeper sails generate more power. Flat sail shapes generate less power (and less drag). Genoa depth is adjusted through a variety of controls, including headstay sage, lead position, and sheet trim. Fig 4.

Twist

A closed leech generates more power. A twisted, or open leech, spills power. Genoa twist is controlled through lead position and sheet trim. Fig 5.

Initially the sheet's primary impact is angle of attack, pulling the sail in. As the sail nears full trim the sheet increasingly pulls the sail down (not in). At this point the primary impact of trim is a change in twist. Fig 6.

Total Power, Mix of Power

The trimmers job is to achieve the correct total power in the sail, and also the correct mix of power from each source.

Sail Selection and Sail Controls

Each genoa control impacts sail power in a number of ways. Of course, the biggest impact on power is the choice of which genoa to fly. The next section will look at sail selection. The subsequent section will cover sail controls one by one.

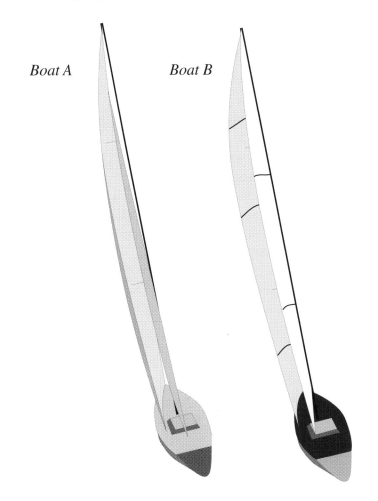

Fig. 3 - Angle of attack changes with trim and steering angle. Here Boat A is trimmed to a narrow angle of attack, while Boat B, with the lead outboard and sheet eased, is trimmed to a wider angle of attack.

Boat A   Boat B

Fig. 4 - Sail Shape: Boat A has deep genoa shape, for extra power. Boat B has a flat genoa shape, preferred for smooth water and heavy winds.

Fig. 5 - Twist: Boat C is trimmed for power, with little twist. Boat D's genoa is twisted open, spilling power.

Fig. 6 - Twist versus Angle of Attack: Boat E has a wide angle of attack - the entire sail is open, while Boat F has twist - the upper leech is open, but the lower part of the sail is trimmed inboard.

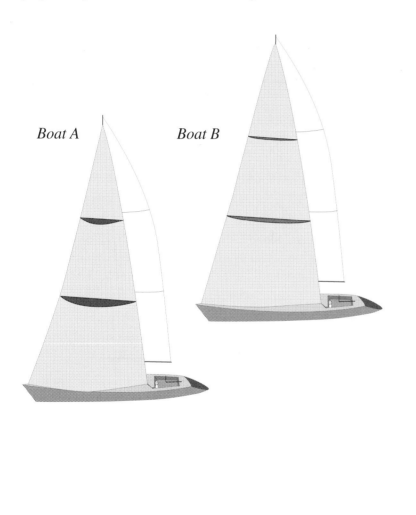

Boat A   Boat B

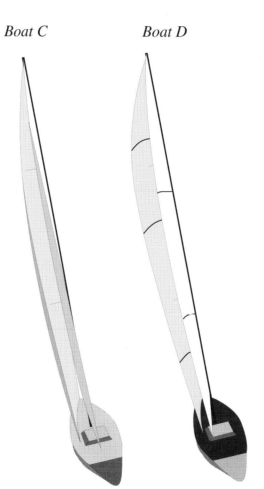

Boat C   Boat D

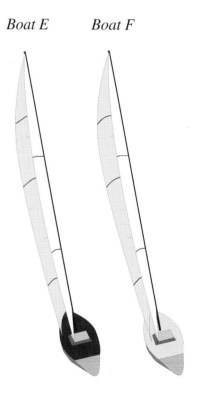

Boat E   Boat F

5.4 Sail Selection

The first step in genoa trim is to choose a sail based on conditions. Each sail has a designed strength and performance range. The optimal safe wind range for a given sail is available from the sailmaker, though with modern materials sail strength is less an issue than size and shape. The sail will be wrong from a performance standpoint before you threaten its strength. [This statement is not a warranty. Do not blow out your sails.] At the crossover between two sails several secondary factors influence the decision.

Sea State

Generally, in waves or chop use the bigger sail for extra power. In smoother water a smaller sail with a shorter overlap is preferred for close sheeting and high pointing ability. In big waves some skippers prefer a smaller jib which allows them to steer around big waves; while others rely on a big jib for power.

Trend of Conditions

No surprises here: If the breeze is building then use the smaller sail. In a dying breeze use the larger sail. Notes that sea state and breeze trend factors tend to coincide. In a building breeze seas will not have built up. In a dying breeze there will be left over seas.

Beware. Do not start with a smaller sail because you anticipate the wind building into its range. Use the smaller sail only if the wind is already in its range and you expect it to continue to build.

Performance Records

The band of uncertainty will become narrower as you become more familiar with your boat. Good record keeping can accelerate this process.

Two notes here: 1) Good record keeping can also help you in subsequent sail purchases. If you find you want to carry one sail up into the range where the next sail would supposedly be better then report this finding to your sailmaker. This information will help in the design of future sails.

Note 2) Once you know the exact crossover wind speed for each sail in your inventory, it is time to get a new boat. Sometimes you can delay this by changing your sail inventory.

Testing

Prior to a race test your options before making a decision. Head out to the starting area an hour early to test out different headsails. Tuning up with both sails against another boat is particularly valuable.

Better still, do your testing in practice against a well sailed sistership. You should sail with different sails, and then both switch. When you find which sail is faster do further testing to optimize performance with both boats using the same sail. Fig. 7.

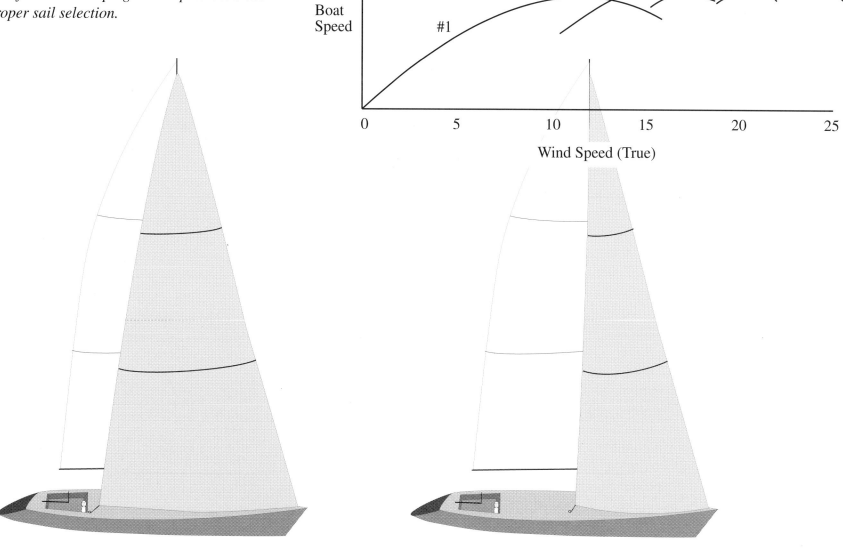

Genoa Selection

Fig. 7 - Sail selection is based on wind strength, sea state, and the trend in conditions. Careful record keeping can help us know the proper sail selection.

Boat Speed

#1   #2   #3   #4

0   5   10   15   20   25

Wind Speed (True)

5.5 Genoa Controls

From our initial set we can fine tune shape to suit conditions. Each control can be fine tuned; and as we adjust one we will need to check the impact on others. As stated above, genoa trimming is a never ending process.

Genoa Sheet

Sheet trim is the primary control of jib shape. The sheet effects the depth, power, angle of attack, and the shape of the slot. When the sheet is properly trimmed the genoa will have smooth even shape, parallel to the main. The main may show the first signs of backwinding.

Initial trim

Initial trim will put the upper genoa leech a few inches off the top spreader as the foot nears the shroud. (Obviously this is a rough approximation - yours may vary.) You will find you point higher and lose speed as you trim.

When additional trim does not improve pointing the sail is overtrimmed. Ease slightly and continue the search for the best mix of pointing and boat speed. Play the sheet constantly to keep optimum speed and pointing.

One or Two Inches

The difference between fair trim and good trim is only an inch or two of sheet. *About right* does not cut it. Two inches too tight and you will be slow. Too loose, and your pointing will suffer.

The difference between good trim and great trim is effort. Get good speed and test extra trim. Try for extra pointing without sacrificing speed. If speed suffers ease for a moment to build speed, and try again. Fig. 8.

The genoa sheet must be played with each fluctuation in conditions or performance. In a lull, or when the boat is slow, the sheet should be eased. As a puff hits the sheet may need an initial ease, and then trim as the boat accelerates.

Keep working, and remember - speed first, then pointing.

Secondary Affects

Sheet trim must be checked after every other adjustment or change.

Raising the halyard raises the head of the genoa, and increases the distance from the clew to the head of the sail. To keep the same leech shape the sheet would have to be eased as the halyard is raised. The reverse would hold if the halyard were eased.

Tightening the headstay is similar to tightening the sheet, except the sail is pulled from the luff rather than the clew. To maintain trim as the headstay is tightened the sheet must be eased. If the sheet is not eased the entire sail will be trimmed in. (And vice versa for more headstay sag.)

Adjusting the sheet lead directly affects the sheeting angle. Any lead adjustment will require some sheet adjustment. As the lead is moved forward the sheet may need a slight ease; as the lead is moved aft the sheet generally needs trim.

Never Relent

Don't cleat the jib sheet, and don't hang out to leeward.

The jib trimmer should be the last crew to the rail. As long as conditions allow, keep the jib trimmer to leeward, working on trim. Once the rest of the crew are fully hiked the jib trimmer should hike too. But don't cleat the sheet. Bring the tail along. That way the sail can be eased without delay, and without the trimmer moving off the rail.

Fig. 8 - The genoa sheet is the primary sail control. The sheet affects power, shape, and angle of attack. Trim the sheet so the genoa shape balances speed and pointing, and play the sheet with each change in conditions or performance - easing to build speed and trimming to point higher when speed is good. Be prepared to check the sheet trim with every change in secondary controls. Any change in the halyard, headstay, or lead will affect the sheet.

In final trim the difference between fast and slow is only a couple of inches. Here, Boat A is eased for acceleration. Boat B is fully trimmed for high pointing.

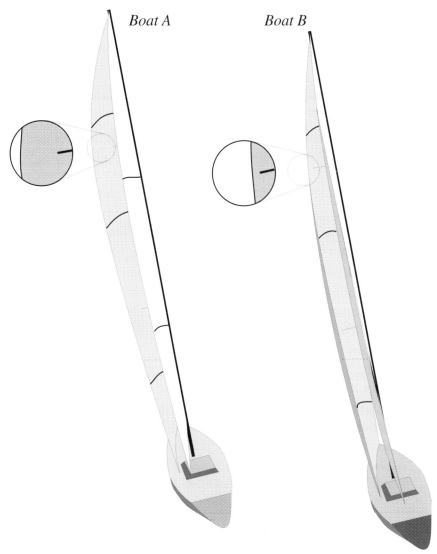

Boat A   Boat B

Halyard

The halyard is used to position the draft. Working from our initial trim settings, this is a two part process.

Initial Trim

Set the halyard to remove wrinkles from the luff of the jib. In light to moderate conditions it is better to leave the halyard too loose - leave a few wrinkles. In heavier air a firmer halyard is needed - remove the wrinkles.

Draft Maintenance

As wind strength changes halyard tension is adjusted to keep the draft in position. As the draft blows aft halyard tension is increased to hold the draft forward. As the breeze dies the halyard is eased to match the reduced loads in the sail. Our goal in this first stage is simply to keep the draft in its designed position.

Draft Tuning

Once we have finished draft maintenance we can fine tune our sail shape to suit conditions. More halyard tension will pull the draft forward. This creates a rounder entry shape which makes steering easier, particularly in waves.

Easing the halyard will allow the draft to move aft, resulting in a flatter, or 'finer' entry. This fine entry will result in a closer pointing shape, but with a narrow steering groove. In easy steering smooth water conditions this softer halyard will allow for better pointing.

To achieve proper halyard tension we must balance pointing ability with groove width. A flat entry which we cannot steer to will be slow; a round easy-to-steer entry will not allow us to point. Fig. 9.

Fig. 9 - Boat A, with the halyard eased, has a narrow angle of attack, which points high, but is difficult to steer. Note the varied behavior of the genoa telltales
Boat B, with a tight halyard, has the draft pulled forward for a wider angle of attack and easier steering.
Fig. 10 - To duplicate halyard settings align a mark on the sail to a mark on the headstay foil.

Measuring and Duplicating Halyard Settings

The best way to measure halyard settings is with a mark on your headstay and corresponding marks on your sails. This is easier and more accurate than number strips on deck matched to marks on the halyard. It also encourages pit crew to keep their heads up, looking forward during the hoist, which is good.

First, put a one inch wide mark on your headfoil six or more feet above the deck - as high as you can reach conveniently. (Your headfoil should be fixed in place. If properly installed it should not move up and down on your headstay.) Next, set each jib (in appropriate conditions) and set the halyard tension properly. Mark the jib luff to match the mark on the headstay. At the sail's upper end you may need to pull a little above the mark, and at the low end you will want the halyard slightly eased from this setting. Fig. 10.

These marks are particularly valuable when setting the jib prior to a spinnaker takedown. It is very hard to judge appropriate upwind halyard tension with the sail loosely sheeted on a reach.

One more trick: Overhoist the sail slightly and ease down to the mark. This helps assure even cloth tension over the length of the luff.

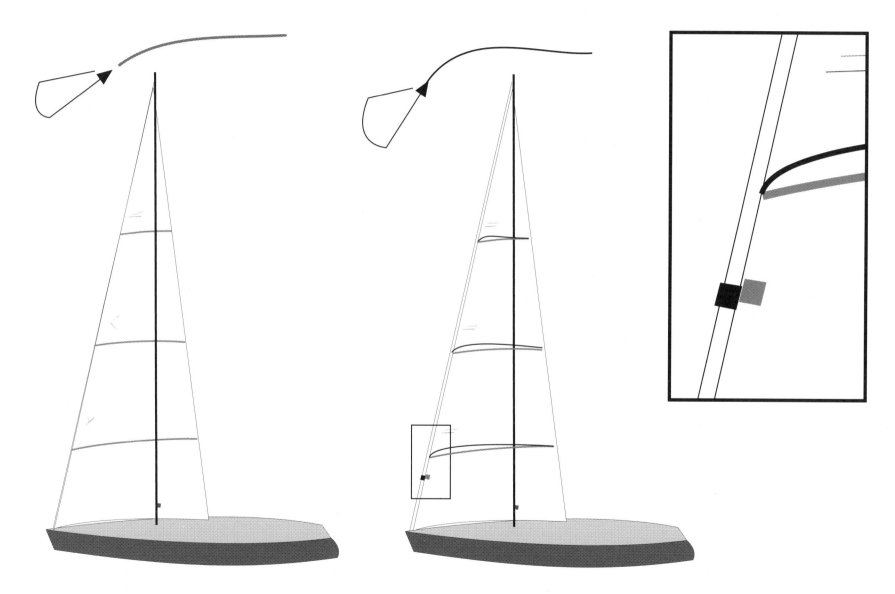

Fig. 9 -
Boat A - Draft aft creates narrow angle of attack.

Boat B- Draft forward and wide angle of attack.

Fig. 10 - Use marks on the sail and foil to set halyard tension.

Headstay Sag

Headstay sag controls depth of draft, particularly in the forward part of the sail. As with halyard tension and draft position, controlling depth is a two stage process.

Initial Trim

Set the headstay sag with backstay or running backstay. Set at one quarter max tension in light air; progressively more for stronger breeze.

Depth Maintenance

As the wind strength changes loads in the sail change, and sag changes. As the wind builds we must add headstay tension to keep the same sail shape. Similarly, as the wind dies the headstay must be eased.

Depth Tuning

More sag adds depth and power; for extra speed in waves, and better acceleration. A tight headstay creates a flat shape. The flat shape will be faster and higher pointing in smooth water. Fig. 11abc.

A secondary affect of headstay sag is a change in entry shape, similar to halyard control. More sag creates a rounder entry; a tighter headstay creates a flatter entry. Consequently any adjustment in sag should be followed by a check of halyard tension to be sure entry shape is proper.

Tightening the headstay flattens the entry; and the halyard may need to be snugged to put some shape into the front of the sail. Sagging the headstay rounds the entry. A matching ease on the halyard can prevent the entry from becoming too round.

Fig. 11a - A tight headstay creates a flat, closewinded, low drag shape best for heavy air and smooth water.

Fig. 11b - A sagged or loose headstay produces a deeper, more powerful shape, best suited for light to moderate winds and chop.

Fig. 11c - This figure shows a deep sail shape silhouetted over a flat shape. As the breeze changes the headstay sag will change due to changing sail load. Adjustments will first be needed simply to maintain shape. From there sail shape can be fine tuned to the conditions.

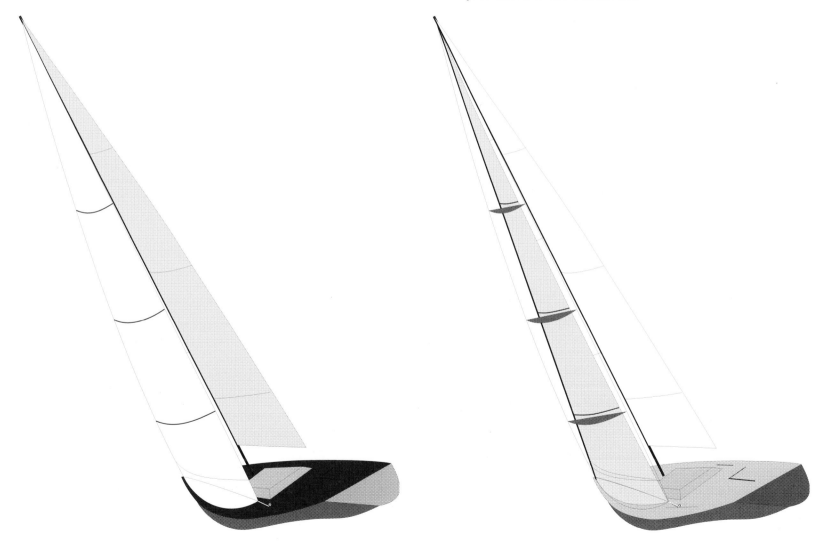

Genoa Leads

Moving the fairlead changes genoa shape and power. The goal of initial trim is to achieve the designed shape. We'll fine tune from there

Initial Trim

Set the jib fairleads so the sail has a fair curve and even shape from top to bottom. When the sheet is trimmed the jib telltales should break evenly from top to bottom. (As you pinch up above closed hauled the upper telltales will luff before the lower ones.) The leech of the jib should match the shape of the main.

NO, the telltales will not all break together. The upper telltales will luff first, and the break will spread down. Fig. 12.

Balance of Power

The jib leads balance high and low shape in the sail. Our goal is to set the lead so the sail shape matches the wind from top to bottom. When the lead is set properly the inside telltales will break smoothly, starting from top and moving down.

Moving the lead forward makes the sheet pull down more on the upper part of the sail, trimming in the top. Moving the lead aft will cause the sheet to pull back on the foot, like an outhaul, without trimming the upper part of the sail as much.

Tuning to Conditions

In waves and chop pulling the lead forward adds power throughout the sail. The top of the sail is trimmed fully, and the foot of the sail takes on a round, powerful shape. In moderate winds the leech will trim within a few inches of the top spreader, while in light air it may be as far as a foot off. The foot of the sail will carry perhaps two feet of depth over a ten foot chord length. Only when the lead is in its forward most position will the entire luff break at once - the way basic sailing texts say they should.

In smooth water move the lead aft to open up the sail. This allows the genoa to be trimmed in closer to the main without clogging up the slot. The foot is stretched flat. Over-

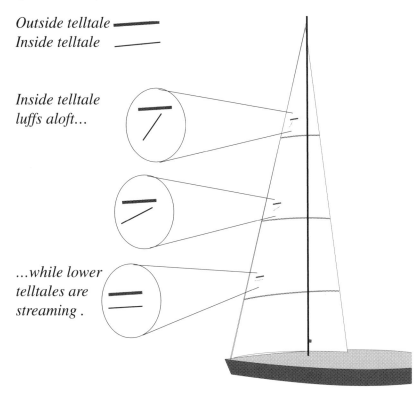

Fig. 12 - The jib telltales will NOT all break at the same time. The upper part of the sail will break first, and the luff will spread down from there.

Outside telltale
Inside telltale

Inside telltale luffs aloft...

...while lower telltales are streaming .

lapping genoas will trim against the shroud base. The telltales break first aloft, and the lower telltales may even be partially stalled while the uppers spin. This flatter shape allows harder trim and thus higher pointing.

In over powering conditions move the lead aft to flatten the foot of the sail and spill open the top; reducing power throughout. Fig. 13.

Fig. 13 - Moving the genoa leads changes the shape and power of the foot and leech of the genoa.
Boat A - Moving the lead aft flattens the foot and opens the leech, reducing power. Move the lead aft to reduce heeling when overpowered and for closer pointing in smooth water.
Boat B - Moving the lead forward adds shape and power in the foot and up the leech. Move the lead forward for extra punch in waves.

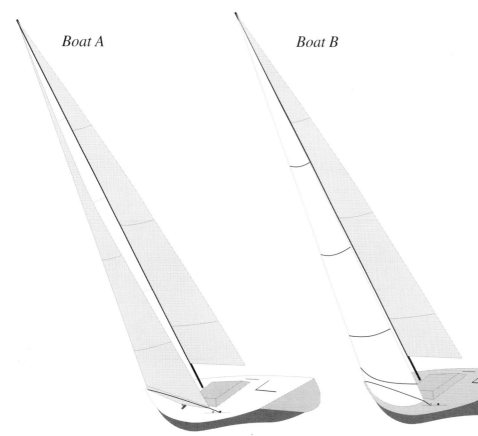

Boat A   Boat B

Adjustable Jib Leads

Adjustable jib lead systems allow you to adjust the lead position on a loaded jib lead. This allows the lead to be adjusted to changing conditions and situations. For example, the lead can be pulled forward for extra acceleration out of a tack. As speed builds the lead is eased to its normal position. Similarly, the lead can be pulled forward to add power when approaching a tough set of waves, or the lead can be eased aft to spill power in a puff.

Inboard and Outboard Leads

An inboard lead position allows for closer pointing in ideal *smooth water moderate air* conditions. With the main and jib both trimmed flat move the lead inboard a few inches. (Drag it inboard with a hook around the sheet.) Your goal is to improve pointing without any sacrifice in speed. Be prepared to ease out immediately if (when) you lose speed. Speed first - pointing second. Keep speed, then try to squeeze up. On many boats it is difficult to improve pointing due to limitations of the keel.

In heavy air an outboard lead de-powers the slot. With an overlapping genoa and the main traveler down the slot will be clogged. Move the lead outboard to open the slot for speed and to reduce heeling. The danger here is a loss of pointing ability. Before moving the lead outboard try first to de power by easing the sheet a few inches while leaving the lead in its regular (aft) heavy air position. Only in extreme conditions - when you ought to have a smaller sail - is an outboard lead effective.

In *very* light air an outboard lead prevents the slot from being clogged and eases flow. Hold the lead outboard and reach off to build speed. Once you have speed then try pointing (back to the harbor). Repeat from above: Speed first.

5.6 Jib Reaches

A high clewed *Reacher* or *Jib Top* is designed for jib reaching, with extra roundness and power forward. Lacking such a specialty sail, you will have to make do with a standard genoa, trimming it as best you can for the reach.

Barber Hauling

Using a standard genoa on a jib reach the lead **must** be moved outboard and forward. You chase the clew of the sail with the lead. It also helps to keep the halyard firm to hold the draft forward and too prevent the back of the sail from becoming too round. Fig. 14.

If the lead is not moved as the sheet is eased, then the top of the sail will twist open, spilling power, and the bottom of the sail will hook in toward the boat, creating excess drag.

At the Cusp

There is a limit to how low you can reach effectively with a genoa. As you push the lead forward in an effort to keep the top of the sail trimmed you make the foot increasingly round.

As you reach the lower limit of effective reaching trim you have two choices: One is to set your spinnaker - particularly if you carry an asymmetrical spinnaker. If the angle is too close for a chute then the alternative is to head up slightly to keep the jib working effectively. As you gain height you will eventually be able to reach down and set a spinnaker. *This is the only time a direct route is not fastest on a reach.*

Reacher

If you carry a high clewed *Reacher* or *Jib Top* the exact lead position depends on the wind angle. Set the sheet lead well aft, and rig a choker to pull the sheet down. Adjust the choker

Fig. 14 - As the genoa sheet is eased on a jib reach the genoa lead must follow the sail outboard and forward.
Boat A - If the lead is not moved the jib foot will be too round, and the leech will spill.
Boat B - A proper lead position will keep the top of the sail from spilling open and move the genoa foot outboard, allowing the main to be eased properly.

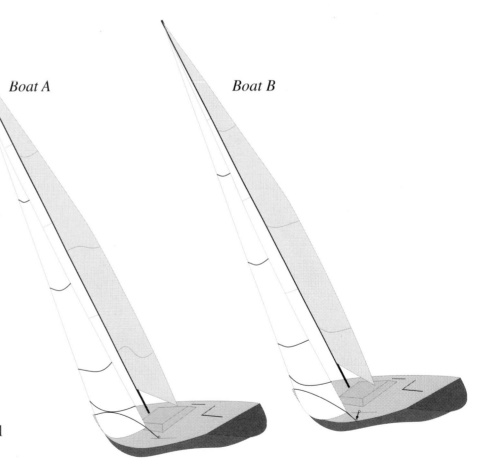

Boat A   *Boat B*

so the sail luffs evenly from top to bottom. This arrangement is better than a fixed lead, as it allows easy adjustment as wind angle and wind speed change. Fig. 15.

Genoa Staysails

Although they have gone out of fashion, some old IOR boats with huge J dimensions still carry genoa staysails. The genoa staysail can be set between the jib and main, creating a double head rig. Tack it on the centerline at 40 - 50% of J aft, and sheet it evenly between the main and genoa. Try it. If you go faster keep it up; if it makes you slower take it down. (WOW!)

If you own one of these relics take care of it - you certainly don't want to have to replace it. It may also be time to think about a newer boat, where you don't need to carry so many sails to sail fast. Fig 16.

5.7 Conclusion

Genoa trim is a never ending battle to match sail shape to the conditions of the moment. The genoa trimmer leads the boat upwind, guiding the driver up or down, depending on performance.

Later, in Chapter 8, we will revisit genoa trim as we consider overall upwind trim solutions in a variety of sailing conditions.

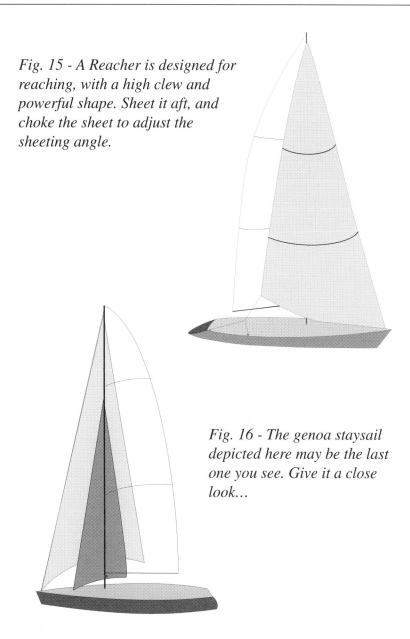

Fig. 15 - A Reacher is designed for reaching, with a high clew and powerful shape. Sheet it aft, and choke the sheet to adjust the sheeting angle.

Fig. 16 - The genoa staysail depicted here may be the last one you see. Give it a close look...

CHAPTER 6 - MAINSAIL TRIM & CONTROLS

6.1 INTRODUCTION

6.2 THE MAINSAIL TRIMMER

6.3 MAINSAIL POWER

6.4 CONTROLS

SIDEBAR - VANG SHEETING

6.5 REACHING & RUNNING

6.6 CONCLUSION

ADDENDUM:

  FULLY BATTENED MAINS

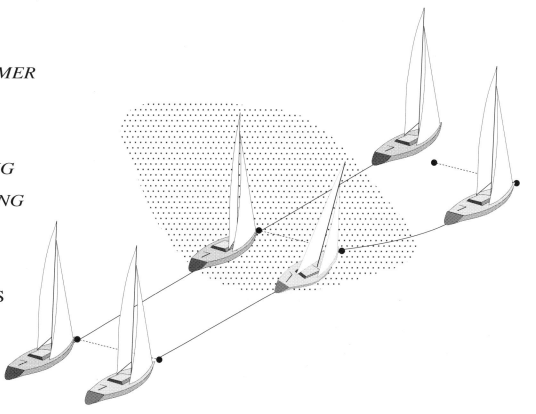

CHAPTER 6 - MAINSAIL TRIM & CONTROLS

6.1 Introduction

The jib leads the boat upwind; the mainsail provides balance and control. Proper main shape is a shape which complements the jib, and balances the helm, while pushing the boat to the proper mix of pointing and speed.

We have more control over mainsail shape than we do genoa shape; and we are required to do more with it. After all, we have all those genoas, but only one main. Having so many controls is a double edged sword; sometimes it is hard to know what to use when. Fear not. If things don't work out, blame the tactician. Fig. 1.

In this chapter we will look at the role of the mainsail trimmer in upwind performance, and the various sources of power for the main. Next, we will consider each mainsail control and how it impacts sail shape and power. We'll look at initial trim settings for upwind sailing, and refinements for varied conditions. Reaching and running trim will be covered in a separate section. Later, in Chapter 8 we will integrate main trim, jib trim and driving techniques in a variety of sailing conditions

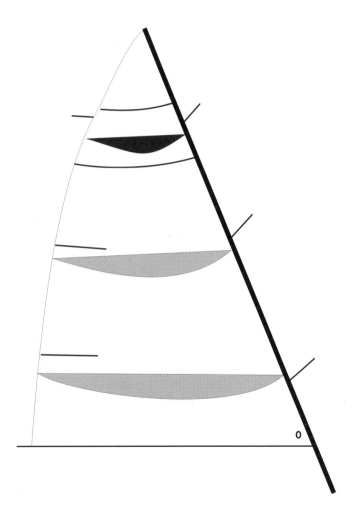

Fig. 1 - A well trimmed main will provide speed, pointing, and balance to our upwind performance.

6.2 The Mainsail Trimmer

The mainsail trimmer is responsible for monitoring the boat's upwind performance, trimming to keep the boat sailing fast, pointing high, and in balance. Fig. 2.

Monitoring performance involves information from on and off the boat. Performance against adjacent boats is one key input. Boat speed and apparent wind angle provide additional information. Also important are the helm balance, heel, and path of the boat through water. For example, if the boat is pitching or the course unsteady the main trimmer can make adjustments to help.

The ability to make quick adjustments to the main in immediate response to changing conditions distinguishes it from the jib. Jib trim is trimmed to an average, with small, incremental adjustments to changing conditions. By virtue of the ease with which the main can be adjusted, and because of its effect on balance, the main is played much more aggressively. This is particularly true in puffy or wavy conditions.

The main trimmer has more control over shape and power than the headsail trimmer. In the next section we will take a look at each source of mainsail power. Following that we will look at each mainsail control.

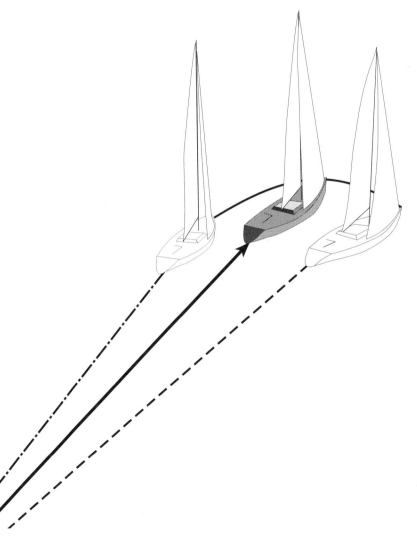

Fig. 2 - The mainsail trimmer works with the jib trimmer and driver to keep the boat sailing fast and pointing high.

6.3 Mainsail Power

There are three sources of mainsail power, as with any sail: Angle of attack, shape, and twist.

Power through angle of attack

The main derives power first through angle of attack. Trim the sail in, and you add power. Let the sail out and you reduce power. Heading up also reduces angle of attack and power.

Angle of attack is increased by trimming the sheet, raising the traveler, or falling off. Fig. 3.

Power through shape

Deeper sails generate more power. Flat sail shapes generate less power (and less drag). Sail shape is adjusted through a variety of controls. Mainsail shape is controlled by mast bend and outhaul tension. Fig. 4.

Power through twist

A closed leech generates more power. A twisted, or open leech, spills power. The mainsheet is the primary controller of main twist. Fig. 5.

Initially the sheet's primary impact is angle of attack, pulling the boom in. As the sail nears full trim the sheet increasingly pulls the boom down (not in). At this point the primary impact of trim is a change in twist.

Controls

The mainsail trimmer has an array of controls available to control each source of mainsail power. The next section will look at these controls one by one.

Fig. 3 - Angle of attack is the first source of mainsail power. Boat A - Power is reduced by easing the sail out or by heading up. Boat B - Angle of attack is increased by trimming the sail in, or by falling off.

Boat A   *Boat B*

Fig. 4 - Another source of mainsail power is sail depth.
Boat C has a deep, powerful mainsail.
Boat D has a flat sail, which generates less power (and less drag).

Fig. 5 - Twist is the third control over sail power.
Boat E has an open, or twisted, mainsail, which spills power.
Boat F has a closed leech, with little twist, for maximum power.

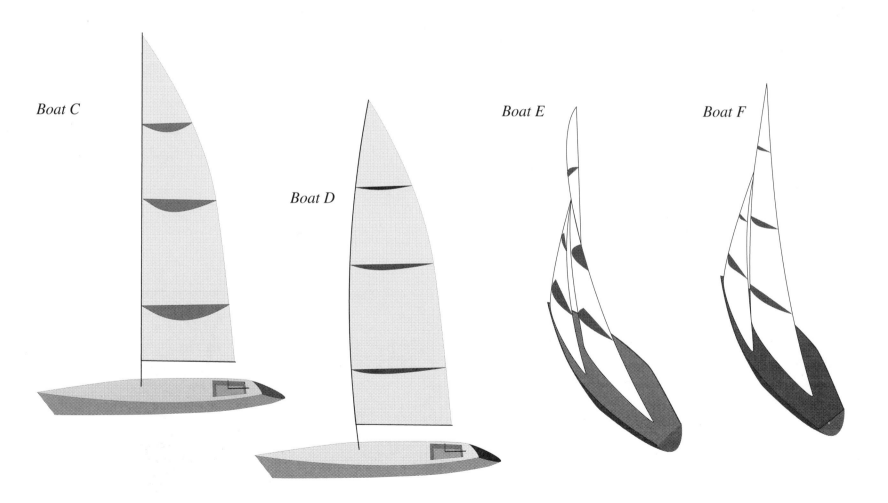

Boat C

Boat D

Boat E

Boat F

6.4 Mainsail Controls

In this section we will review each mainsail control, how it will be used to alter mainsail shape, and how it will impact the power of the sail.

Mainsheet

The mainsheet is the primary mainsail control. The sheet controls twist and leech tension; which affect power and pointing. Trimming the main also changes angle of attack and overall sail depth. The mainsheet should be trimmed so the leech end of top batten is parallel to the boom. Fig. 6. When the boom is on center line the end of the batten should point straight aft. Fig. 7.

Leech Telltales

From this initial setting the sheet can be fine tuned to keep the upper leech telltales flowing, with an occasional stall. Usually this telltale behavior achieves the best mix of speed and pointing.

There are conditions when performance will improve with the main slightly eased or trimmed compared to the settings described above. You never know until you try.

If the sheet is eased slightly, so the telltales never stall, then speed may increase without any loss of pointing ability. At other times, trimming to the point of stalling the telltales half the (or more) time may result in higher pointing, though the added drag will usually cause some sacrifice of speed.

Secondary Controls

As you make adjustments to the secondary controls described below you will need to check and recheck sheet trim.

Never relent. You can always go faster.

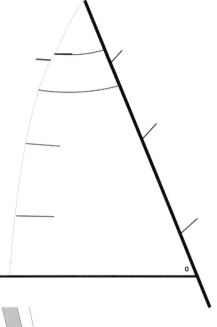

Fig. 6 - Trim the mainsheet to put the upper leech parallel to the boom, and the telltale flying most of the time.

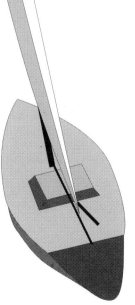

Fig. 7 - With the main at full trim the boom should be on the centerline.

More on the Mainsheet

In light air over-trimming the sheet will stall the sail. We seek all the power the sail can generate. This means trimming just short of a stall. Fig. 8, Boat A.

In more moderate conditions, higher pointing is possible by trimming the main hard, to the point of a partial stall. There are of course limits on how hard you can trim without a sacrifice of speed. The sheet should be eased to twist out the upper leech of the main when the boat is slow. Fig. 8, Boat B.

In heavy air over trimming the mainsheet will create excess weather helm. Some backwinding in the luff of the main is to be expected. Don't let a little backwinding trouble you - it is fast. . Fig. 8, Boat C.

Boom Vang

The boom vang is primarily an offwind control. Upwind a very tight vang can add extra bend in the lower section of the mast. Snugging the vang upwind can also help control twist.

In light air a tight vang will close the leech, stall flow, and wreak havoc on performance.

We'll see more on the vang in the Reaching and Running section, below. At the end of this section we will also look at an alternative trim technique known as *Vang Sheeting.*

Fig. 8 - Twist and power change with wind speed.
Boat A, in light air has a deep shape for power, with enough twist to ease flow.
Boat B is trimmed for moderate winds, with a tight leech and moderate depth.
Boat C is set up for heavy air, with a flat sail shape and twist to spill excess power.

Mast Bend

After the mainsheet, mast bend is the second most powerful controller of mainsail shape. Mast bend is used to change the shape of the middle and upper portions of the sail. Mast bend is controlled by the back stay and/or baby stay and running back stays.

Mast bend flattens the sail by increasing the distance from luff to leech. Use bend to reduce power as the breeze builds, and for reduced drag and extra speed in smooth water. Use less bend (a straighter mast) for extra power in chop, or when sailing downwind. Fig. 9.

As secondary affects, mast bend also impacts twist and draft position. Concurrent to a change in bend the mainsheet should be adjusted to retrim leech tension; and luff tension must be checked as well.

Outhaul

The outhaul controls depth in the lower portion of the main. The more we pull on the outhaul the flatter the foot of the sail becomes. On mains rigged with a flattening reef, think of the flattener as an extension of the outhaul, which takes over the outhaul function when the outhaul is at its limit.

The outhaul should be on part way whenever you are sailing upwind. As the breeze builds from light to moderate air the outhaul should come on all the way. The foot of the main should be stretched flat as the boat is over powered. In chop and waves the sail should be fuller for more power; in smooth water it can be set flatter for closer pointing. Fig. 10.

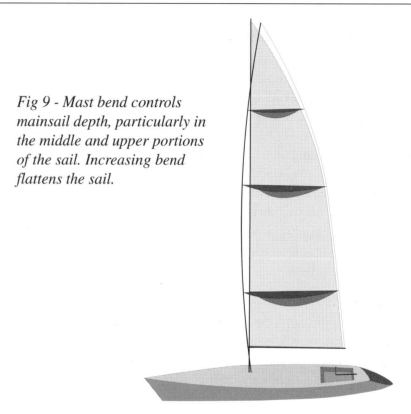

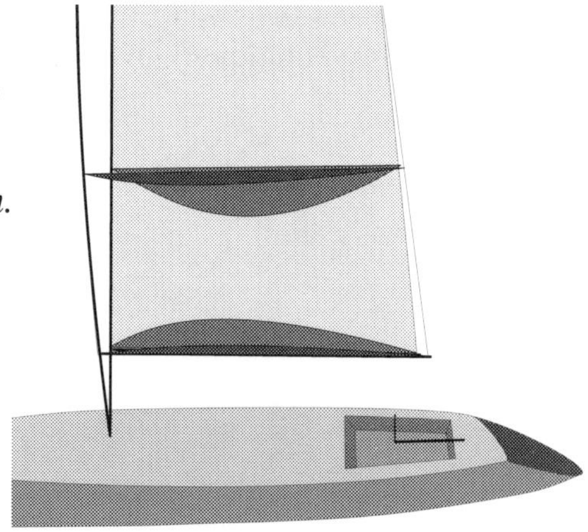

Fig 9 - Mast bend controls mainsail depth, particularly in the middle and upper portions of the sail. Increasing bend flattens the sail.

Fig. 10 - Use the outhaul to control shape in the lower portion of the main.

Traveler

The traveler positions the boom, controlling angle of attack. Keep the boom centered (traveler to windward) until overpowered. Fig. 11.

Gradually lower the traveler to leeward to control heeling as the wind builds. The boom should start centered with the #1 genoa. As you reach the upper end of the #1 the traveler may need to go down a foot or so. As the wind builds the range of play in the traveler increases. With a #3 the boom main be centered, or it may be eased to the quarter.

The traveler should be played constantly in puffy conditions to control heel and weather helm. Once the sail shape is set for the average conditions the traveler is used to make quick adjustments to overall power. Fig. 12.

There are times when it will be faster to leave the traveler set and play the mainsheet, adjusting twist, when overpowered. The preferred method depends on:

Sea State - In more waves playing twist is preferred, in puffy, smooth water conditions the traveler is preferred.

Boat Design - Heavier, smaller keeled, smaller rigged boats respond well to traveler play. Lighter, deep keeled, over canvassed boats respond best to twist adjustments.

Ease of Use - If one is easier to adjust, and the other is a pain in the... I mean difficult, then you'll probably go faster using the control that works - until you can fix the one that doesn't!

Testing - Try both techniques. Which provides better performance for you, today, in these conditions?

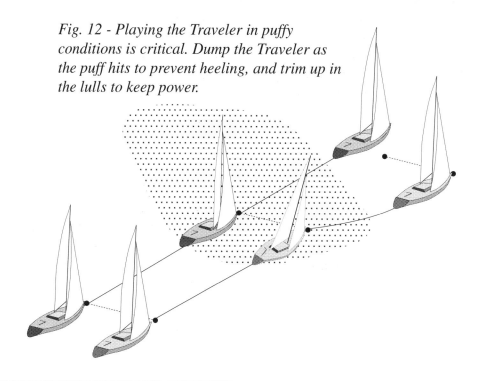

Boat A   *Boat B*

Fig. 11- The Traveler controls the angle of attack of the mainsail.
Boat A - In moderate conditions position the boom along the center line of the boat.
Boat B - In heavier air lower the traveler to control heel and reduce weather helm.

Fig. 12 - Playing the Traveler in puffy conditions is critical. Dump the Traveler as the puff hits to prevent heeling, and trim up in the lulls to keep power.

Luff Tension

Luff tension adjusts draft position. Adding tension pulls the draft forward. The main halyard and cunningham control luff tension. Use the halyard until you reach its legal limits, then use the cunningham. Fig. 13.

Draft position is not so much a power control as it is a drag control. If the draft moves too far aft it creates too much drag. As the draft is pulled forward drag is reduced, with some loss of power.

The draft should be just forward of the middle of the sail, at 40-45%, most of the time. When overpowered try to pull the draft further forward with extra luff tension. In light air chop a more draft aft shape can help add power.

Mast bend pushes the draft aft. As you add bend add luff tension to compensate. Also, don't forget to ease luff tension when you straighten the mast. Fig. 14.

Full length battens also impact draft position. For more on the relationship between draft position, luff tension, and battens, see the addendum to this chapter.

Fig. 13 - The main halyard and cunningham control luff tension and draft position. More luff tension pulls the draft forward, less tension lets the draft move aft.
Sail A shows the draft where we want it - just forward of the middle of the sail.
Sail B shows the draft too far forward. This happens when the wind drops, or you turn down to a reach. To correct this the cunningham or halyard should be eased.

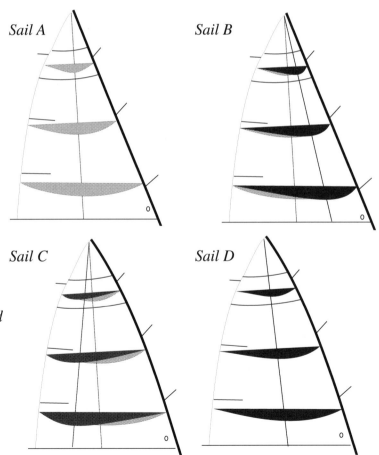

Fig. 14 - The draft moves aft as we bend the mast and as the wind increases. Sail C is a draft aft sail. Sail D shows a sail with added luff tension to compensate for the impact of mast bend.

Mainsail Controls - Conclusion

Our goal in mainsail trim is the extract the appropriate power from the main - in balance with the jib. We also seek the optimum mix of power from the three sources of sail power - angle of attack, shape, and twist. With impact on all three facets, the mainsheet is the primary control of overall mainsail power. Fig 15.

Our secondary controls influence the depth, angle of attack, and overall power of the main. As adjustments are made to any one control they impact the settings of other controls.

In Chapter 8 we will look in detail at the balance between the sails and the balance among the various sources of sail power.

Fig. 15 - Changing conditions call for changing mainsail shapes. The mainsheet remains our primary sail control.

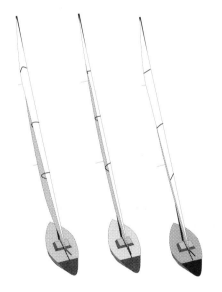

SIDEBAR - Vang Sheeting

Vang Sheeting is an alternative mainsail trimming method.

Conventional Trim

In conventional trim the mainsheet controls the angle of attack, and it controls twist. That is, the mainsheet pulls the boom **in** and **down**. As you near full trim the emphasis is on the down component - adjusting twist. The traveler takes over the in and out component - moving the boom to center line once the desired twist is achieved, or playing the main in and out in puffs. This technique does not rely on the boom vang as an upwind trim control.

Vang Sheeting

In *Vang Sheeting* the boom vang takes over the mainsheet's up / down control over the boom, and the mainsheet handles the in / out trim which is the traveler's domain in our conventional upwind arrangement. This technique does not require a traveler.

Vang Sheeting requires a very powerful boom vang, capable of handling the entire leech load. *Vang Sheeting* is particularly popular on two person dinghies and other boats without back stays. When there is no back stay the vang controls mast bend as well as twist. (The vang pulls the boom down and thrusts it forward. The forward force of the boom bends the mast.)

We all Vang Sheet

On reaches we all vang sheet. On boats using conventional trim methods upwind the vang takes over control of twist once the sheet is eased, and the sheet moves the boom in and out. *Vang Sheeting* simply uses this trim method for upwind trim as well.

6.5 Reaching and Running Trim

Reaching

Upwind trim demands a balance of speed, power, and pointing. Reaching trim is simplified by eliminating concerns over pointing. Reaching trim calls for more power. Ease the outhaul and ease the back stay to add power. Don't get carried away easing the outhaul. Don't sacrifice area as you add shape.

Reduce luff tension for the lighter apparent winds and straighter mast relative to upwind sailing. Set the boom vang to control the leech of the sail. Keep the top batten parallel to the boom and try to keep flow off the leech telltales.

Most importantly, ease the sheet. Ease until the sail luffs, then trim to stop the luff; ease and trim. An overtrimmed main is slow.

In heavy air reaching dump the vang to spill the leech when overpowered, and be prepared to dump the sheet to prevent a broach. If the boom is close to the water ease the vang and keep it from hitting water. When the boom hits the water it can't be eased properly.

Running

On a run don't forget the main. While everyone fusses over the spinnaker the main is often neglected. Ease until the sail luffs or until it rests against the rig. There is no harm to the sail or rig - let it out. Since there is no flow on a run don't worry about the rig interfering with shape. Ease the back stay to straighten the mast for a powerful sail shape. Ease the outhaul to add shape without sacrificing area Set the vang to keep the top batten parallel to the boom. Ease the vang if the batten hooks in, tighten when the batten spills out. Fig. 16.

Fig. 16 - Reaching and Running
Don't neglect your main downwind. Let it out. Ease 'til it luffs, and trim. On a run ease the sail out against the rig.
Outhaul: *Eased for power.*
Mast Bend: *Straight for power.*
Luff Tension: *Eased - draft at 50%.*
Traveler: *Down.*
Sheet Trim: *Ease to luff, then trim.*
Vang: *Top batten parallel to boom, try to keep flow.*

6.6 Conclusion

The mainsail is critical to the trim and balance of the boat. Use your mainsail to keep a balanced helm. When there is excess weather helm and heel de-power the main. When the helm is mushy and the boat lifeless power-up. The helmsman and mainsail trimmer must work together to optimize performance. The helmsman is at the mercy of the mainsail trimmer.

The next chapter covers helming. After that we'll look at trim solutions integrating the main, jib, and driver.

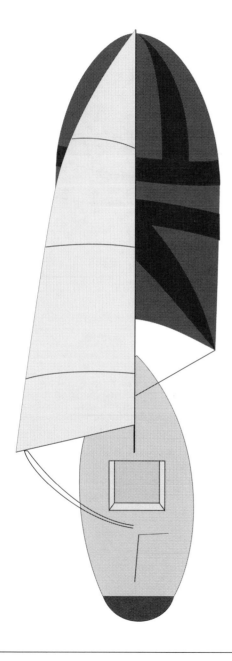

Fig. 16

Addendum: *Fully Battened Mains*

Fully Battened Mains are Good

Full battens improve both the performance and the racing life of main sails. Full battens change some of our control and trim techniques, and they generally make mainsail trim easier.

Full battens eliminate some of our control over draft position. The battens' curve determines the draft position, and luff tension has little impact. At the same time, the battens prevent the draft from moving out of position, so our need for control is diminished. We can still pull the draft forward with extra luff tension, but the propensity for the draft to move aft with mast bend is reduced.

Tapered upper battens give us a sail with self correcting draft position. As the sail loads up and the draft starts to drift aft the battens soft forward section bends to hold the draft forward.

No More Poke!

The nagging problem in mainsail design and trim has been batten poke - the sharp crease and kink which develops at the inboard end of conventional battens - particularly the top batten. With full battens batten poke disappears. Kinked upper leeches are replaced by smooth even shapes. Fig. 17 - next page.

Full battens also provide a more stable platform for main sails and reduce wear from luffing and flogging. Since fully battened sails do not flog the life of a racing main will be extended enough to cover the cost of a proper set of tapered full length battens.

Fig.17 - Full battened mains hold their shape better than traditional mains, they are easier to trim, and they eliminate batten poke.

Not only that, but they overcome the age old problem of batten poke, which gave mains a kink at the inboard end of the upper battens. And not only that, they last longer too!

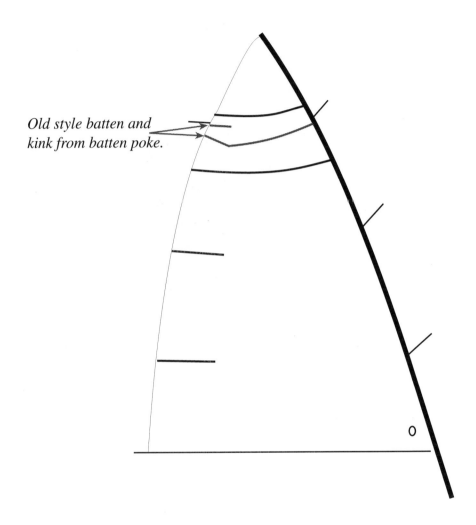

Old style batten and kink from batten poke.

One or Two?

Not all your battens need be full length. Depending on the size and roach of your main only the top one or two battens need be full length. While you're at it, make sure they are tapered. It is worth the additional cost to get tapered battens.

Not Quite Full Length Option

An alternative to full length battens is longer but not quite full length battens. These avoid the compression and loading along the luff which full length battens create. These are an alternative to consider, particularly on boats which luff slugs or slides, although they do not provide all the benefits of true full length battens.

Keep It Loose

Some sailors complain of difficulty flattening their fully battened mains. This is most often due to putting the batten in too tight. The full length batten should be inserted *with no compression.* Better the batten be too loose than too tight.

Another cause of trimming difficulty is soft battens. Get stiff, tapered battens.

Conclusion

If rule makers are preventing the use of fully battened mains in your area or fleet, join the lobby in favor of full battens. They are better. Catamarans, dinghies, and windsurfers have known it for years.

CHAPTER 7 - UPWIND HELMSMANSHIP

7.1 INTRODUCTION

7.2 GARBAGE IN...

7.3 STEERING UPWIND

7.4 CALLING TRIM FROM THE HELM

7.5 DRIVING AT STARTS

7.6 CONCLUSION

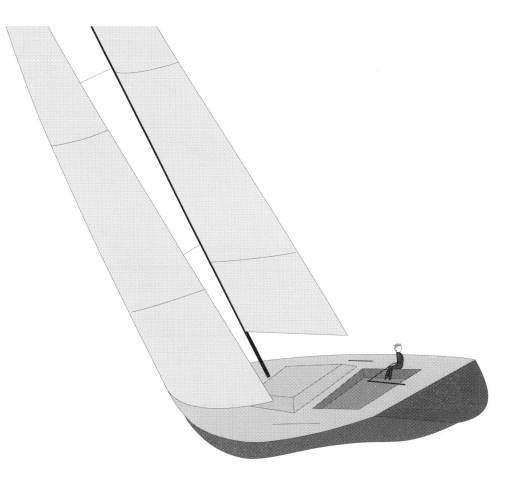

CHAPTER 7 - UPWIND HELMSMANSHIP

7.1 Introduction

Helmsmanship.* One of the most important and least tangible elements of boat speed. Experience and concentration are important performance factors. The ability to stay calm in situations which scream out for panic is another trait. The truly excellent helmsman not only drives fast, but is also able to call trim through the feel of the helm. The driver is often also the skipper. In that role the helmsman must surround himself with trusted crew. The helmsman must be confident in those around him so he can concentrate on sailing fast.

In this chapter we will discuss helmsmanship upwind in various conditions. We will also look at driving at starts. Chapter 13, later, covers Driving Downwind.

7.2 Garbage In...

To be a great driver you must first be able to feel how the boat is performing. Once you have that information you can respond to improve performance. There are many sources of information to draw from. The importance of each source varies with conditions. Fig. 1.

Driver info...

Boat speed

Our boat speed is the first critical piece of performance info. The best source is comparison to nearby sister ships. In

---

* Don't be misled by the implications of helmsman. Many of the fastest drivers are women.

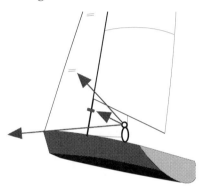

Fig. 1 - The driver uses information from the seat of his pants, boat speed, jib telltales, and wind and waves ahead; along with information passed along by the trimmers and crew; to guide him in steering.

mixed fleet racing this is not often available. We must make do with speed from our instruments, and comparisons to boats of similar design.

Obviously, if we are slow then we've got to do something about it. The first response at the helm is to foot off. We'll explore possible reasons for *the slows* in more detail below.

Pointing

If your speed is OK but pointing is a problem then changes in trim are called for. As driver you may be able to help decide what trim changes are needed based on the feel of the boat.

Seat of the pants "feel"

If the boat feels mushy, slow, or unresponsive you may be over trimmed. You should also be able to feel the boat lose power before it loses speed. You can respond and reestablish power. Ease the sails, and bear off if necessary.

Feel of the wind

As with seat of the pants feel, you can often feel changes in the wind before they show up as changes in performance. In a lull drive you can expect power and speed to drop. Retrim for lighter air while maintaining the best performance you can.

Feel of the helm

Weather helm is a key trim guide. If you are carrying more than 4° of helm, the boat is out of balance. (*Note:* On tiller boats 5° of helm is about 1" of helm per foot of tiller length. i.e. For a four foot tiller four inches of helm equals 5°. On wheel boats you will have to measure the ratio of wheel rotation and rudder turn.) Fig. 2.

Angle of heel

Once you are fully powered angle of heel becomes a key performance guide. Steer and trim to maintain a constant angle of heel. Too much heel will mean too much helm and leeway.

Jib telltales

Jib telltales are a valuable trim and steering aid. You can use them a couple of different ways. The most common method is to correlate telltale behavior to performance gears, ranging from acceleration to speed, pointing, and pinching. We'll look at that in more detail in the next section.

A second way to use telltales is somewhat the reverse. When the boat is performing well look at the telltales. Steer to maintain that behavior, whatever it is.

If there is a problem with jib telltales it is that some drivers rely too heavily on them, while ignoring many of the other inputs described here.

Fig. 2 - When trim is properly balanced you will have less than 5° of weather helm. By coincidence, for a tiller X feet long X inches of weather helm is 5°

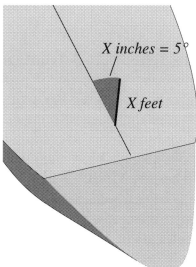

Info from trimmers

Much of the information discussed here you gather yourself. Other information can be passed to you by your trimmers. For example, you should not be looking at other boats to compare performance - the crew should gather and pass along this information. Rather than take a barrage of info from all sides it is best to pass all the info through one or two people - the jib trimmer and either the main trimmer or the tactician, for example.

Comments from the rail

Rail crew can call incoming puffs and waves. They can also provide critical information about other boats. Of course, given the state of crew today, the information must be viewed with a high degree of skepticism.

7.3 Steering Upwind

As you tune in to the your performance information you should respond as necessary to anything which seems amiss. Your jib telltales can help you fine tune your steering to improve performance.

Using Jib Telltales to Advantage

One valuable tool for upwind performance is genoa telltales. Genoa telltales serve as a trim guide and as a steering guide. Once the trimmer has set the sail to proper shape the driver can fine tune his course to suit the boat's needs. There is more to it than simply keeping the telltales streaming. Fig. 3.

Full Speed Mode

The baseline is sailing at full speed, with the telltales streaming. This course will hold full speed. Fig. 4.

Acceleration Mode

Slightly lower than a full speed course, in Acceleration Mode the *outside* telltales will dance. By "pressing down" against the jib the boat will be fully powered. This extra power improves acceleration out of tacks and through chop. Fig. 5.

Point Mode

Slightly higher than Full Speed Mode is Point Mode. Here the inside telltales will rise (but not luff). The goal is to hold this slightly higher course without sacrificing speed. At the first sign of a loss of speed it is best to slide back down to Full Speed Mode. If you are slow to respond the bottom will fall out, and you'll need to fall all the way down to Acceleration Mode to rebuild speed. Fig. 6.

Pinching and Feathering

Higher than Point Mode is *pinching*, with the inside telltales luffing. You are pinching if you force the boat up and lose speed. More time and distance is lost through pinching than through any other single flaw in driving. Don't do it.

Feathering, on the other hand, is OK. The telltale behavior is the same as for pinching - the inside telltales luff. The difference is that you feather as a way to depower in heavy air. You are feathering if you don't lose speed. If you slow down you are pinching. Fig. 7.

Gentry Tufts

Gentry Tufts are a string of several short telltales used in the place of a single lower telltale. They provide more subtle information about where on the sail flow is becoming attached. Use them to more narrowly define your steering groove. If you find you have a great balance of speed and pointing when the front tufts are luffing, and the aft tufts are streaming then steer to maintain that behavior. Fig. 8.

Tacking

A slow smooth turn initially, coasting upwind to carry speed; with a faster turn through the second half. Settle immediately and drive off slightly to accelerate. Work with your trimmers to quickly get back up to speed. Keep it smooth.

In waves a sharper turn is needed to get the bow around. First look for a smooth spot. Start the turn heading into a wave trough. The bow will pop out as you hit the crest of the wave and (hopefully) cross the wind before the next wave hits. This way the next wave helps you complete the turn rather than pushing you back onto the old tack. (See figures in Chapter 4 - Upwind Boat Handling.)

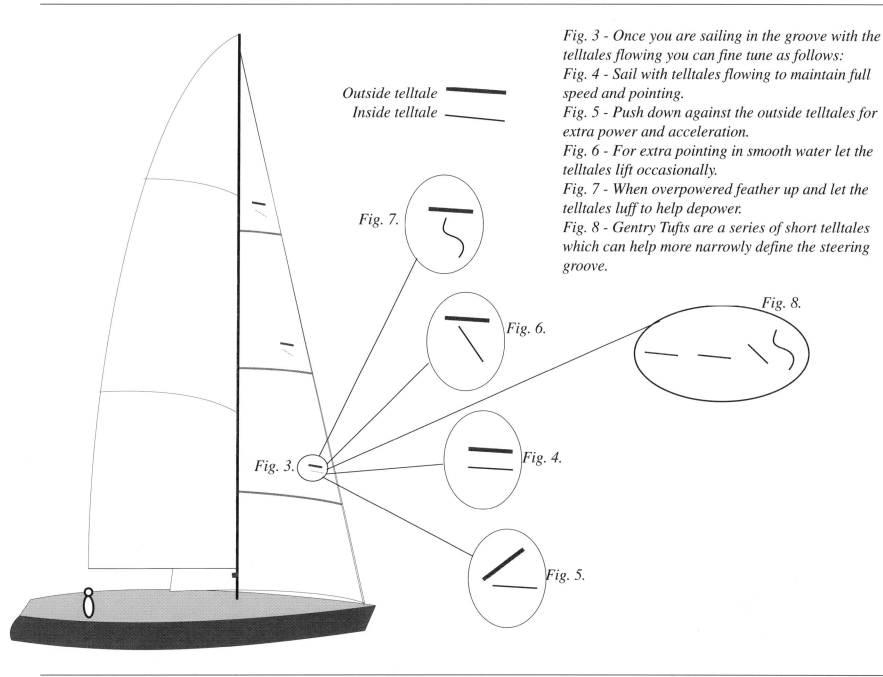

Outside telltale
Inside telltale

Fig. 3 - Once you are sailing in the groove with the telltales flowing you can fine tune as follows:

Fig. 4 - Sail with telltales flowing to maintain full speed and pointing.

Fig. 5 - Push down against the outside telltales for extra power and acceleration.

Fig. 6 - For extra pointing in smooth water let the telltales lift occasionally.

Fig. 7 - When overpowered feather up and let the telltales luff to help depower.

Fig. 8 - Gentry Tufts are a series of short telltales which can help more narrowly define the steering groove.

Fig. 7.

Fig. 8.

Fig. 6.

Fig. 3.

Fig. 4.

Fig. 5.

7.4 Calling Trim from the Helm

It is not enough to simply steer fast. A good driver will also provide feedback to the trimmers to assist in improving trim.

The helmsman has the most direct feel of how the boat is performing. He must help call trim by giving details of the feel of the boat. Is the groove to narrow or too wide? Do you have enough punch in the waves? Do you feel you should be pointing higher? Is the helm properly balanced?

For the trimmers to trim properly the helmsman and trimmers must communicate and understand the relationship between trim, helm, and performance.

Narrow or Forgiving

If the steering groove is narrow and the telltales won't settle down then the jib may be over trimmed or too flat for the conditions (or the helmsman). The easiest way to widen the steering groove is to ease the sheet an inch or two. You can also create a rounder, more forgiving entry shape by tightening the halyard, or sagging the headstay. Fig. 9.

Of course, if you are going fast and pointing high, who cares that the boat is hard to settle. Live with it.

If the steering groove is wide and the boat is not pointing well try a flatter entry shape and narrower slot. Trim the sheet, tighten the headstay, and/or ease the halyard. In smooth water you will be able to steer to a narrower groove than in wavy conditions. Fig. 10.

Proper Power

If the boat feels sluggish, and lacks punch in the chop, the driver must call for more power. Conversely, if the boat is overwhelming the helm you are overpowered.

There are many ways to change the boat's power - through sail shape, twist, and angle of attack for each sail. In Chapter 8 we will look at how to balance each type of power.

Weather Helm

If you are carrying more than 4° of weather helm your trimmers need to know. To reduce weather helm flatten your sails, add twist, or reduce angle of attack by easing the traveler. (Which to do? - see Chapter 8, next for ideas)

Wind & Waves

In heavy air and waves we want to keep the boat in the water and prevent it from pounding through the seas. You do not really steer through the waves. Set the boat up with proper trim and it will find its own best path. Fig. 11.

Weather helm can be used to head the boat up for each face. Rather than force the boat up with the helm the boat should be trimmed with enough weather helm that it heads itself up for each wave. In order to bear off the weather helm will have to be relieved for a moment by lowering the traveler or easing the sheet. To head up pull the traveler up, or trim the sheet. Steering with the sails and using the natural weather helm of the boat is much faster than pushing the boat around with the rudder.

Angle of heel is an excellent guide for steering in these conditions. The proper angle of heel will create appropriate weather helm to match the size and period of the waves.

In short chop it is not possible to get the bow up for each wave. Crank up the power, put the bow down, and crush the chop.

Fig. 9 - With the halyard eased and the sheet trimmed hard the sail will have a narrow high pointing angle of attack.

Fig. 10 - A tighter halyard (and eased sheet) will create a more forgiving angle of attack for easier steering in wavy conditions.

Fig. 11 - A properly trimmed boat will almost steer itself through waves. Trim in enough weather helm to bring the bow up for each swell. In chop this won't work. Just crank up the power, put the bow down, and crush the chop.

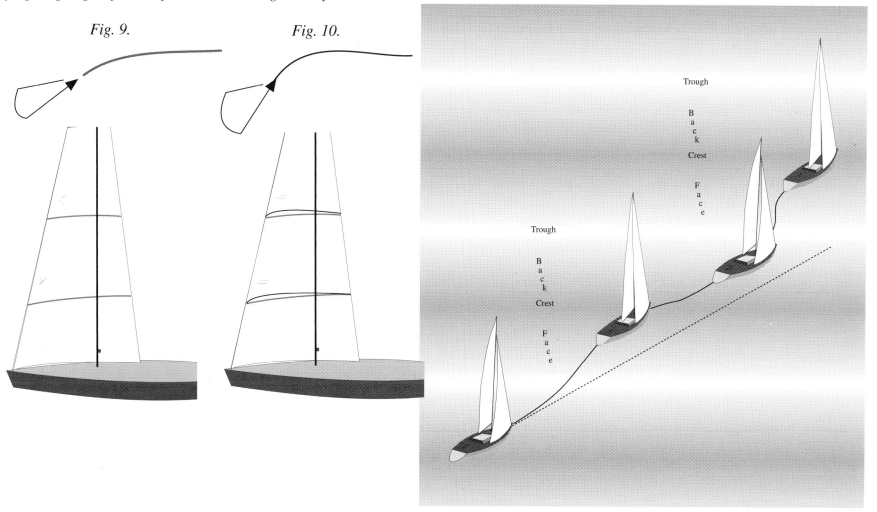

Fig. 9.   Fig. 10.

Turbo Sailing

Point higher without giving up any speed! Enjoy the rewards of Turbo Sailing!

In smooth water beating with the crew on the rail try forcing the boat to point higher. It will, without any loss of speed. Turbo Sailing works best in ideal sailing conditions - smooth water and enough breeze to get the crew fully hiked without being overpowered. Get your boat sailing at normal speed and angle, and then head up slightly. Turbo Sail until the first sign of diminished speed or power; then bear off immediately to power up and rebuild speed. Experiment with trim to find out if extra mainsheet tension or flatter shapes helps you hold the higher angle. And beware the first sign of a lull or chop. Nothing is as slow as trying to Turbo Sail in Non-Turbo conditions.

Turbo Sailing offers improved performance in special conditions. The next time you're racing upwind in smooth water with the crew on the rail give it a try. But don't try to force it when the conditions aren't right. Fig. 12.

7.5 Driving at Starts

Starts are chaos. Driving at starts requires that you focus on factors affecting your start. You should know which way you want to go after the start, and you should know which end of the line is favored. You need to anticipate and keep clear of crowds.

You need proper position against the boats closest to windward. You need to create a space to leeward. You need to keep clear air, and judge the time, speed, and distance to the line. Fig. 13.

Make a Plan

You need a starting plan, and your crew need to be ready to put the plan into play. You must pick a spot on the line, select an approach that will get you there.

Starts require free form boat handling - you never know what will happen next. A well organized and prepared crew will allow you to take advantage of opportunities as they present themselves.

Sail Your Boat

Don't be distracted by the madness around you. Sail your boat. Don't talk to other boats - assign that chore to someone else. Sail your boat. Don't be late, don't be timid, don't worry about the crowds. Work with your trimmers. Sail your boat.

Your tactician should look ahead and tell you where crowds are forming, and what to expect in the next 30 seconds or minute. He should also look behind, and warn you of following traffic.

Your foredeck crew should call the line, signalling distance to go. Trimmers should keep the boat at full speed, and

Fig. 12 - Turbo Sailing involves trimming hard and flat, and sailing slightly higher without any sacrifice in speed. It only works in ideal, smooth water, moderate air conditions.

Fig. 13 - Driving at starts requires timing, judgement, and teamwork. It also requires focus. Sail your boat. Ignore the chaos around you.

avoid the common mistake of overtrimming in the confused seas and disturbed air of the start.

Practice Drills

Starts are hard to practice. It is tough to get enough boats out to get a realistic set up. There are several drills you can use to train for starts.

Stop and Go

From a close hauled course luff you sails and coast to a stop, then trim and accelerate to full speed. How long does it take? How much distance do you cover? Obviously that will vary with the wind and seas. Fig. 14 - next page.

Trimming from a stop it is best to trim the jib first, and following with the main. If the main is trimmed first it tends to push the bow up into the wind, and you will need to pull the bow down with the rudder, which is slow. Trimming the jib first holds the bow down, for better acceleration.

Variations on Stop and Go

Once you are comfortable with the Stop and Go try these variations:

Try trimming while holding hard on the wind, as though there were a boat close to leeward. Also try the Go-Stop-Go. From full speed stop as quickly as you can - push out the main as an air brake - and then accelerate

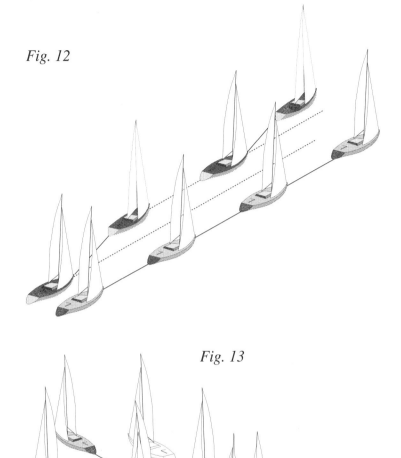

Fig. 12

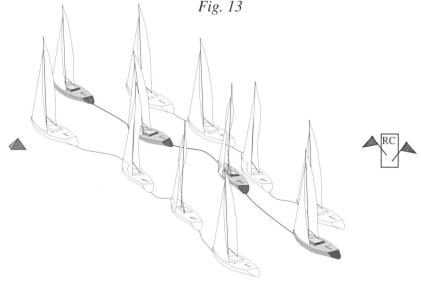

Fig. 13

to full speed again. This can be a handy way to kill time, or to break an overlap so you can dive below a leeward boat.

Practice Approaches

Use a buoy as your chosen starting spot, and practice various approaches to it. From a distance try to guess how long it will take to get to it. With a little practice you can become quite good at this skill, and it is a great help at starts.

More Practice

Try a 360° turn, and see how long it takes. Do you end up where you started?

Also pretend you were over early, and circle back for a restart.

7.6 Upwind Helmsmanship - Conclusion

Helmsmanship is a subtle skill requiring practice and concentration. A relaxed yet acute awareness is needed to be able to sense what is going on with the boat. To build sensitivity practice steering with your eyes closed. Feel the boat through yours hands, seat, hair, feet, and inner ear. Go ahead and laugh, but try it.

The best helmsmen are those who have surrounded themselves with great crew, so they can focus their attention on driving. If you want to be driver, tactician, and sail trimmer then race single handed. If you really want to look around and do tactics, get off the helm. Fig. 15.

If you want answers to the most perplexing problems in upwind performance… turn the page!

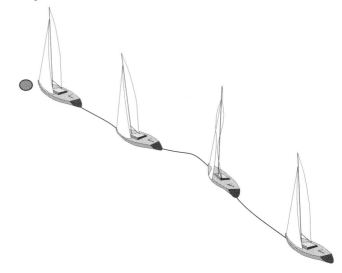

Fig. 14 - The Stop and Go drill is used to practice trimming and accelerating at starts. How long will it take to accelerate to full speed from a luff? How much distance will you cover? Practice to find out.

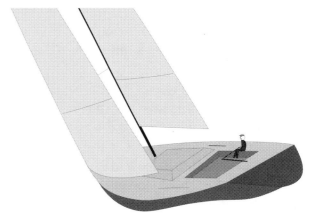

Fig. 15 - The best drivers focus their full attention on driving, and trust their crew to take care of everything else. Great drivers require great crew!

CHAPTER 8 - UPWIND TRIM SOLUTIONS

8.1 INTRODUCTION

8.2 TOTAL POWER TRIM

8.3 MODERATE AIR TRIM

8.4 LIGHT AIR SAILING

8.5 HEAVY AIR TRIM

8.6 TRIM AND TACTICS

8.7 TRIM SOLUTIONS

8.8 SO MANY CHOICES...

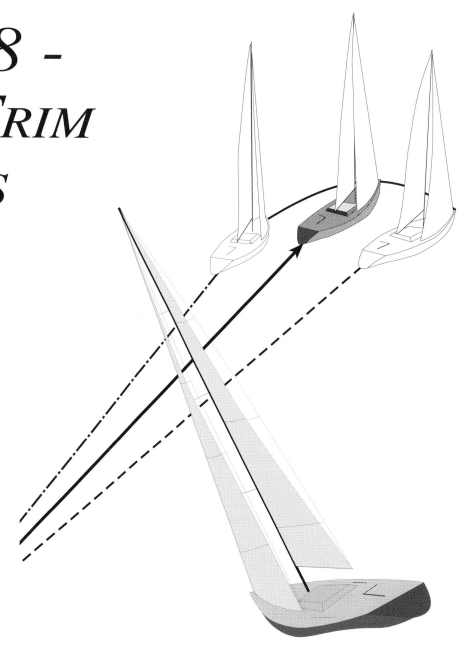

CHAPTER 8 - UPWIND TRIM SOLUTIONS

8.1 Introduction

In this Chapter we will look at various sets of sailing conditions and consider how to trim and steer through them. Our goal is to integrate the ideas of the previous three chapters, on genoas, mains, and driving.

First we will elaborate on the approach to performance which we call *Total Power Trim*. *Total Power Trim* considers the total power generated by the sails, and the three sources of power from each sail. Our trim goal is to generate not just the correct total power, but also the correct mix of power.

We will then apply *Total Power Trim* to moderate air performance. Following that, we'll consider light and heavy winds and various sea states, and how trim will change to suit each. That done, we will also consider special tactical situations - such as starts and bad air - and how to trim for them.

8.2 Total Power Trim

Total Power is the sum of the power from the main and jib. As we will see, the power from each sail is the sum of the power from three sources: angle of attack, sail shape, and twist.

Angle of Attack

This is the first kind of sail power you learn in basic sailing. Trim the sail in, and you add power. Let the sail out and you reduce power. Let it all the way out and it luffs. Turn the boat into the wind and you stop.

A wider angle of attack adds power. Angle of attack is increased by trimming sheets, raising the main traveler, or pulling the jib lead inboard. Angle of attack is also changed through steering. Falling off increases the angle of attack, and power. Heading up reduces the angle of attack, and reduces power.

Angle of attack is our first source of sail power. Fig. 1.

Sail Shape

Deeper sails generate more power. Flatter sails generate less power (and less drag). Sail shape is adjusted through a variety of controls. Mainsail shape is influenced by mast bend and outhaul tension. For jibs, headstay sag and lead position are the controllers of sail depth.

Sail shape is the second source of sail power. Fig. 2.

Twist

A closed leech generates more power. A twisted, or open leech, spills power. The mainsheet and jib sheet are the primary controllers of twist. Initially the sheets' primary impact is angle of attack. As sails near full trim the sheets increasingly pull the clew down (not in). At this point the primary impact of trim is a change in twist. (This assumes the boom vang is not loaded upwind.) The jib lead position also changes twist, for a given sheet tension. To a lesser degree, mast bend, headstay tension, and luff tension also affect twist.

Twist is our third source of sail power. Fig. 3.

Trimming for Total Power

Good sail trim changes with conditions. In Moderate conditions we trim to maximize speed and pointing. Changes in trim often trade one for the other.

THREE SOURCES OF POWER

Fig. 1 - Angle of attack is the first source of power.

Boat A has tight trim, which creates a wide angle of attack, and lots of power.

Boat B's sails are eased, for a narrow angle of attack, which generates less power, and less heeling force.

Fig. 2 - Sail shape is the second source of power.

Boat C has deep sails, for extra power.

Boat De has flat sails, for less power, and less drag.

Fig. 3 - Twist is the third source of power.

Boat E has tight leeches, with little twist, for maximum power.

Boat F has open leeches, or lots of twist, which spills power, and eases flow.

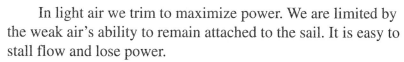
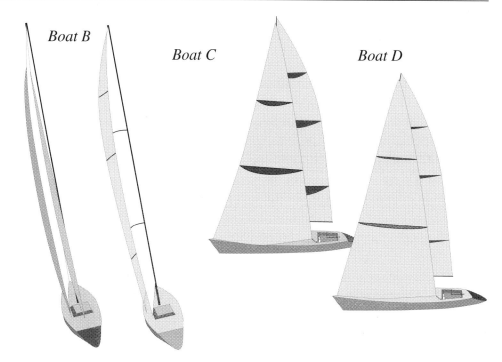
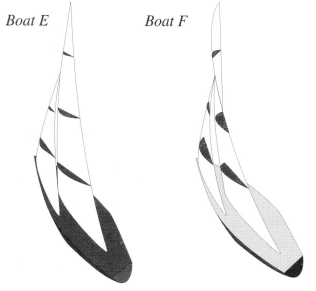

In light air we trim to maximize power. We are limited by the weak air's ability to remain attached to the sail. It is easy to stall flow and lose power.

Heavy air requires that we depower to achieve the correct *total power* and the correct *mix of power*. The mix of power involves the balance of power from the main versus the jib, and the power from each source within each sail.

One general trim note as we head into the details: Match your sails. As you change trim in one sail a similar change should be made in the other. A deep, twisted jib and a flat, tight leeched main won't work well together.

8.3 Moderate Air Trim

We define moderate air as winds which are strong enough to get the crew fully hiked. For some boats this is as little as seven knots of wind. For others a full ten knots is required. Trim becomes a game of trade-offs - maintaining full power by maintaining sufficient total power - trading one source of power for another.

Sail Trim

Angle of attack is managed by the driver in moderate conditions, as we shall see, below.

The trimmers make trade-offs involving sail shape and twist. They will affect our speed and pointing ability. A tight leech (less twist) will add power and improve pointing, but hurt speed. A deeper sail will add power at a sacrifice of pointing. A deep sail with little twist will stall - you can't have it all. A flat, open sail will provide neither speed nor pointing ability.

Across the spectrum of moderate winds sail trim options improve as the breeze increases. At the upper end of the moderate range you can have it all - sailing at full speed and pointing well. Trim here requires sufficient depth to keep the crew fully hiked, with the leech as tight as possible short of a stall.

The optimum mix of shape and twist is a function of sea state. More shape will be needed in more chop. A flatter, tight leeched sail will provide both full speed and great pointing in smooth water. Similarly, coming out of tacks, extra shape will help the boat build speed, and extra twist will be needed to prevent a stall. As full speed is achieved the sail can be flattened and the leech closed to carry the speed closer to the wind. Fig. 4.

Driving

Moderate air driving revolves around subtle efforts to cheat up slightly without loss of speed. The driver manipulates angle of attack to attempt to sail up - carrying speed and remaining sensitive to any loss of power. As power slips the driver pushes the bow down to widen angle of attack, rebuild power, and maintain speed.

The driver is guided by the feel of the boat and by the jib telltales.

Jib Telltales

The sailing groove in moderate winds is divided into acceleration, full speed, and high point sections. Fig. 5.

The acceleration sector is the lowest pointing sector. The driver pushes the boat down - for a wider angle of attack, and extra power - whenever the boat is slow. Coming out of tacks, or after bashing a bad set of waves, the driver will sail with the telltales flowing and the *outside telltale* dancing. By pushing down until the outside telltale is active (not stall) you maximize sail power. In addition to sailing low the sheets may be eased slightly in this mode.

As you approach full speed the driver brings the boat up slightly. The sheets should now be fully trimmed. With the telltales flowing straight back the boat will maintain full speed.

Once at full speed the driver can sneak the boat up slightly into point mode. The inside telltale will lift and the boat will lose some degree of power. If the power loss is not too great you will be able to hold full speed at this higher angle. If not, then slide back down to speed mode and try again. Don't get too greedy in point mode. You don't want to lose speed, and be forced all the way down to acceleration mode to rebuild speed - you'll be giving back all the height you gained.

If the inside telltale starts to dance and spin then you are not in point mode - you are pinching. Stop it.

Fig. 4 - In moderate winds we trim to a narrow angle of attack - pointing high, with the boom to the centerline. Changes in sail depth and twist control the mix of power, with flatter shapes with closed leeches in smooth water, and extra depth and twist in waves.

Boat A - In smooth water trim with flatter sails and little twist.
Boat B - In chop add depth for power, and add twist for consistent power as the boat pitches in the waves.

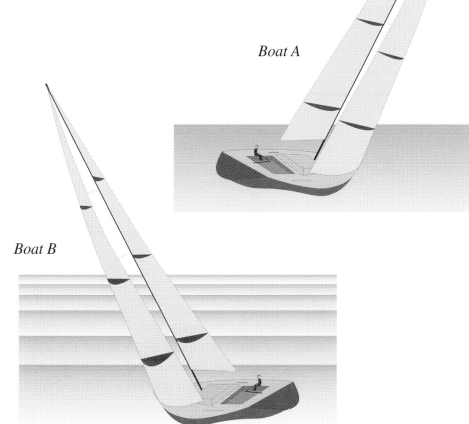

Boat A

Boat B

Fig. 5 - For full speed sailing the telltales will be streaming. For extra pointing the inside telltale will lift. For extra power drive down until the outside telltale starts to dance.

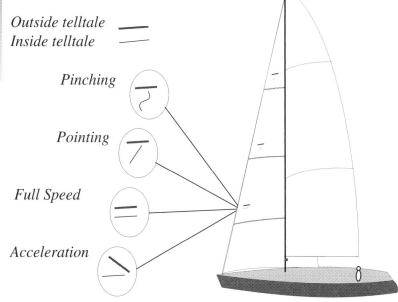

Outside telltale
Inside telltale

Pinching

Pointing

Full Speed

Acceleration

8.4 Light Air Sailing

In light conditions, with crew inboard, we seek all the power we can get. In more moderate winds the trimmers can guide the driver, and assist in the subtle improvements which differentiate good from the great performance.

In light air the driver leads, and the trimmers follow - adjusting to changes in sailing angle, true wind, and apparent wind, which are too severe for the driver to keep up with.

Driving

Our first goal is speed, and the lighter the winds the more aggressive the driver will need to be to increase angle of attack to add power. After you foot off to build speed you can come up to try to point as well.

Sail the telltales in the full speed mode - both sides flowing - when sailing in light air. Don't try to point. Footing off into acceleration mode can easily lead to a stall. It is best to ease the sail as you bear off, rather than push the low end of the sail.

Sail Trim

The big variable is angle of attack. Depending on how light the wind, the sheet may be eased a foot or more from full moderate air trim. Build speed. Sail fast. Normally we'd say *speed first, then pointing*. In light air its, *speed first, speed second, and then pointing*

Wind speed and angle are volatile in light air. The trimmers will be busy with the sheet trying to keep up. The goal is to maximize power while maintaining flow. An over trimmed sail with a wide angle of attack will stall at the luff, with no air flow. If the sail is too deep, the flow will not hold. Likewise, if the leech is too tight, the flow will stall. You can trade one

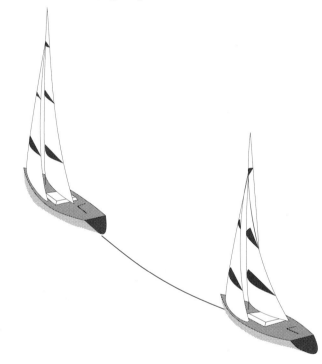

Fig. 6 - In light air use a deep sail shape to generate power, sufficient twist to prevent a stall, and a wide angle of attack for acceleration. As speed builds head up while trimming to reduce twist and maintain angle of attack.

power for the other. In light air an emphasis on deep shapes and open leeches is the place to start. Fig. 6.

As the wind diminishes flatter shapes are called for. You read right. *In extremely light air flatter sail shapes are needed*, as the wind will not have the strength to remain attached to a deep shape.

8.5 Heavy Air Sailing

Strong winds, beyond those needed to fully power the boat, provide small incremental improvements in upwind performance. In fact, at the very high end, you reach a point where upwind VMG goes down as the wind goes up, due to increased windage and seas. Once we are fully powered performance improvements hinge on the ability to reduce drag.

Fighting Drag

Deep sails, luffing sails, and overtrimmed sails are all sources of drag. Excess weather helm creates enormous rudder drag. Likewise, excess heel is a source of increased drag. Flat sails, trimmed to avoid luffing, are the lowest drag configuration.

Backwinding, as differentiated from luffing, is not a problem. At times the main can carry a bubble in excess of half its area. This is preferable to trimming out the bubble and generating excessive heeling force. At the point where the choice becomes flogging the main or carrying excess heel and helm, then less sail area would be more efficient. Try lots of twist, and perhaps an outboard jib lead, until you have a chance to change down.

Total Power

Correct total power can be achieved a number of ways. As winds increase sail power will need to be reduced. First try flatter sails, then increase twist, finally, reduce angle of attack. Fig. 7.

For a given wind speed trim balance will vary based on sea state. In smoother water flat sails with closed leeches provide the lowest drag, best speed, and highest pointing. In wavy conditions more sail shape is needed for power through the waves. More twist widens the sailing groove and prevents being overpowered.

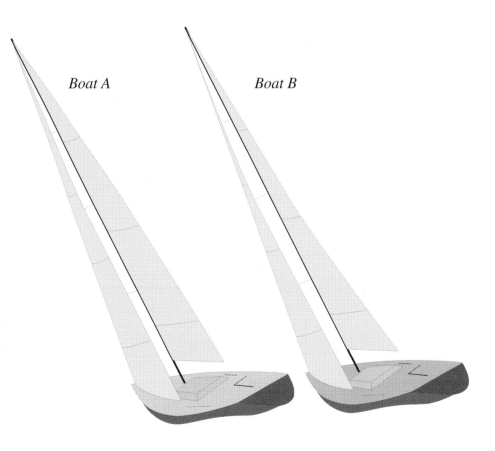

Fig. 7 - In heavy air we reduce power, first by flattening sails, then through twist, and finally by reducing angle of attack. The exact balance of each source of power depends on the characteristics of the boat and the sea state.
Boat A has flat sails and little twist. As winds increase twist is increased to spill power, as on Boat B.

Boat A   Boat B

Correct trim is found through testing, trying to maintain as much speed and height (pointing) as conditions allow. If pointing is poor try more sheet trim, particularly on the main. If the boat is pitching the quickest solution is to foot off while adding shape and twist.

Try to achieve proper power without compromising angle of attack. Focus on flat sails and twist before dumping the traveler (or moving the leads outboard). Reducing angle of attack often results in lower pointing. Keep control, while keeping the boat up on the wind. Fig. 7.

Driving

Driving in heavy air centers on feathering to reduce power while keeping speed. The jib telltales should stand up, or even luff, on the inside. The boat should be sailed at a constant angle of heel to control weather helm. This is much more critical than the telltale activity.

If the boat is very hard to steer it is out of trim. The section below on *Trim Solutions* addresses many types of steering problems, and possible solutions.

8.6 Trim and Tactics

There are plenty of occasions when the trim you might use for best straight line upwind performance will need to be altered to suit the prevailing tactical circumstances. We'll look at few such situations here.

Starts

Disturbed air, chopped up water, changing speeds. All suggest adding power. A deeper sail shape will give you power, while extra twist will help with acceleration. As the boat reaches full speed and clear air off the line, flatter, less twisted shapes will provide better pointing while maintaining speed. Fig. 8.

Pinch Mode

There are plenty of times when height becomes the priority - either because there is a boat threatening to leeward, or you want to squeeze off a boat to windward.

Trim the sheet, *but do not flatten the sails.* Deep, closed leech sails will point high, though you will sacrifice speed. (Yes, in full power conditions flatter sails have less drag and higher pointing potential than deep shapes, but if you have the correct shape for the prevailing conditions adding mastbend and reducing sag will open your leeches - which hurts pointing.) Trim harder - which adds power. Rather than balance that through flatter sail shape reduce power by reducing angle of attack instead - pinch up! You'll be slow, but high. Fig. 9.

Bad Air

When footing out from bad air your interest is speed, not height. Add twist as you bear off, and add depth to compensate for the lighter (disturbed) air. Fig. 10.

Fig. 8 - Starting trim requires extra power. Deeper sails, with extra twist, create the best shape for acceleration.

Fig. 9 - Boat A: To pinch up trim the sheets to reduce twist.
Fig. 10 - Boat B: To foot out from bad air add twist and depth.

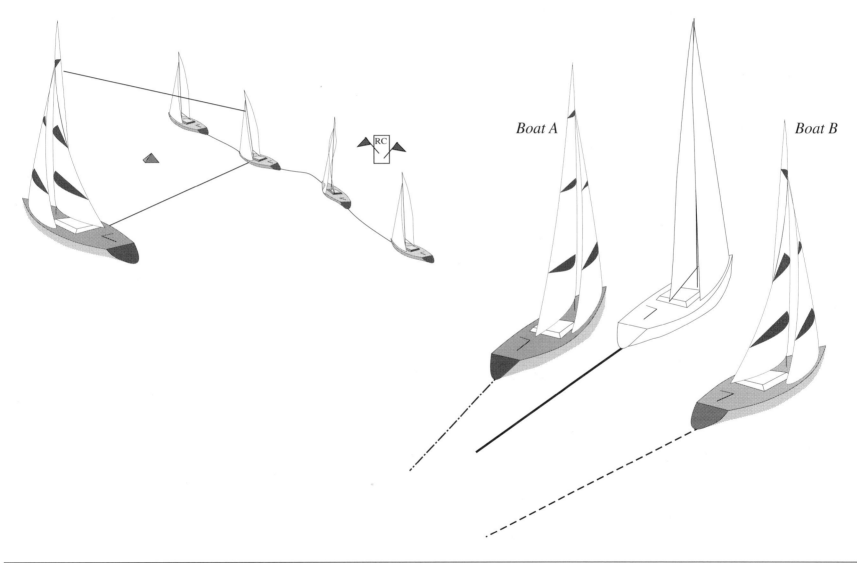

Boat A

Boat B

8.7 Trim Solutions

Following are a guidelines for dealing with performance problems. There are lots of variables to wrestle with; the answers here may *not* be right, but we hope the approach is. Keep trying, keep testing, keep searching for the mix which matches the sailing conditions. Once you find it congratulate yourself, take a deep breath, and get back to work - conditions have changed.

If you are…

…Slow - pointing OK, but not going fast.

Then try adding depth for extra power, and perhaps add some twist for easier flow….

Or try sailing with fairly deep sail shape and hard sheet trim. This is a max power setting. Carry this trim to the point of nearly stalling the main. Generally, anything which adds power will be a performance improvement - if you can control it. 110% hiking effort helps here, as does careful feathering to keep the boat fully powered, and no more. Fig. 11.

Slows may be due to excess drag, from too deep a sail shape. Flatter sails, sheeted harder, may give you the same power, with less drag.

Try pushing more load to the jib by trimming a little harder on the jib sheet (while perhaps dropping the lead aft slightly). Then sail a touch low in the groove. Press down until the *outside* lower telltale begins to dance. With extra power in the jib (through wider angle of attack) the main may need to be flattened or twisted to compensate.

In light air foot off to build speed, and then work your way up.

Fig. 11 - Slow?
Boat A is slow.
Boat B has increased power with more sail depth. They may also need to add twist.
Boat C is trying more jib trim and less main.

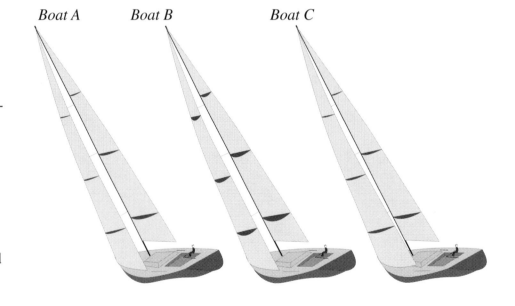

Boat A   *Boat B*   *Boat C*

...Low - and just can't point

Then sheet harder - you have too much twist. You may
need to flatten the sail shape as you trim out twist.

Try more main and less jib. It is common, when overpowered, to spill power by lowering the main traveler. The
danger here is a loss of pointing ability. It is better to
keep the main trimmed and feather the boat, or depower
the jib while keeping the main leech firm. Boats with
relatively small keels are particularly susceptible to
pointing problems when the main is dumped. Playing
the traveler in puffy conditions can be effective, but you
must be sure to pull the main up again after the initial
blast of each puff. Fig. 12.

Change to a bigger genoa. At the low end of a genoa you
can keep speed, but lack the power to point. Change up.

...Slow and Low -

Then start over. Usually this is a sign of being over
trimmed. The first step out of this mess is to get speed,
so you are low and fast. Then you can work on pointing.
Ease the sheets to build some speed. You may also have
too much sail shape and the jib leads may be too far
forward, creating too much drag. Fig. 13.

Is your bottom clean? Is your driving coaching the spinnaker hook up, or calling tactics?

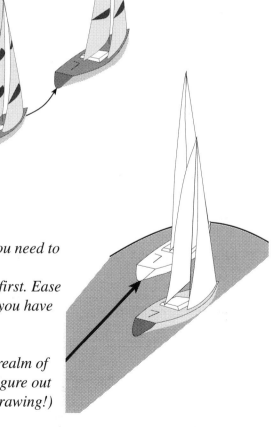

Fig. 12 - Can' Point?
Less twist should help. Trim the sheets. You may need to flatten
sail shapes as you reduce twist.
Or try more main and less jib. Trim the main harder - or pull
up the traveler if you are below centerline - and sail with the
jib telltales a little soft.

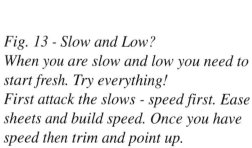

Fig. 13 - Slow and Low?
When you are slow and low you need to
start fresh. Try everything!
First attack the slows - speed first. Ease
sheets and build speed. Once you have
speed then trim and point up.

(No diagram can capture the realm of
possibilities here. When you figure out
the solution insert your own drawing!)

...Rounding Up

Then you are overpowered. Reduce power one way or
    another. The source you reduce depends on your speed
    and pointing between roundups.
Try more twist for starters, as twist will reduce the helm
    load right away. Fig. 14.

...Mushy Helm

Add speed, add power. Often a mushy helm makes it
    difficult to point. Ease sails for speed, and then trim up.
    Add more sail shape to the point of nearly stalling the
    main. If the main does stall try a little twist to encourage
    flow. Fig. 15.
If you've got a bigger jib available, then change.
If your performance is good, then live with it.

*Fig. 14- Boat A is overpowered and rounding up
uncontrollably. Boat B, with more twist, is under control.*

Boat A   Boat B

*Fig. 15 - Mushy Helm.
Add power. In light air it can help to add
heel. Or, if performance it good, live with it.
(Welcome to J-Boat racing.)*

Fig. 16 - Hyper critical groove.
If you can't settle the boat in the groove ease the genoa sheet a couple inches, tighten the halyard, or sag the headstay. (Or change drivers.)

Boat A: Narrow steering groove. Boat B: Wide steering groove

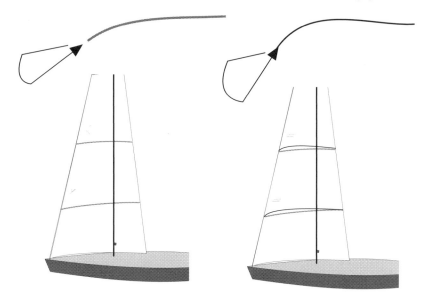

Fig. 17 - Hyper critical power.
Upright and slow one moment, slammed down the next? Try more twist. Twist allows power to come on and off more gradually. With insufficient twist you get all or nothing.

…Hyper critical groove, with the inside telltales spinning one moment, and the outside telltales dancing the next.

There are two ways to widen the steering groove. The textbook solution is a tighter halyard, to pull the draft forward and round the entry. Fig. 16.

Often a more effective solution is to ease the genoa sheet a couple of inches. Sagging the headstay can also help. Of course, if you are pointing high and going fast you might want to consider another alternative: Live with it.

…Hyper critical power. Slammed down one moment, upright and luffing the next? Just can't settle on a constant course and angle of heel?

Then try more twist. What is happening is that the entire sail plan is filling and dumping. Adding twist will give a more gradual onset of power. Move the jib leads back and ease the main sheet (while pulling up the traveler).

In puffy conditions aggressive sheet or traveler work can also make the difference. Sometimes the genoa alone is too much sail in a puff. Try a smaller jib and more powerful main; then play the main aggressively in the puffs. Fig. 17.

If a jib change is inconvenient at the moment try extreme twist, with the leads way back and the top of the genoa completely open.

…Pitching

Then you need more power. You are sailing too high or your sails are too flat. Foot off. Adding speed is the surest way to power through waves. Add depth in the sails for extra punch, and add twist to create a wide sailing groove and control heel. We assume here that you have already done all you can to get weight out of the ends of your boat - particularly the bow and rig. You still have an anchor and sails in the bow? Never mind… Fig. 18.

…Pounding in the waves

Try adding twist to provide power through the entire range of motion of the boat, and try moving crew weight around. The crew should be packed together, hip to hip, on the rail. Adjust fore and aft positioning. Often moving crew weight forward will keep the bow in the water and reduce pounding. At other times moving the crew aft will alter the pitching moment of the boat and reduce the pounding. Fig. 18 (again).

…Unable to point in bow-on waves

Waves often don't run square to the wind. At times, one tack you will be more bow-on to the waves, while the other tack will be beam-on. Trim will differ.

Generally, in wavy conditions, you need twist to keep power through the pitching. Tight leeched sails have a narrow working range. Twisted sails can handle the variable apparent wind angles which result from the motion of sailing through waves. Fig. 19.

For pointing trouble in bow-on waves one trick is speed. Trim with twist to keep speed, and you will may solve you pointing problems. If the wave length is long enough then foot off and build speed on the back of the waves, and then head up to make quick work up the face of the waves. Truth is, this rarely works, as the wave length is often too short to allow so much steering. You'll read about this technique more than you'll actually do it.

Weather helm can help you point in waves. When you can't steer through every wave you want to trim the boat to steer itself. *A properly trimmed boat will find its own best path through the waves.* The trick is to trim with enough weather helm for the boat to head itself up in balance to the force of the waves pushing the bow down.

Even if you can't steer through the waves you may be able to trim through them. Play the traveler (or mainsheet if it is fast enough) to steer the boat. You want to generate weather helm as you approach the face of each wave, to counter the force of the wave pushing the bow down. Ease trim and reduce weather helm to foot off between waves and build speed (and power). You can trim through chop which is too narrow to steer through.

Another solution: Never mind pointing. Sail fast and crush the waves. You'll make up for the extra distance with the extra speed.

…Unable to point in beam-on waves

When the waves are from the beam, or nearly so, the bow tends to wash down with each passing wave. To hold the bow up, and maintain pointing ability, add weather helm. The weather helm will hold the bow up. You add helm by adding power, particularly to the main. Either extra depth or extra sheet trim may do the trick. In lighter winds extra heel will induce helm - move some crew inboard. Once you are fully powered generate helm with trim, and generate all the power you can control with the crew fully hiked. Fig. 20.

Fig. 18 - Pitching and Pounding.
When you are pitching you need to add power to push through the waves. You need to conquer the up and down forces with forward force. You may need to foot off to build speed. Twist gives consistent power through the full range of motion.

When pitching results in pounding the boat can stop dead in its tracks. You need all the power you can muster. Also, move crew weight around to change the pitching moment of the boat. Keep everyone packed together, and move them fore and aft as a group.

Fig. 19 - In Bow-on waves, trim with plenty of twist and depth. Twist to equalize power as you pitch, and depth to provide sufficient power to fight the waves.

Fig. 20 - In Bean-on waves, trim with less twist, particularly in the main. You must maintain sufficient weather helm to prevent the bow from being washed down with each passing wave.

8.8 So Many Choices...

One lesson of this exercise it to provide specific solutions to particular performance problems. The more general (and perhaps enduring) message is that there are plenty of variables to work with - keep fiddling. Remember that you want not only correct *total power*, but the correct *mix of power* as well. Fig. 21.

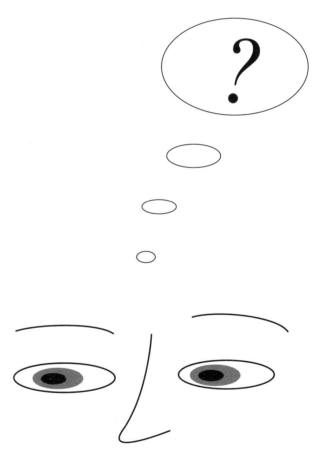

Fig. 21 - Say What? With so many choices it is impossible to remember exactly what to do when. Who knows what will work, anyhow? Just remember, you can change the power three ways in each sail, and you can change the balance between the main and jib. And you can change your driving style. Keep juggling until you figure it out...

CHAPTER 9 - DOWNWIND BOAT HANDLING

9.1 INTRODUCTION

9.2 SPINNAKER SETS

9.3 SPINNAKER JIBES

9.4 SPINNAKER TAKE DOWNS

9.5 SPINNAKER PEELS

9.6 NOTES ON HALYARDS

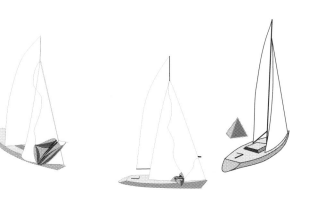

CHAPTER 9 - DOWNWIND BOAT HANDLING

9.1 Introduction

Nothing takes as much teamwork and practice as spinnaker handling. This chapter covers the skills and techniques needed to handle and control the beast. Later, in Chapter 11, we'll look at how to trim it.

This chapter is devoted to conventional spinnakers, set from poles. The next chapter covers asymmetrical spinnakers set from sprits. After reading that chapter you may well decide to switch.

Throughout the discussion the *Divide and Conquer* approach to boat handling will be central: One team sails the boat with the sails you've got, while the other team handles the mechanics of the set, jibe, or douse. Fig. 1

Note: The material presented here is so accurate and complete that no practice is necessary. Simply read the appropriate section aloud to your crew, and you will be ready to go.

Fig. 1 - One key to successful boat handling is the Divide and Conquer approach: One group sails the boat with the sails you've got, while the other team handles the set, jibe, or douse.

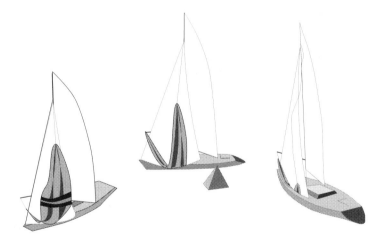

9.2 Spinnaker Sets

All spinnaker sets starts with careful packing and proper hook up. Most spinnakers can be packed by running the luff tapes to make sure the sail is not twisted as it is packed into the turtle. Large spinnakers and heavy air spinnakers can be set in *stops*. Stops are rubber bands or weak yarn placed around the spinnaker at three foot intervals. To use rubber bands the spinnaker is fed through a *spinnaker gun*, or bottom-less bucket, loaded with rubber bands. Fig. 2.

Regardless of how the spinnaker is packed the head and two clews should be secured at the top of the turtle. The hook up requires check and rechecking to make sure the halyard and sheets are not twisted or fouled. Fig. 3.

Bear Away Set

A bear away set is the simplest. You set the pole as you approach the mark close-hauled, bear away to a reach, and hoist.

On most boats the sail is set from the leeward rail, forward of the shrouds. On some boats the spinnaker can be rigged to hoist from the companionway or forward hatch. Do not hoist from the bow. Setting the spinnaker from the bow moves too much crew and equipment weight forward.

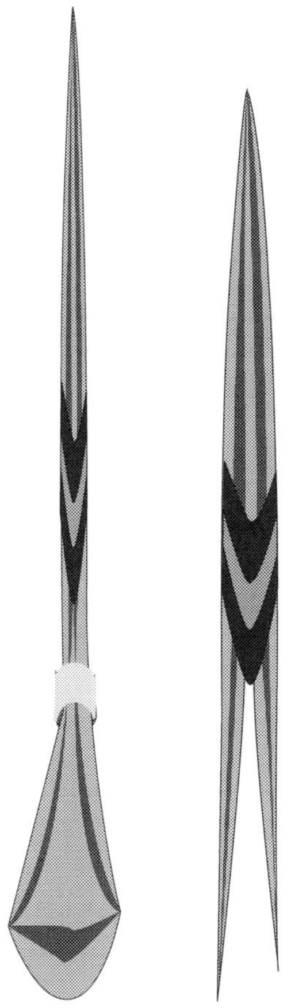

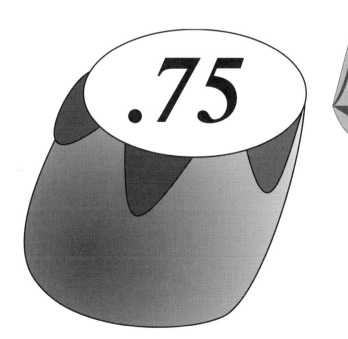

Fig. 2 - Pack your spinnaker carefully. Heavy air spinnaker can be set in stops, which prevent them from filling during the hoist. Stops can be set straight, or in a "frog leg."

Fig. 3 - Pack the chute in a turtle, with the head and clews secured at the top.

Pre Rig

Prior to the start of the race, or during the windward leg of a race, you should position the spinnaker sheets and halyard to the appropriate side for the hoist, and pre rig the spinnaker pole. The pole should be positioned on the bow with the guy, topping lift, and downhaul/foreguy pre-rigged.

The pole can be set to the mast track if the track runs all the way to the deck, so as not to interfere with tacks. Otherwise, the pole can be secured to the shrouds. Fig. 4ab.

Pre-rigging the guy simply means setting the guy through the pole jaw, making sure it is not twisted or macramed through the lifelines.

Pre-rig the downhaul with a preset amount of slack so that when you pull up the pole to take out the slack the pole will be at a good height for the hoist.

Pre-rig the topping lift to the pole and pull it back against the rig to keep it clear of the jib during tacks. Secure the pole through the jaw at the inboard end of the pole. If there is no inboard jaw (as on a dip pole rig) then you'll have to fashion another way to hold the toppinglift back. A shackle or sail tie can work fine. Avoid hooks, which may grab things other than the toppinglift.

Set Up

The hook up should be carried out with a minimum of disruption. If you pre rigged carefully there will be no need to slack sheets to hook up. The pit crew should bring the halyard tail to the rail so it can be eased as needed with a minimum of crew movement. Your spinnaker gear should be set up so you do not need to involve the trim team in your efforts. If you need to ask the driver or trimmers to ease the spinnaker gear then change your set up. Divide and Conquer. Fig. 5a.

Hook up the spinnaker sheets and halyard while in proper hiking position to windward. Usually this means the final port tack for a starboard tack set. Hook up the halyard at the same time you do the sheets. There is a danger, when you tack, that the genoa will fetch up against the spinnaker halyard and pull the spinnaker out of the bag. To prevent this pull lots of slack in the halyard. Prior to the tack hold the slack to keep the halyard from fouling on the spreaders. As you tack the slack halyard will sag out to leeward, clear of the genoa.

In heavier going the sail may wash out of the bag on a long approach tack. Try securing the spinnaker bag to the middle of the foredeck or at the mast base to keep it out of the water, and tie the bag securely shut after the hook up. Open the bag just prior to the hoist.

When you tack on the layline *do not immediately set the pole*. If time allows, hike out (or lie still) until the boat is up to full speed, then set the pole. Once you are up to speed (and you are sure you will fetch) the foredeck crew can go forward and lift the pole into place. The pit crew, working from the rail with the toppinglift tail in hand, should pull the slack out of the topping lift. *There is no need to get off the rail to tail the toppinglift. Bring it with you on the last tack and tail from the rail*. Fig. 5b.

A couple of additional details deserve mention: It is a good idea to review who will do what on the hoist, just to be sure; and make sure the jib halyard is cleared, flaked, and ready to drop.

Fig. 4a - Pre-rig your spinnaker gear. Position your sheets and halyard for the expected hoist, lead the guy through the end of the pole, attach the topping lift and downhaul, and secure the pole either at the base of the shrouds (as shown here), or at the bottom of the track on the mast (fig 4b).

Fig. 4b - On boats with double sheets and guys the guy should be shackled to the sheet, with the sheet eventually attached to the spinnaker. Here we see the pole pre-rigged to the mast track. Note also the slack in the foreguy, preset to a proper initial setting.

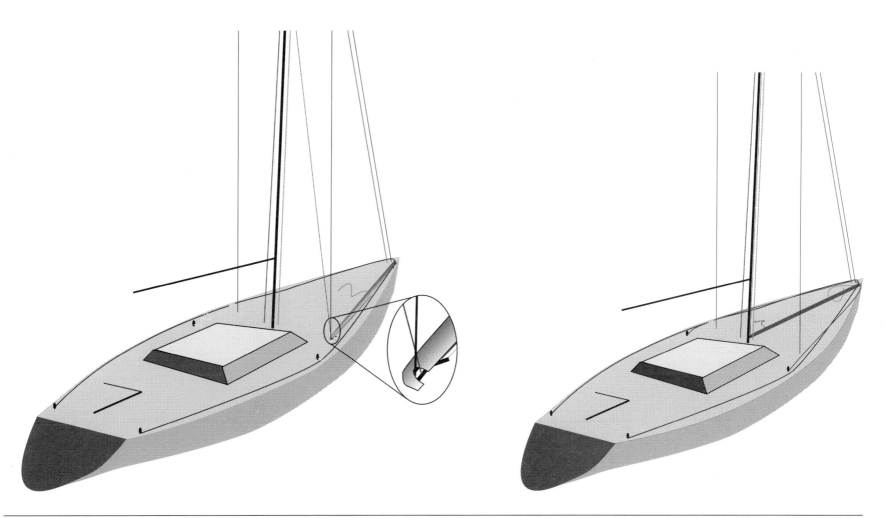

The Hoist

Coming into the mark you will need to decide if an immediate hoist is correct tactically, or if there would be an advantage to close reaching initially with the jib. If you are going to close reach then keep hiking until the hoist is called.

On the hoist the guy must be pulled aft to prevent twists as the sail goes up. If you are going for an immediate hoist at the mark, you can pre-pull the guy as you approach the mark. Fig. 5c.

The sheet should not be trimmed until the halyard is at full hoist. As you near full hoist the guy can be trimmed off the headstay to a position perpendicular to the wind. During the hoist the main and jib must be eased to maintain proper trim and speed. Fig. 5d.

Once the chute is up the jib should be dropped. In light to moderate air the genoa should be on its way down as the spinnaker hoist tops out. In heavy air simply ease the jib sheet and wait until the boat settles with the spinnaker. When the boat is under control go forward and douse the jib - or leave it flying as a staysail is if adds speed! Fig. 5e.

If there is a delay with the spinnaker hoist, keep sailing with the main and jib and the loss will be minimized.

FIG. 5 - BEAR AWAY SPINNAKER SET

Fig. 5a - Hook up the spinnaker prior to your last tack into the mark. Note the extra slack in the halyard, which prevents the jib from pulling the spinnaker out of the bag on the tack.

Fig. 5b - If time allows, allow the boat to get up to speed out of the tack before you set the pole. The pit crew should carry the tail of the topping lift to the rail so it will not be necessary to leave the rail to raise the pole lift.

Fig. 5c - As the bow reaches the mark pre-pull the guy to the pole.

Fig. 5d - Do not trim the spinnaker sheet until the spinnaker is all the way up. Be sure to ease the main and jib - sail fast with what you've got!

Fig. 5e - In light to moderate conditions drop the genoa as soon as the spinnaker is all the way up. In heavy air ease the jib sheet, but don't drop it right away. Don't venture forward until the boat is under control.

BEAR AWAY SPINNAKER SET

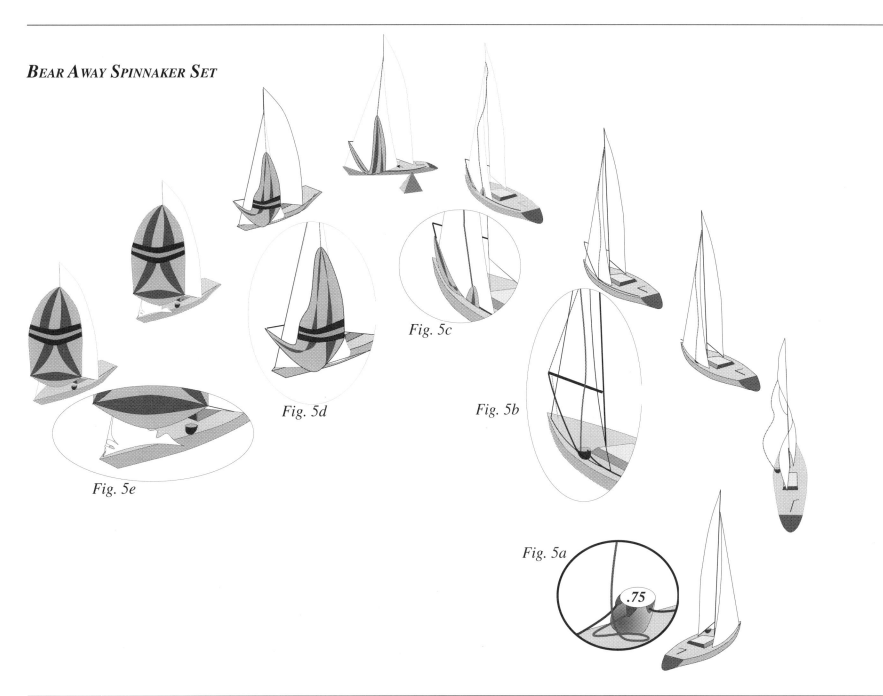

Fig. 5c

Fig. 5d

Fig. 5b

Fig. 5e

Fig. 5a

.75

Jibe Set

Use a jibe set when the spinnaker leg is on the opposite tack as the rounding. For example, marks to port leading to a port tack spinnaker leg. Jibe sets are more difficult than bear away sets because you cannot preset the pole. You must wait until jibe. There are several additional details critical to a successful jibe set.

We'll assume here marks to port. We'll be approaching the mark on starboard, bearing away, and jibing to sail the next leg on a port broad reach.

Hook up the spinnaker just aft of the bow pulpit, on the starboard rail. The pole should be set up on the port side of the forestay - for port tack - with topping lift, downhaul, and guy in place. Take care to make sure the guy is not fouled. The topping lift can be rigged under the jib sheets, as it typically is in pre-race set up. (Alternatively, it can be rigged outboard of the jib to port - if it is long enough.)

As you round the mark and bear away start the hoist. At the same time, pull the sheet (on the starboard side) just far enough to separate the spinnaker clews. Wait to trim to fill until the sail is up and the guy is trimmed. Continue to bear away, and jibe. Make sure you jibe the jib and ease the old (port) jib sheet so you will be able to raise the spinnaker pole.

Once the jib is jibed, raise the pole as you continue to hoist. Once the pole is up, trim the guy square with the wind. As soon the halyard tops out, trim the sheet, and drop the jib. Fig. 6.

Sample Seven Crew Jibe Set Plan

A jibe set requires carefully coordinated crew work. Many crew have two tasks in the process. Practice is suggested.

Following is a sample list of how a seven person crew might make it work. Govt. warning: Obviously the details depend a little on how the boat is laid out - your performance may differ.

Foredeck: Make sure the set up is clean. Pull the jib through the jibe, and then lift the spinnaker pole into place. Finally, pull down the jib.

Mast: Jump the spinnaker halyard. Help gather the jib.

Pit: Hoist the spinnaker, drop the jib.

Port Trimmer: Ease the jib sheet as you bear away, dump it on the jibe. Tail the topping lift.

Starboard Trimmer: Trim the jib sheet on the jibe. Pull the spinnaker sheet to separate the clews on the hoist, and then trim the sheet at full hoist.

Main Trimmer: Ease, and then jibe, the main. Trim the guy once the pole is up.

Driver: Drive. Jibe and settle. Watch for traffic.

No Pole?

You can execute a jibe set with no pole rigged. Sometimes it is faster and cleaner this way, particularly if the decision to jibe set was a late one, and you don't have time to make sure the pole is hooked up cleanly.

In this variation the foredeck crew acts as the pole, hand holding the guy outboard until the mast crew can hook up and set the pole.

Tack Set

Tack sets are similar to jibe sets, as they do not allow complete preparation before the set. When tacking around the mark the spinnaker pole cannot be set until the tack is complete. Fig. 7.

Prepare the spinnaker as usual, and hook up the pole but do not raise it. Set the heel of the pole on the mast, but leave

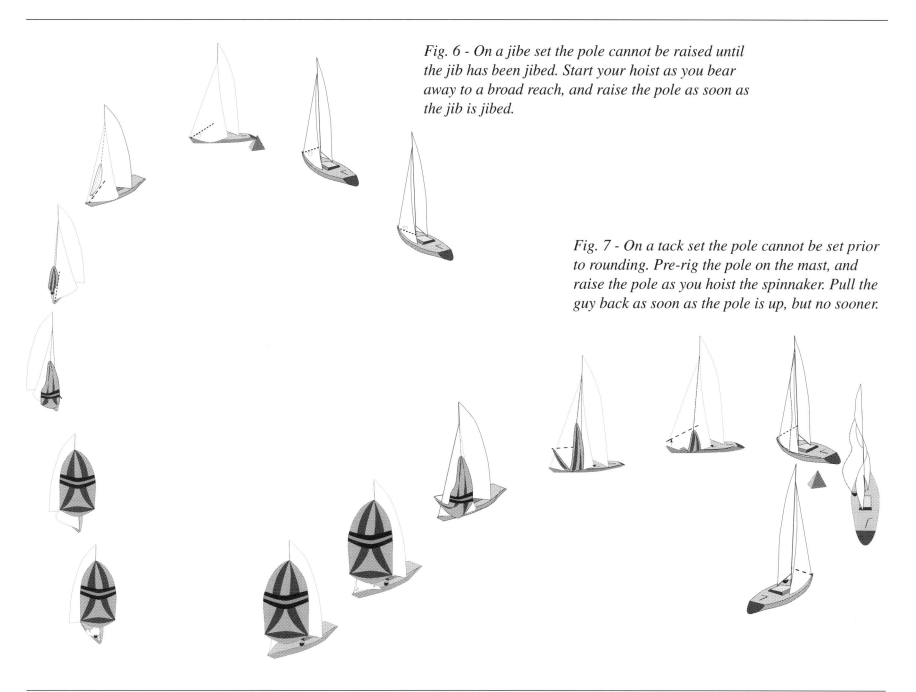

Fig. 6 - On a jibe set the pole cannot be raised until the jib has been jibed. Start your hoist as you bear away to a broad reach, and raise the pole as soon as the jib is jibed.

Fig. 7 - On a tack set the pole cannot be set prior to rounding. Pre-rig the pole on the mast, and raise the pole as you hoist the spinnaker. Pull the guy back as soon as the pole is up, but no sooner.

the nose on the deck so the jib can be tacked over it. As you round the mark coordinate to raise the pole and hoist the spinnaker simultaneously. Have the foredeck crew lift the pole while the guy trimmer tails the topping lift. Tension on the guy will prevent the pole from going up, so do not pull the guy until the pole is set. Meanwhile, the mast crew can jump the halyard while the pit crew tails.

Building speed with the main and jib as you hoist the spinnaker is critical to a successful tack set. Proper trim can prevent you being passed by boats carrying a full head of steam into the mark.

Bow Tricks

When working the bow there are many details which can make you job safer and easier. Here are a few:

Pulling down a genoa: The foredeck crew should pull the sail down at the luff so it will drop quickly. The mast crew should *sit down* on the foredeck at mid foot and gather the sail on board. Do not grab the clew, as it can pull you overboard, and don't worry if the clew hangs over the lifelines. Pull it aboard after you get the entire sail down.

Hoisting a genoa: Drape the clew over the leeward lifelines just prior to starting the hoist. As the sail goes up it will luff, making for an easy hoist. With the clew inside the lifelines the sail will start to fill as it blows against the lifelines, slowing your hoist.

9.3 Spinnaker Jibes

Practice, practice, practice.

There are two basic jibing techniques: End-for-end jibes for smaller boats and dip-pole jibes for larger boats. For boats at the transitional size a third alternative is also available.

Our *divide and conquer* approach provides a good framework for analyzing jibes. The job of the trim team - driving and trimming through the jibe - changes little from technique to technique, while the foredeck squad's job - jibing the pole - changes significantly. The foredeck team often get the brunt of the blame when problems occur, but more often than not it is the work of the trim team which makes or breaks a jibe. We'll look first at the driver and trimmers functions. Then we will look at the various techniques used on the foredeck to jibe the spinnaker pole.

Regardless of method, practice is a key ingredient to develop the coordinated effort behind any smooth jibe.

Trimming and Driving Through Jibes

The driver must pace his turn to the crew work; and the crew must rotate the spinnaker and free fly it as the boat turns. This means trimming the (old) guy and easing the (old) sheet as the boat turns downwind.

Driving

The helmsman should make a smooth turn from broad reach to broad reach. The turn must match the trim as the spinnaker is trimmed around the boat.

Do not hold the boat dead downwind. Stay on a broad reach on one jibe, and then turn smoothly to a broad reach on the other jibe as you put the main across. Avoid centering the

Fig. 8a - Proper trim is the key to good jibes. The spinnaker must be trimmed (rotated) to the new leeward side as the boat turns. It is better to over-rotate.

Fig. 8b - If the spinnaker is not rotated it will collapse.

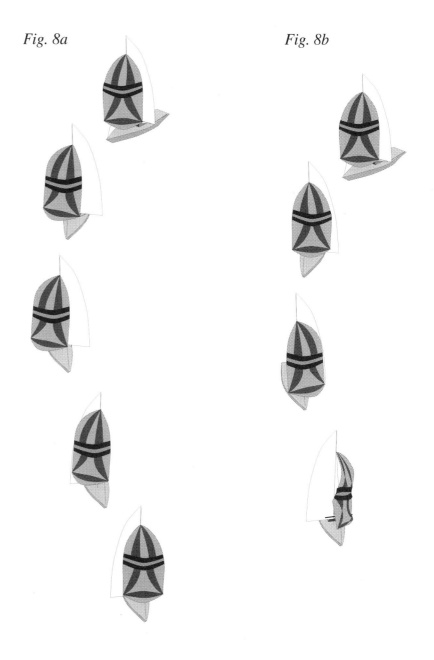

main and avoid a dead downwind course - keep the air flowing across the spinnaker in one direction.

Trimming

As the boat turns from broad reach to broad reach the spinnaker must be trimmed around the boat. This trim during jibes is referred to as *rotation*. You must rotate the spinnaker around the boat as the boat turns. The spinnaker has to stay on the downwind side of the boat. This means trimming the guy and easing the sheet as you turn downwind. It is best to trim too far - *over-rotate* - the spinnaker, and then correct your trim. If you *under-rotate*, and do not trim far enough around, the spinnaker will collapse.

Over rotate until the tack is nearly at the headstay - get 90% of the sail around the boat. Then trim back as the pole work is completed. Fig. 8ab.

No, No, No

Often you will hear that you should *Keep the spinnaker in front of the boat* and *Steer to keep the boat under the spinnaker.* These suggestions are misleading. You don't necessarily want the spinnaker in front of the boat. You really want to *Keep the spinnaker on the downwind side of the boat.* The only time the spinnaker should be in front of the boat is when you are dead downwind. And although you will often hear that you should *Hold the boat dead downwind while you jibe,* this is in fact wrong, and dangerous! In a dead downwind position air circulates behind the main and can cause wraps in the spinnaker. Sailing dead downwind will also induce the boat to roll, making steering and crew work very difficult. Fig. 9.

Jibing Practice

In practice, the crew should free fly the spinnaker without a pole. As the driver turns from broad reach to broad reach rotate the spinnaker to keep it flying. Play the curl on both luffs to keep the sail full. Trim both sides if the sail gets away from the boat; and ease both sides if the spinnaker is strapped too tight. Keep the spinnaker downwind of the boat, and keep it full. Incidentally, foredeck crew are particularly fond of this drill.

The key to successful jibes is coordinating the trim and the turn. Once you do that it matters little what happens on the bow. Fig. 10.

Fig. 9 - Do NOT hold the boat dead down wind during a jibe. When the boat is dead downwind air circulates around both sides of the spinnaker, which can cause headstay wraps. Sailing dead down wind also induces the boat to roll, which makes steering and crew work difficult.

Fig 10 - Take down your spinnaker pole and practice, practice, practice, jibing without it. With coor-dinated trim and driving you don't need a pole.

Fig. 9

Fig. 10

End-for-End Jibes

The fastest and easiest jibe for boats without large numbers of crew is the end for end jibe. While the cockpit crew sail the boat and fly the spinnaker the foredeck crew jibe the pole.

The foredeck technique depends as much on quickness as it does on strength. With good technique - and a little cooperation from the back of the boat - end for end jibes are pretty straightforward. Fig. 11.

Twings are often helpful during end for end jibes. Twings are used to choke down the spinnaker sheet to a lead block along the rail amidships. The twing is a line with a block on one end. The spinnaker sheet is lead through the block. One twing is rigged to each sheet. The windward twing is choked down to the rail to improve the working angle of the guy. The leeward twing is left free or trimmed down part way to create a proper sheet lead. During jibes both twings can be snugged down to control the spinnaker and keep the guy within easy reach.

FIG. 11 - END FOR END, STEP BY STEP

1) As the boat turns downwind the trimmers should start spinnaker rotation, trimming the guy and easing the sheet.

2) Snug the twing on the spinnaker sheet and ease the topping lift or downhaul about six inches.

3) The foredeck crew should take a position with his back against the mast, to windward of the pole.

4) As the boat turns square downwind release the pole off the mast. The best timing for the release is the moment the spinnaker rolls to windward, so there is no load on the pole. This makes the pole easier to handle. At this point in the jibe the spinnaker is also easy to fly free, with no pole.

5) With the pole off the mast open the outboard jaw. Twist and lift the inboard end to clear the guy off the outboard end. Meanwhile, it is time for someone in the back of the boat to jibe the main.

6) Grab the new guy and put it into the pole. With proper rotation the guy should be within easy reach.

7) Push the pole out and forward to the get the new end to the mast. Once again, stand to the (new) windward side to avoid being speared if the pole slips. If the foredeck crew is struggling to force the pole onto the mast ring, the trimmers can help by giving a quick ease on the sheet and guy.

In boats at the large end of the end for end size range, and in heavy air, a second crew handling the pole can speed up the process. One crew takes the pole off the mast and goes for the new guy. The other crew makes sure the old guy is cleared out of the pole, and both push the pole out and put the jaw to the ring.

Dip Pole Jibes

Larger boats with unmanageable spinnaker poles must resort to dip pole jibes. A proper dip pole jibe requires two sets of spinnaker sheets and guys. When sailing under spinnaker the leeward sheet and windward guy are *working*, while the leeward guy and windward sheet are *lazy*. The spinnaker pole is rigged with an internal control so the outboard end can be released from the guy by a crew member working at the mast.

During a jibe the end of the pole which is attached to the mast remains in place, while the outboard end is *dipped* under the forestay as it swings from one side to other.

FIG. 12 - DIP POLE JIBE, STEP BY STEP

1) Prior to jibing the lazy spinnaker gear must be readied. Lay the tail of the lazy guy onto the leeward primary winch with a single wrap, and pull sufficient slack forward to allow the foredeck crew to take a bite of the line to the bow. Flip the lazy sheet on top of the spinnaker pole so it will not be trapped under the pole when the pole is dipped. (Once the spinnaker sheet is on top of the pole the sheet can be wrapped on the working guy so it will stay in place until the jibe.)

2) At the command, *"Prepare to Jibe"* the driver turns the boat downwind while the trimmers rotate the chute to windward by easing the sheet and trimming the guy. The foredeck crew takes the lazy guy forward and positions himself in the bow pulpit, facing aft, while the mast crew raises the inboard end of the pole on the mast so the outboard end will be able to swing under the forestay.

3) As the turn and rotation continue the spinnaker will roll to windward. At that instant the mast man trips (releases) the old guy from the pole, and the pit crew

Fig. 12

lowers the topping lift.

4) The mast crew can then give a yank on the foreguy to swing the pole over the deck. (Don't use the trip line to swing the pole - you will jam the jaw open. Either grab a bite of the foreguy or put a sail tie around the pole adjacent to the trip line and use that to swing the pole.)

5) As the pole swings over the deck the foredeck crew puts the new guy into the end of the pole, being careful to make sure it is not twisted. To avoid twists make sure the guy runs directly from the guy block to the pole jaw. Never mind the route from the pole to the spinnaker - that piece of the guy runs the wrong way.

6) When the foredeck crew calls "*Made*" the new guy is then trimmed aft and the pole raised. Make sure the pole goes aft before it goes up. If the pole is raised before the guy is trimmed the pole can poke a hole in the sail. The old sheet is eased as the new guy is tensioned.

7) The transition from the old guy to the new sheet can be executed at any time. Sometimes it is best to tension the new sheet as the pole is tripped off the old guy to keep the old guy from binding on the pole. At other times it is easier to wait until the jibe is complete before making the switch.

Notes, Details, and Complications

A complication arises at step 3 when the new sheet is under the pole as you start to jibe. When this happens fly the spinnaker on the old guy and leave the new sheet slack. The foredeck crew will have to clear the sheet off the end of the pole before it can be used.

At step 6 - *Made* - the foredeck crew should not push the pole away. It is better to control the pole and let the trim of the guy pull the pole aft. If you push the pole aft before the guy is trimmed the slack in the guy can wrap around the pole.

Marks on the mast and topping lift can help set the proper dip for the pole during a dip pole jibe. It is also important to keep the spare halyards forward during jibes. The jib halyard should stay forward at the jib tack at all times to prevent it from being trapped at the mast after a jibe.

Often the jib sheets are tied together and left over the pole. That way, when the pole is lowered the jib is free to tack over the pole. Trouble is, during dip pole jibes, the jib sheets have a tendency to slide off the tip of the pole - or worse yet - fall into the open jaw! Clear the jib sheets off the topping lift. Set them over the pole *at the mast*. This will leave the jib sheets under the topping lift, but over the pole. When the chute is dropped and the pole lowered the topping lift will have to be cleared behind the jib sheets. If the topping lift is long enough it can be run slack to wind around the leech of the jib if an immediate tack is necessary after the take down.

Foreguys and Downhauls

The terms *foreguy* and *downhaul* are often used interchangeably. While they perform the same function they are not exactly the same thing. Strictly speaking, a *downhaul* is used on end for end poles, which are rigged with a bridle on the pole. The *downhaul* thus pulls down on either end of the pole from a lead somewhere in the middle or aft part of the foredeck. A *foreguy* is used on dip pole jibe poles. It is rigged directly to the outboard end of the pole, and leads to a block just aft of the jib tack fitting. The foreguy thus pulls the pole forward, in opposition to the *guy* (more accurately called the *after guy*) which pulls the pole aft. When the *guy* is trimmed or eased a corresponding adjustment of the *foreguy* is necessary.

Hybrid Jibes

Lazy Guy End for End Jibes give the best of both worlds for many boats

Traditionally small boat spinnakers are jibed end for end, while big boats use dip pole technique. As long as the spinnaker pole is manageable, and the spinnaker not too big, the end for end jibe is quicker. As the spinnaker pole gets too large to grip, too long to manage, and too heavy to handle the switch is made to dip pole jibes. Recently the crossover size for switching from end to end to dip pole has been pushed up, from the low 30 foot range to about 40 feet. The lazy sheet and guy technique has been used on a number of moderate to large boats, such as the J-35, New York 36, Mumm 36, One Tonners, and even the Swede 55. Why the change in size limits, and how does the technique work on larger boats?

New Materials, New Techniques

The reasons for the push to end for end jibes on larger boats can be traced to several phenomena. Part of the shift is due to new materials - specifically carbon fiber spinnaker poles, which are substantially lighter than the aluminum poles they replace. Another issue is foretriangle size. The revival of fractional rigs has resulted in smaller spinnakers and shorter poles. Even masthead rigs are being designed with relatively larger mains and smaller fore-triangles than similar length boats of earlier design. An additional factor is the lighter weight of the newer boats. The resultant lighter loads make sails easier to handle, and spinnaker poles smaller and lighter. Finally, as small boat sailors move into these larger boats they bring with them small boat techniques. This technique transfer is not limited to spinnaker work - roll tacks, pumping, and added attention to weight and balance have moved up as well.

Lazy Guy End for End Jibes

Jibing the spinnaker end for end on a moderate sized boat can be a struggle, particularly when it blows. Releasing the pole from the mast against the compression of the guy is tough, and handling the pole is a challenge. Tougher still is the task of wrestling the pole back onto the mast to complete the jibe. As the jaw at the end of the pole gets closer to the pole eye on the mast, resistance builds. The difficulty in these jibes is due to the compression on the pole from the loaded spinnaker guy.

End for end jibes with lazy sheets and guys eliminate the compression. The principle behind the technique is borrowed from dip pole jibes: You fly the spinnaker with one set of lines while jibing the pole with another set. The foredeck crew no longer have to fight the load of live lines. By doing the pole work on slack lines the jibe can be accomplished easily.

Lazy Sheet and Guy Technique

The set up calls for spinnaker sheets lead aft and guys lead near the point of maximum beam. When setting the spinnaker on starboard tack, the pole is attached to the starboard guy, and the port sheet is used to trim the spinnaker. The starboard sheet and port guy are slack, or "lazy". The setup for port tack would be just the opposite.

As the boat is turned downwind to jibe from starboard to port, the starboard sheet is trimmed, taking tension off the starboard guy. With both guys now free, the spinnaker is flown on the sheets while the foredeck crew jibes the pole. The pole is taken off the mast, and placed on the port guy; the old guy is then removed from the starboard end, and the pole reattached to the mast. Fig. 13.

Before starting the pole work the foredeck crew should have the new guy in hand, with plenty of slack. After dropping the new guy into the jaw he (or she) will be able to push the

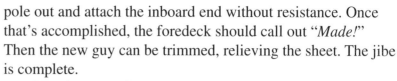

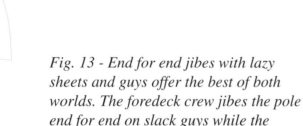

Fig. 13 - End for end jibes with lazy sheets and guys offer the best of both worlds. The foredeck crew jibes the pole end for end on slack guys while the trimmers fly the spinnaker on the sheets.

pole out and attach the inboard end without resistance. Once that's accomplished, the foredeck should call out "*Made!*" Then the new guy can be trimmed, relieving the sheet. The jibe is complete.

During the jibe

A few additional details can help assure smooth jibes. One issue revolves around when to initiate the pole work. As the boat squares away and the spinnaker is rotated to windward the time will come when the spinnaker will roll to windward and the pole will unload. That is the appropriate moment to tension the new sheet and release the old guy. Once the guy is unloaded pole work can proceed quickly.

Drive and Trim

Regardless of technique, the truth is that more jibes are messed up by the trimmers and drivers than by the deck crew. Coordinated trimming and steering are essential to successful jibes. As the boat turns through the jibe the spinnaker must be rotated to keep it downwind.

Trim the guy/new sheet and ease the old sheet as you turn downwind. Watch the curl and rotate as fast as you can without luffing the spinnaker. Keep rotating until the clew is within a few feet of the head stay. Play the curl. Both sides should be eased if the chute is strapped against the forestay; both should be trimmed if the chute is rolling from side to side or flying far in front of the boat. It is better to be aggressive and over-rotate than to under rotate. An under rotated spinnaker will collapse and blow through the foretriangle, creating a mess (and possible head stay wraps).

Crew Organization

Your crew organization will vary with the number of crew, but the general principle is to have one trimmer on the old sheet, one trimmer on the new sheet, and a third trimmer moving from the old guy to the new guy. The transition from the old guy to the new sheet is a matter of trimming the new sheet to take load off the old guy as you initiate the jibe, as described above. Once the new sheet is trimmed the old guy is free, and the guy trimmer can stand by the new guy, ready to trim when the foredeck calls, "*Made*." The trimmer on the old sheet should stay on the job until the pole work is done and the new guy is trimmed to take the load.

In Heavy Air

When jibing in heavy air less rotation is called for because the apparent wind angle changes less. In extreme conditions align the centerline of the spinnaker in front of the boat and choke down the sheets. Over-rotation can cause a roundup in a big blow. But over-rotation is still better than under-rotation. An under-rotated spinnaker will round you the wrong way - onto the old tack. Over-rotation rounds you onto the new tack - so at least the jibe is done when you crash. In severe conditions jibe the boom first, before starting the pole work.

In heavy air we are often told the driver must sail the boat under the spinnaker, but this only works if the sail is first trimmed in front of the boat. Since the foredeck crew will be jibing the pole on slack lines, he'll be finished quickly, and the time spent free-flying the spinnaker will be brief. For consistent jibes it may be helpful to have two crew handle the pole - particularly in breezy conditions.

In light air

In light air set the spinnaker without a lazy guy. If the breeze remains light you can jibe in the traditional end for end style - directly onto the sheet. If the breeze builds you'll need to pull down the clew and attach the lazy guy before jibing.

Boat Handling is your foundation

Racing success starts with good boat handling, and good boat handling requires teamwork. Regardless of the jibing technique you choose - traditional end for end, dip pole, or end for end with lazy sheets and guys - practice is essential. To coordinate trim rotation and steering try a series of jibes - 20 or 30 of 'em should do - with no pole. Once you are able to fly the spinnaker through the jibes the pole work will be a snap.

Side Bar: The Equipment

End for end jibes with lazy sheets and guys require a hybrid of the equipment required for dip pole and end for end jibes. In addition to carrying two sheets and two guys the pole must have jaws at both ends. Triggered ends, which lock open and close automatically, are preferred. The pole must also have a bridle system so the topping lift and foreguy/downhaul will support and control either end of the pole. The lead position for the downhaul can remain near the stem, though it is more effective further aft, near the middle of the foredeck. Finally, the mast will need a ring to accept the pole jaw.

On weight-sensitive boats (what boat isn't?), double sheets and guys offer an opportunity to lead both sheet and guy to winches on the windward side, positioning crew weight to weather. As you work out your rigging try to create fair leads for cross sheeting which will not create havoc. One common solution is cross sheeting to a cabin top winch. Assuming the winch is large enough for the job this often provides a good grinding position and clean leads from the sheet block to the winch and on to the trimmer.

Fig. 14 - Reach to reach jibes require fast trim to rotate the spinnaker and keep pace with the turn. Set up high if you can, and allow a few boat lengths for the turn.

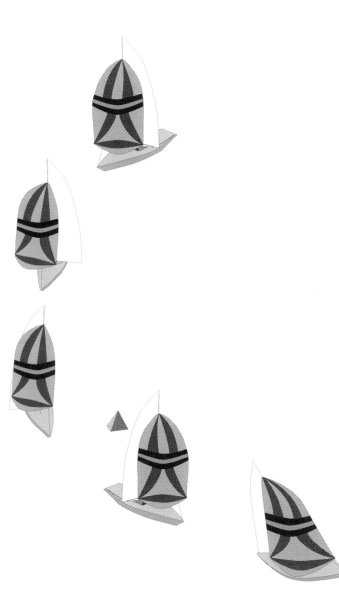

Jibing in Special Conditions
Reach to Reach Jibes

When jibing from beam reach to beam reach the spinnaker must be rotated all the way around the boat. It takes aggressive trimming to get the sail around. The driver should help as much as possible by easing into the turn to allow the trimmers a chance to keep up, but there are times when tactics dictate otherwise.

When tactics force an in close / out close jam turn it is suggested that the driver apologize in advance to the rest of the crew: *"This is gonna be ugly - do the best you can to keep up."* As you start into such a jibe ease the sheet way out and grind the guy around. You'll probably collapse the chute, but if you're going to have any chance of coming out clean you'll need to force the rotation early. If the rotation is late you'll end up with a collapsed spinnaker that is blown back through the foretriangle - a real mess. Fig. 14.

Light Air Jibes

In light air all jibes are reach to reach, and it is difficult to get the sail to move around the boat. As you turn downwind you over run your apparent wind, and the spinnaker collapses. We've done extensive research in these conditions due to circumstances beyond our control. Here is what we've found:

We call this a three step jibe. First, bear away smartly, and as you bear away grab sheet near the clew of the sail - *and run it forward*. (Yes, you need to physically drag it forward. Simply easing does not move the sail fast when the friction is stronger than the wind.) By running the clew forward you can rotate the sail fast enough to allow the driver to turn as quickly as she would like. In the meantime trim the guy back *a little* and start the pole work. This will put the spinnaker well out in front of the boat.

Step two: Now hesitate for a moment in your turn, slightly by the lee. During this hesitation the flow across the spinnaker will stall. Finish the pole work now.

Third, turn up smartly onto the new course as you snap trim the new sheet, and establish flow across the sail on the new tack.

We tried a quick turn all the way through in light air and found the reversal of flow would collapse the sail. By hesitating momentarily during the turn that problem was eliminated. Try it. Hum a waltz. Fig. 15.

Heavy Air Jibes

Jibing in heavy air is a challenge. There are several ways to get in trouble, and an equal number of techniques to try to keep trouble at bay. The biggest problems, and best broaches, occur when the sails overwhelm the rudder.

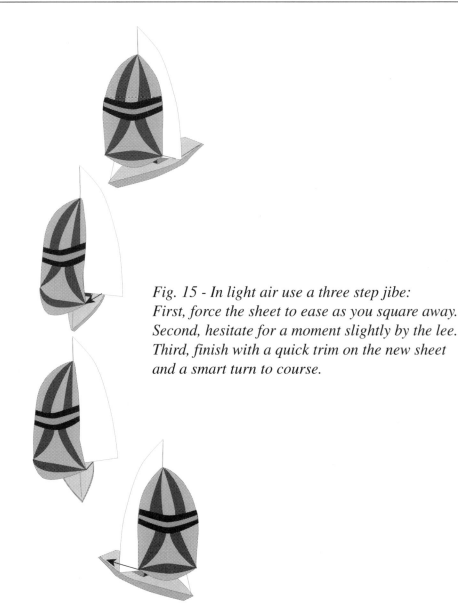

Fig. 15 - In light air use a three step jibe: First, force the sheet to ease as you square away. Second, hesitate for a moment slightly by the lee. Third, finish with a quick trim on the new sheet and a smart turn to course.

Maintaining control while jibing the spinnaker requires putting the spinnaker on a short leash. Choke down the spinnaker with twings and over trim to keep the spinnaker from rolling around. Center the spinnaker in front of the boat as you square downwind. Initiate the pole work when the sail is pulling to weather and the pole is unloaded. Keep the chute in front of the boat, and trim to stay ahead of the roll.

Often the difficulty with heavy air jibes is caused by the main, not the spinnaker. As the main is trimmed it loads the helm, and the inevitable puff which comes as you try to drag the main across can overwhelm the rudder. Either that, or your pushing down by the lee to help urge the main across, but it goes back out on the old tack and starts you rolling and rounds you up or you manage to finally throw the boom across and it runs out part way and fetches up (either against the runner, or the sheet tangles or…) and your round up - but at least this round up is on the new jibe, so you won't have to start over or …

One option on heavy air jibes is to jibe the main first, and then jibe the spinnaker. This is the method used on two person dinghies, and it works on bigger keelboats as well. Turn by the lee, rotate the spinnaker, and jibe the main. Once you are more or less under control crew can go forward to jibe the pole. Fig. 16.

When you jibe the main in heavy air you'll need to trim it in until it jibes, and then let it run out fast - as fast as it can go. To make sure it runs out bypass the cleat when you trim it. For a block and tackle system trim directly off the last block on the boom, and avoid the ratchet block and cleat which will slow the ease on the flip side of the jibe.

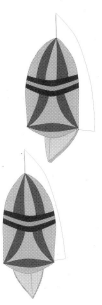

Fig. 16 - Heavy air jibes put the driver at the mercy of the trimmers. The sails can overwhelm the rudder. Often the problems are due to difficulty jibing the main. One option is to jibe the main first, and then do the pole work.

9.4 Spinnaker Take Downs

There are several variations for take downs, depending on the approach to the mark and the plans for the next set, but in the end they boil down to a choice between two preferred methods. The choices are the *Stretch and Blow* and *Pole Down, Chute Down*. As stated, your choice depends on several factors. We'll take a look at the two preferred methods, as well as some that we aren't fond of. We'll look at technique and also the circumstances which would guide our selection.

The *Divide and Conquer* framework guides us in crew organization for spinnaker douses. One team should takes down the spinnaker while the other team sails the boat around the mark. Divide and Conquer.

Stretch & Blow

A *Stretch and Blow* take down allows for fast spinnaker take downs on the bow. It is the preferred method when you approach the mark on a reach and must trim up as you round.

FIG. 17 - STRETCH AND BLOW, STEP BY STEP*

* Disclaimer: The times offered here are approximate. Yours may vary.

2 minutes from mark: Make sure your spinnaker halyard is ready to run. Ease it a couple of inches, and belay your coils to clear kinks and bends. If it is jammed this will give it time to work free. Also, a few inches ease will give some play and keep it from jamming if mast geometry changes slightly when the backstay is tensioned.

1 minute: As you approach the mark hoist your jib and set your controls for upwind work.

30 sec.: Ease the spinnaker pole to the forestay and overtrim the spinnaker sheet so the sail is pulled against the back of the genoa - the *Stretch*.

10 sec.: As you start your turn, and the spinnaker collapses, let the halyard go. That's right: Let it run - the *Blow*. Now we are sure that the spinnaker is coming down. It floats out over the water, like a leaf in the wind.

At the Mark: Crew on the bow gather the spinnaker, and stuff it down the forward hatch. As the sail is pulled aboard the sheet and guy are eased. Leave the halyard, sheets, and guys attached for now. Go hike out.

On the Escape: Lower the pole and make sure the jib sheets are clear for a tack. Hail the after guard to announce, *"Clear to tack."*

At Your Leisure: After the boat has settled and escaped from the mark you can do your house keeping, clearing the running gear off the sail and repacking.

The advantages of this technique are that it is fast, it allows the spinnaker to be carried to the very end of the leg, and it keeps extra crew out of the cockpit.

Just Let it Run…?…!

Yep, just let the halyard run! Make sure you rotate the spinnaker first by putting the pole forward and over trimming the sheet, then let 'er rip! If you *Blow* before your *stretch* then you will run over the sail. Remember, *Stretch & Blow*. No, the sail will not fall in the water - it will float out to leeward until you gather it in. The exception is light air, where the wind may not hold it up. Then you'll want to half dump the halyard, and ease the rest.

Gather the Sail

On the gather the crew should reach under the genoa and grab the foot of the spinnaker, the spinnaker sheet, or the lazy

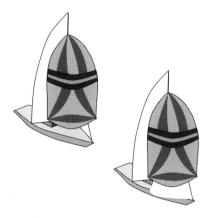

Fig. 17 - The Stretch and Blow take down is the preferred leeward take down. The spinnaker is first overtrimmed into the back of the genoa. Then the halyard is released completely, and the sail is pulled onto the foredeck.

guy if one is rigged. Pull the spinnaker down *under* the genoa foot, *not* behind the leech. Also, sit down to gather the sail. The foredeck crew should have their butts firmly planted on deck as they gather the spinnaker. If you don't like getting wet take up golf.

Heavy Air Take Downs

The Stretch and Blow is great because it works particularly well in lots of wind. Once you blow the halyard the spinnaker blows out to leeward and is easy to gather. In a big breeze don't carry all the way to the mark. Dump the halyard a 30 seconds shy of the mark so the sail can be gathered and stowed before you round. Ideally you'll have crew on the rail as you trim up. If possible position yourself just high of the mark on your approach so you can turn down briefly just after the halyard is dumped. This makes the sail easier to gather.

One more detail: Beware a broach as you put the pole forward and trim the sheet. If you start to round up, then dump the halyard to relieve the load.

Fast, Easy, Effective

The *Stretch and Blow* is preferred because it is fast, reliable - even in heavy air, and especially because it keeps the spinnaker gatherers out of the cockpit. By moving the spinnaker gather to the bow it leaves the trimmers free to trim, without the spinnaker draped over their work.

Pole Down, Chute Down

The alternative to the *Stretch and Blow* is the *Pole Down, Chute Down* method. This method, with variations, is used for jibe take downs, windward take downs, and leeward take downs. As the name suggests, the pole comes down before the spinnaker, and you free fly the spinnaker briefly. This works best when the approach is a broad reach or run. The advantage is that you have the pole out of the way. As you turn up wind you have crew on the rail, not running around stowing the pole.

Step by Step

2 minutes from the mark: Make sure your spinnaker halyard is ready to run. Ease it a couple of inches, and belay your coils to clear kinks and bends.

1 minute: Hoist the jib and set your controls for upwind sailing.

30 seconds: Trip and drop the pole. Stow it.

Free fly the spinnaker. The foredeck crew can serve as a temporary pole, and hold the guy outboard, while the mast crew stows the pole.

Clear the jib sheets. Make sure they are over the pole and in front of the topping lift.

15 sec.: Pull the spinnaker down. Grab the sheet, and pull the sail down on the bow. Ease the guy and then the halyard.

At the Mark: Leave the halyard, sheets, and guys attached for now. Go hike out.

At Your Leisure: After the boat has settled and escaped from the mark you can do your house keeping, clearing the running gear off the sail and repacking.

Variations

Windward Take Down

We use a windward take down to position the spinnaker and spinnaker gear for the next spinnaker set. By pulling the spinnaker down on the side where we will want it next we save the trouble of re-leading the gear later, while racing upwind.

The windward take down works best when we approach the mark on a broad reach or run. Use the procedure listed above except in #6 you grab the guy and pull the sail down while easing the sheet and halyard.

As always, keep the spinnaker and spinnaker pole under the jib sheets so you will be clear to tack.

Jibe Take Down

Use a jibe takedown whenever jibing is part of your mark rounding. For example, broad reaching on starboard when approaching a mark to be left to port. You can douse the spinnaker to either side of the boat, depending on where you would like the spinnaker gear to end up.

The jibe takedown is just another form of *Pole Down, Chute Down*. With a good crew in moderate conditions it goes as described in Fig. 18.

You Don't Say?

Spinnaker take downs requires hundreds of coordinated crew movements. Practice is suggested.

Pre Positioning for the Next Set

Using the variations of *Pole Down, Chute Down* allows you to pull the spinnaker down in position for your next set, saving you from having to re-lead the spinnaker gear as you sail upwind.

Fig. 18 - Jibe Take Down

2 minutes from the mark:

Make sure your spinnaker halyard is ready to run. Ease it a couple of inches, and belay your coils to clear kinks and bends.

1 minute:

Hoist the jib and put on upwind sail controls. Make sure the jib sheets are over the spinnaker pole. Sheet the jib loosely to port.

45 seconds:

Square away. Trip the pole off the guy and lower it to the deck. Free fly the spinnaker. Clear the topping lift behind the jib sheets.

30 seconds:

Turn by the lee and jibe the jib, forcing it over the spinnaker pole. Jibe the main.

20 seconds:

Douse the spinnaker. Take it in on either side. Just be sure to decide in advance where that will be. The port side is probably easiest.

10 seconds:

Make a smooth turn to the mark, and trim up to close hauled.

At the Mark:

Mark at the bow, boat on course, spinnaker below, crew on rail, pole stowed, big smiles.

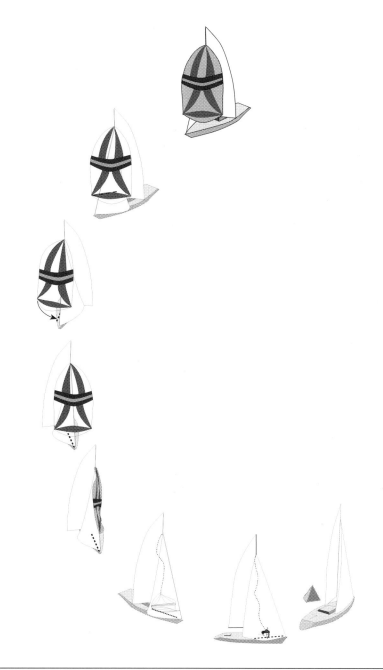

Traditional Leeward Take Down

A conventional leeward takedown pulls the spinnaker in along the leeward rail. We don't recommend it. Here is how it works:

After the jib is set pop open the guy shackle or let the guy run. Gather the spinnaker foot, and lower the sail into the cockpit and down the companionway. Fig. 19.

There are several drawbacks to this takedown. First, it is slow. Second, the sail usually comes down on top of the genoa trimmer, obstructing his efforts; third, it puts too much crew weight to leeward; and fourth, the sail often blows out the back of the boat, like a huge air brake. In addition, it often requires releading much of the spinnaker gear. If the guy is run then it may pull all the way out and need to be re-lead. If the guy is tripped then the guy is left at the bow. Eventually it will have to be retrieved.

Last, but not least, these takedowns are dangerous. If the guy is run, it can whip crew. If it is tripped someone must go forward and release a very heavily loaded shackle at the tip of the spinnaker pole. With the foot gathered the sail can fill and pull crew overboard.

We don't like this method. There are better ways to take down spinnakers.

Fig. 19 - The conventional leeward takedown has several drawbacks: It is slow, it puts too many crew on top of each other to leeward and aft, and it requires too much re-rigging to prepare for another spinnaker set.

9.5 Spinnaker Peels

The true wind speed was only 8 knots, and on the run it seemed like nothing. We'd jibed our 1/2 oz chute repeatedly, trying to catch the shifts and puffs downwind. The next leg would be a close spinnaker reach - with an apparent wind angle of 70 to 80 degrees. In 8 knots of true wind it would be too much for the 1/2 oz. Approaching the mark we rigged the .75 using the starboard spinnaker halyard, a spare sheet, and a changing pennant at the bow. About 5 lengths from the mark we hoisted the .75 inside the 1/2 oz. Once it was set we eased the spinnaker pole forward to the headstay and the bow man released the tack shackle from the 1/2 oz. As the 1/2 oz. luffed on its sheet to leeward the bow man secured the tack of the 3/4 oz. to the guy shackle and hailed aft, "Made." The guy was trimmed aft and the bow man released the changing pennant before moving aft to help retrieve the old chute, which was just starting down. As the helmsman brought the boat up to course and rounded the mark the peel was complete. The 1/2 oz. was safely below, and the .75 was drawing firm in 11 knots of apparent wind.

Spinnaker Peels

Changing conditions call for changing sails. Upwind a new genoa is hoisted before the old sail is dropped. Changing spinnakers we use a similar technique, hoisting the new sail before dousing the old. Spinnaker peels, as such changes are called, require teamwork and attention to detail. You will need a spare sheet, a second halyard, and a temporary substitute for the guy. For details read on.

The Set up

The new chute should be set up with its own sheet and halyard, and a changing pennant which will be a temporary substitute for the guy. Take the new chute forward and set it up on the leeward rail near the bow pulpit. Lead the sheet aft through a spinnaker block and to a winch. (Often you can double up the new sheet into the same sheave as the working spinnaker sheet.)

The halyard must be lead so as not to foul the other halyards. The basic principle is to always keep your port halyard to port of your starboard halyard. Hoist the new sail inside or outside the old one to keep the halyards on their proper side. (For more on halyards see details below).

The tack of the new spinnaker should be secured to a changing pennant. The changing pennant should be tied to the jib tack horn and hitched to the forestay about six feet above deck. If you are using a sail tie attach it to the spinnaker with a slip knot. Fig. 20.

The Change

Hoist the new spinnaker to full hoist and trim it. Fig. 21. Ease the guy and /or topping lift forward so the foredeck crew can release the guy shackle from the old chute. Fig. 22. The old sail will luff harmlessly to leeward. Next attach the free guy shackle to the new spinnaker tack and release the changing pennant. Fig. 23 - next page. Trim back the guy and topping lift for proper trim. Retrieve the old sail after the new sail is set and trimmed; and repack it promptly. Fig. 24 - next page. You may need it again soon. When you do an outside hoist the old sail may try to blow around the front of the new sail when you release the guy. Grab the clew of the old sail and pull it down inside.

If Your Pole is Rigged with a Foreguy

If your spinnaker pole is rigged with a foreguy (as opposed to a downhaul and bridle) there is a better alternative to the changing pennant. The tack of the new spinnaker can be shackled to a snatch block which is free to run up the foreguy to the pole. Put the block of the snatch block around

Fig. 20 - To set up for a spinnaker peel rig the replacement spinnaker with a spare sheet and extra halyard. Rig a bow pennant as a temporary substitute for the guy.

Fig. 21 - Hoist the new sail, and trim the sheet. You can hoist inside or outside, depending on sailing conditions and the halyard arrangement.

Fig. 22 - Ease the guy to bring the pole to the headstay, within reach of the foredeck crew, so the foredeck crew can release the old spinnaker tack from the guy.

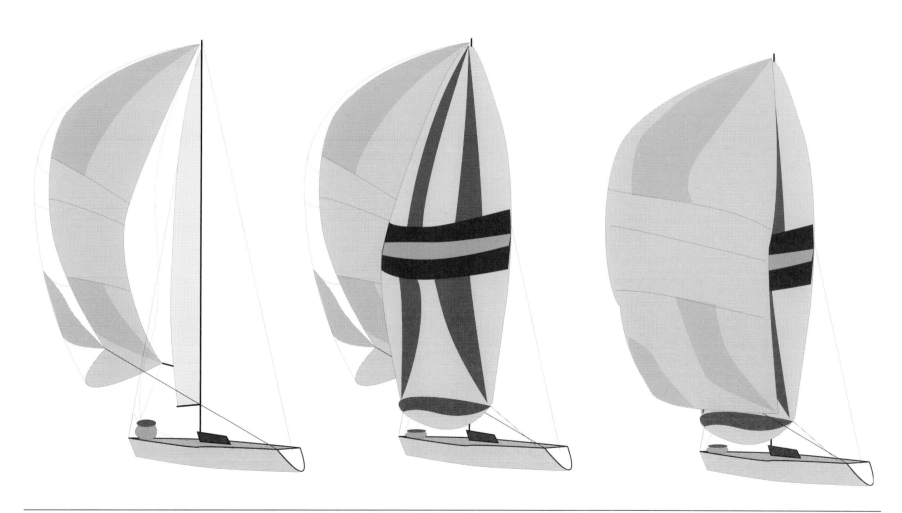

the foreguy, and attach the shackle to the spinnaker. As you hoist the new sail the shackle will run up the foreguy to the pole.

Once the new sail is set ease the pole to within reach of the foredeck. Be sure to keep the foreguy tight as you ease the pole or the new spinnaker tack will sag to leeward, out of reach. Trip the old spinnaker guy, secure the new spinnaker to the guy shackle, and release the snatch block shackle from the spinnaker.

On America's Cup boats and some Grand Prix racers it is common to see the bow crew out at the end of the pole with the tack of the new sail in hand. He then uses a double ended shackle (or second guy shackle) to secure the new tack. While this may be the correct technique for a Grand Prix crew it is faster and safer (though admittedly less dramatic) for most of us to ease the pole to within reach of the deck, rather than send a crew member outside the lifelines.

Never Cross Your Halyards

"Never cross your halyards, keep your port halyard to port of the starboard halyard." Here's what we mean by that:

If you are on starboard tack and your spinnaker is up on the port halyard bring your starboard halyard around the forestay and directly to the head of the new sail. Hoist the new spinnaker inside the old one. On starboard tack with the spinnaker on the starboard halyard bring the port halyard outside the spinnaker sheet and then to the head of the new sail. The new sail will then go up outside the old one - keeping the port halyard to port of the starboard halyard. Always keep a genoa halyard secured at the jib tack horns. Even if the other halyards are fouled you want to have one that is not twisted, trapped, or locked out.

Heavy Air Peels

Inside hoists are easier, so in heavy air use an inside hoist on any peel. For example, on starboard tack with the spinnaker on the starboard halyard you can hoist the new chute inside the old spinnaker using the port halyard. When you pull down the old spinnaker the starboard halyard will be trapped aft of the new chute. This will not twist the halyards, but it will trap the starboard halyard aft to port. The starboard halyard is available for an outside hoist should you need to peel again. Otherwise *the starboard cannot be used until the spinnaker comes down and the starboard halyard is cleared around, outside the port halyard and the forestay.* Do not take the starboard halyard around the bow before first clearing it outside the port halyard, *or it will be twisted completely around the port halyard.*

What About the Genoa Halyard?

When the genoa is down *always* keep a genoa halyard secured at the jib tack horns. Even if the other halyards are fouled you want to have one that is not twisted, trapped, or locked out.

Get Ready to Peel

You will need to peel anytime the wind strength or wind angle changes dramatically. By planning ahead and responding promptly you can save yourself from a hastily executed peel (or blown out spinnaker).

Set up to peel any time you are flying your light chute. You want to be ready to peel on a moments notice so you never learn the true limits of your light sail (by overstepping them- if you know what I mean).

Get Ready for Fall

Once you have mastered light air peels you can test your skill changing from a 3/4 to a 1.5 in a building autumn wind. If you own a 1.5 oz be ready to use it. Don't wait until you are pushing the limits of the 3/4 oz before peeling. A carefully planned moderate air peel is easy; a hurried heavy air peel can be a mess.

Conclusion

A smooth peel will cost you less distance than a tack. Practice peels so you will be ready for light air drifters this summer, and heavy air thrills this fall.

Fig. 23 - *Release the tack of the old sail, and let it luff to leeward from its sheet and halyard. Attach the guy shackle to the tack of the new sail, and release the pennant. Trim the guy to pull the pole back.*

Fig. 24 - *Once the new sail is properly trimmed you can pull down the old sail. Keep track of the halyard. It will either be clear to use, or trapped aft. (See text for details.)*

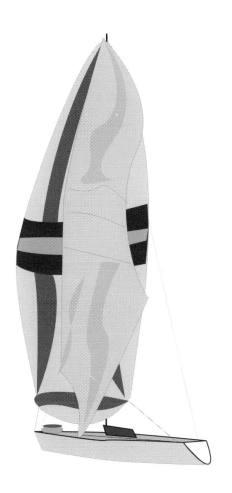

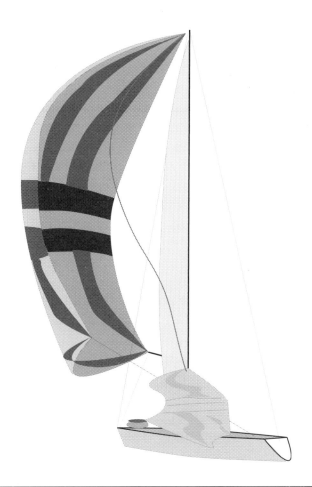

9.6 The Three Halyard System

The most common halyard configuration on racing boats today is the three halyard system with twin grooved headstay. For the foredeck crew, keeping halyards clear and available requires a system and some planning. Overall goals are to keep options open, to be ready for anything, and to anticipate what the next move will be. Immediate goals (during each maneuver) are to be set up to react quickly (but not hurriedly) when a change is called for, to be able to execute with a minimum disruption, and to be clear for any subsequent evolution once the maneuver is complete.

Below are general principles of halyard organization which focus on the overall picture. These are followed by a series of examples which demonstrate these principles and focus on the details needed to succeed.

GENERAL PRINCIPLES

• For an initial jib hoist use the center halyard in the leeward groove.

• For an initial spinnaker hoist use the leeward wing halyard. Keep the weather wing halyard available for spinnaker peels; and the center halyard available for jibs and stay sails.

• Keep halyards forward when sailing downwind. When the jib comes down after a spinnaker set keep the jib halyard forward. Bring the third halyard forward before a jibe. Halyards left aft at the mast will be trapped aft of the spinnaker pole after the jibe.

• Keep halyards at the mast when sailing upwind. Extra halyards stowed forward create measurable turbulence for the jib and hurt performance.

• Keep the starboard halyard to starboard of the port halyard. (This applies primarily to spinnaker peels - see example below.)

• Color code halyards. Color coding the halyard balls, mast exits, winch caps, and line fleck reduces the chances for confusion. Wing halyards need halyard balls to prevent jamming and scoring halyard sheaves.

• Mark the full hoist positions.

The entire foredeck team (Bow, Mast, and Pit crew) should understand the principles of halyard organization. Most maneuvers should be talked through before execution so the plan and sequence are clear. Each team member should watch over the others' efforts to check and double check against twists, raps, and lost halyards. Communications should be by voice and hand signals.

Example 1: 'Round the Buoys

We start a round-the-buoys race using the center halyard and the port groove in the headstay. This saves the port halyard for a leeward spinnaker set (assuming port roundings) and the starboard halyard for a genoa change.

Approaching the windward mark our Pit crew notes the jib halyard setting so it can be duplicated when resetting later. Before setting the spinnaker pole the forward crew checks to be sure the starboard halyard is to leeward of the pole and topping lift so it will be available as needed while the pit crew flakes the jib halyard to assure a smooth drop after the spinnaker hoist. On the hoist we jump and tail the halyard to full hoist before the sheet is trimmed.

With the spinnaker up the jib comes down and the halyard is stowed forward, and the jib set through the pre-feeder, ready to go. Before the jibe the foredeck crew may take the starboard halyard forward as well, so it will not be trapped to windward of the pole. (If a halyard is trapped we can clear it over the pole by shackling it to the jib sheets (which should be over the pole) and pulling it over; but we prefer to avoid trapping halyards).

Approaching the leeward mark the spare halyard is again stowed at the mast base. After confirming the sail selection with the afterguard we set the jib on the center halyard in the port groove. We opt for a leeward takedown, so the spinnaker comes down to starboard and the port halyard is around the forestay. It will be used for the next spinnaker set, either from the starboard rail, or by clearing it around the bow and returning it to port.

Sailing upwind conditions change, and we are overpowered with the #1 genoa; a jib change in called for. The Afterguard agrees to a tack change and the #2 is passed from below in its turtle. The Bow crew secures the Starboard halyard to the head of the sail and drags the sail forward, hooking in the tack and feeding the luff tape. A careful look aloft confirms that the starboard halyard is not wrapped around the forestay or fouled on the port halyard - which is still to starboard after the spinnaker takedown. Sailing through the fleet it is fortunate we are on starboard tack as we set up. With the halyard in place the hoist is started as the lazy jib sheet is secured to the new sail and lead position adjusted. With a clear lane on port we start to tack as soon as the halyard tops out. The foredeck crew moves from the mast into the bow pulpit as the helm goes down. As soon as the jib breaks the halyard is cast off, and with the help of the foredeck crew it is most of the way down before the tack is complete. The luff falls in a pile on deck. A sail tie is tied around the luff, the tack is released, and the sail pulled aft. At the mast the halyard is released and secured to the mast collar. The sheet is removed and secured to the #2, and the lead is set for the new sail. The #1 is passed below. With the luff gathered the sail is ready to go back up if needed.

Approaching the windward mark the Afterguard calls for a bear away set on starboard tack. The port halyard is pulled around the bow with the spinnaker sheets to set up on the port rail. Turning the mark the spinnaker goes up and the jib comes down. The center halyard is brought forward and stowed with the starboard halyard. The jib is re-lead to use the port tack and groove, and the center halyard.

The breeze starts to fade and we jibe. We're now on port, on a broad reach. The breeze fades further and the 3/4 oz spinnaker starts to sag. It is time to peel.

Example 2: Spinnaker Peels

Changing conditions call for changing sails. Upwind we change jibs; downwind we change spinnakers, hoisting the new before dousing the old, as with jibs.

With the spinnaker up on one wing halyard we peel using the other wing halyard. If, for example, the spinnaker is up on the port halyard when on starboard tack, we take the starboard halyard around the forestay and hoist the new chute inside the old one. This will keep the starboard halyard to starboard of the port halyard, as desired.

From port tack with spinnaker up on the port halyard then we would peel to the starboard halyard by taking it outboard and aft of the original spinnaker. The old chute then comes down inside, once again keeping the starboard halyard to starboard of the port halyard. The port halyard would then be available for an inside peel, or it can be cleared around the bow to be used for a jib.

In heavy air an outside set can be difficult. In that case we can hoist inside with the outside halyard. On port tack with the spinnaker on the port halyard we would peel to the starboard halyard with an inside hoist, and pull the old sail down aft. The port halyard will then be trapped aft. This is not a problem unless we try to use the halyard again without clearing it first. If we were to take the port halyard directly forward it would be wrapped around the starboard halyard. We must clear the port halyard outside the starboard halyard before it can be used again.

There are several ways the trapped halyard might be cleared. To peel again the trapped port halyard can be used on the outside and all will be clear once the old sail comes down. Otherwise the trapped halyard can be cleared after the spinnaker is taken down. With the starboard spinnaker halyard stowed the trapped port halyard can be cleared forward and around the bow.

Throughout the peel process (and whenever the jib is down) keep the center halyard forward at the headstay, clear and ready to use.

Example 3: Distance Racing

The objectives when distance racing are not really different than those for round-the-buoys races. The differences are a consequence of the uncertain format of the race. We really don't know what to expect next, and so we must be ready for anything. The best configuration for a change is to have either a jib set on the center halyard and leeward headstay groove or a spinnaker set on the leeward wing halyard.

When starting on a jib reach use the center halyard in the leeward groove. This leaves the leeward wing halyard for a spinnaker set; and the weather wing halyard and inside groove for a jib change. When changing from a spinnaker to a jib return to this configuration.

Upwind starts use the same configuration as round the buoys, except if there is only a short beat followed by a shy (jib) reach. Our upwind jib would be set in the groove which will be leeward on the reach. We can then hoist our reaching jib inside and take down the old sail outside the high clewed reaching sail with little fuss.

Starting downwind under spinnaker it is best to set with the leeward wing halyard and stow our center and weather wing halyards forward where they will be ready for the next change.

When changing watches it is critical that the bow crew pass information on the state of halyards from watch to watch. It is best to leave everything straight; but if anything is out of the ordinary (such as a halyard around the forestay after a spinnaker douse) the new watch must be made aware. Only one crew member on each watch should handle the halyards. Allowing the full crew to take a turns on the bow invites confusion and tangled halyards.

Conclusion

By adhering to the above outlined principles we can take advantage of the flexibility offered by the modern twin grooved headstay and three halyard configuration. The system keeps our halyards clear and our options open, allowing us to set and change sails as necessary.

Of course, if this all seems like more trouble than it is worth you might want to consider a sport boat, with a jib on a roller furler and a spinnaker on a sprit, and one halyard for each.

CHAPTER 10 - ASYMMETRICAL SPINNAKER HANDLING

10.1 INTRODUCTION

10.2 ASYMMETRICAL SPINNAKER HANDLING

10.3 ASYMMETRICAL SPINNAKER SETS

10.4 ASYMMETRICAL SPINNAKER JIBES

10.5 ASYMMETRICAL SPINNAKER TAKEDOWNS

10.6 ASYMMETRICAL SPINNAKERS ON CONVENTIONAL BOATS

10.7 CONCLUSION

CHAPTER 10 - ASYMMETRICAL SPINNAKER HANDLING

10.1 Introduction

The new group of boats is a hybrid between keelboats and dinghies - offering keelboat stability (almost) with dinghy performance (almost). Featuring the latest in design and construction, these boats feature light weight planing hulls, asymmetrical spinnakers mounted on extendable bow sprits, and massive rigs offset by high aspect dagger keels with weighted bulbs.

There are several aspects to these designs which demand special techniques to attain their performance potential. The most obvious is the huge, sprit mounted asymmetrical spinnaker. Also important is the raw power to weight ratio, both upwind and down, and the lightweight, planing hull form.

10.2 Asymmetrical Handling

Rigging and handling asymmetricals is easier than conventional spinnaker rigging. While there are plenty of tricks and subtleties the process is simpler and more straightforward than for conventional spinnakers.

Rigging

The asymmetrical rigs more like a jib than a spinnaker. There are two sheets - which boat attach to the clew. A single tack line holds the tack forward. The halyard runs from the head. In addition to these lines there is a control line to extend the sprit. There are no guys.

10.3 Asymmetrical Spinnaker Sets

Bear Away Set

The spinnaker is typically set from a turtle or bag set in the companionway. On larger boats the sail is set from a bag secured to the leeward rail. Prior to the hoist the pole is extended. The tack line is pulled prior to or simultaneous to the hoist to pull the tack to the end of the sprit. Getting the sail out and around the spreaders will give you a smoother hoist. A quick hoist helps prevent twists, and once the sail is up the sheet is trimmed to fill the sail. As with a conventional spinnaker, a big ease is needed for best acceleration as the sail fills. Fig. 2.

Fig. 2 - On an asymmetrical spinnaker set extend sprit and pre-pull the tack line as you come into the mark. At full hoist, trim the sheet and roll the jib.

Sets - Variations

Jibe sets with asymmetricals are very much like conventional sets. The difference is that you are set up with the spinnaker to windward and bear away to an immediate jibe as you round the mark: Extend the sprit, pre-pull the tack line if time allows, and hoist. You can start your hoist as you bear away, and hoist full speed once you are on a broad reach. For best results make sure the spinnaker is in front of the spreaders before jibing the main.

The only other variation in asymmetrical sets is being set up for a bear away set, and changing tactics to a jibe set. In this case you must hoist quickly and trim the new sheet prior to your jibe. If you jibe without trimming the spinnaker will either blow around out front, with the clew outside the luff, or blow into the foretriangle, rather than through the gap in between the forestay and spinnaker luff.

The only other permutation of spinnaker sets is sailing a bear away set but having the spinnaker gear set up to windward, as though you were doing a jibe set. The best course of action here is to remove the tack line, halyard, and sheets from the sail, tie them all in a bundle, pull them around the boat, and hook them up again on the correct side. Obviously it is best to figure out that you need to do all this well in advance - not on your final dash into the mark.

10.4 Asymmetrical Spinnaker Jibes

Asymmetrical spinnaker jibes are much easier than conventional jibes, but to be done right they require coordinated effort on the part of the entire crew. When executed perfectly the spinnaker pops full on the new jibe with nary a luff, and the boat shoots ahead on the new tack.

Here's how it works:

At the hail of prepare to jibe the driver turns down while the crew hike to weather to roll the boat down. The trimmer overhauls the new sheet and eases the old sheet. At about the time the clew reaches the headstay the spinnaker loses air behind the main. The trimmer keeps pulling while the driver snaps the boat through the rest of the turn, coming to a course with the apparent wind a little aft of the beam. The spinnaker snaps across and fills on the new tack. The trimmer immediately eases the sail as the boat accelerates out of the turn, and the driver pushes the boat down to course.

A couple of details can help assure success. One is loading the new sheet and overhauling as you ease the old sheet. Don't let the old sheet run until the new sheet is loaded. At the same time, make sure the old sheet runs free as you jibe. It is equally important to steer properly through the turn. You want to ease into the turn and then snap through the finish to complete the jibe and quickly get up to speed.

Easing the tack line a few feet is another helpful technique. If you go into the turn from a close reach, with the tack snug to the pole, easing a few feet will let the luff blow forward, and make it easier to jibe the clew inside the luff. Fig. 3.

Here are some problems

Early turn / late trim:

If the boat is turned before the new sheet is overhauled the sail will backwind into the foretriangle. You will then have to pull hard and drag the sail around, or jibe back to blow the sail clear, and try again. Overhauling the new sheet prior to jibing is essential. Fig.

No overhaul:

If you release the old sheet before loading up the new sheet the spinnaker clew will blow out in front of the luff. You will have to try it back in to keep the clew inside the luff before you jibe. If you jibe with the clew out front then you'll either have to jibe back or pull like crazy to flip the clew inside the luff. Fig.

Slow turn:

If you turn too slowly at the end of the jibe the spinnaker will be starved by the main, and won't refill. You need to snap through the end of the turn to get the spinnaker across and full on the new jibe, then drive down.

No ease - stall or round up

When you do snap through the jibe you need to ease the sheet as the sail fills and the boat accelerates. If the spinnaker is overtrimmed, and stalled, you won't jump up to full speed - or onto a plane - as you will with a proper ease out of the jibe.

Fig. 3 - The key to good jibes is an aggressive overhaul of the windward spinnaker sheet, and an equally aggressive ease as the spinnaker fills on the new jibe. Pulling the new sheet early and hard keeps the clew from blowing forward of the luff. Easing out of the jibe provides a burst of acceleration which is missed if the sail is over trimmed.

10.5 Asymmetrical Takedowns

There are countless takedown variations - not all of which are desirable. Among the several you might plan your choice depends on your approach, the conditions, and your needs for the next set.

Conventional

If you will round without a jibe then a conventional leeward drop is the easiest. First, set your jib. Then pull down the spinnaker by easing the tack, gathering the foot, and running the halyard. When the approach is a close reach the driver can ease things tremendously by squaring down to a broad reach momentarily while the sail is gathered and dropped. During the initial phase, easing the tack line, you can also retract the pole. Fig. 4.

If traffic to leeward prevents squaring away the takedown can be challenging indeed. Easing the tackline in these circumstances just allows the sail to blow aft. A better approach is blowing the halyard halfway to start the gather, and then easing the tack line and balance of halyard from there.

Fig. 4 - On a leeward takedown ease the tack line and grab the clew, then run the halyard and gather like crazy.

Jibe Drop

The jibe drop is the easiest way to take down an asymmetrical spinnaker. As you prepare to jibe, set your jib. Next, retract the pole and pull the sail aft. As you square away to jibe, lower the halyard and pull the sail down. As you jibe the sail will be blown on board, where it is easy to gather. Fig. 5.

Windward takedown

There are times when you will need to take the spinnaker down to windward, in anticipation of you next spinnaker set. It is a little ugly, but it can be done; and it is better than releading gear later, or not being ready for the next set.

Here goes: With you jib flying, overhaul the windward spinnaker sheet and drag the clew of the sail around the forestay, and back along the windward side. As you can imagine, performance suffers as the sail backs. As soon as you have cloth (or nearly so), release the tack line and lower the halyard. Drag the sail down.

Before you try this takedown be sure all your pins and fittings are taped to hide sharp edges. Windward takedowns invite snags and tears.

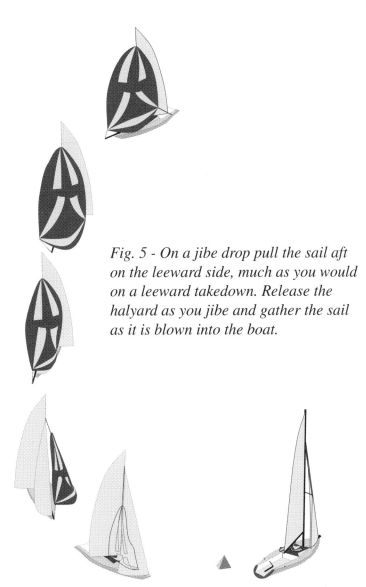

Fig. 5 - On a jibe drop pull the sail aft on the leeward side, much as you would on a leeward takedown. Release the halyard as you jibe and gather the sail as it is blown into the boat.

10.6 Conventional Boats

The reaching performance of asymmetrical spinnakers make them an attractive addition to the sail inventory on conventionally rigged boats. The spinnaker handling requirements are a hybrid of sprit boat and conventional technique. Following are a few details.

Rigging

The spinnaker pole is carried low, and usually well forward. The sails requires two long sheets - both attached to the clew, and two guys - lead well forward, and inside the lifelines. In addition, a tack pennant is needed to hold the spinnaker tack during jibes.

Sets

The spinnaker is hooked up and hoisted much like a conventional spinnaker, although a few details differ. Both sheets are hooked to the clew, and both guys are attached to the tack. If you do not intend to jibe a single sheet and guy will do.

Jibes

Jibing an asymmetrical on a conventional boat differs from sprit boat jibes in two ways. First, the spinnaker clew jibes around the front, outside the luff. Second, the pole must be jibed.

The spinnaker sheet must be eased way out as the boat turns downwind to get the spinnaker out in front of the boat. The new sheet must then be trimmed to drag the spinnaker around the front and in on the new side. Fig. 6.

In the meantime, the pole is jibed from one side of the headstay to the other. The easiest method for jibing the pole is to rig a pennant from the jib tack fitting to the tack of the spinnaker. Fly the spinnaker from the pennant while you dip the pole.

Take Downs

When dousing a conventional asymmetrical you can use the *Stretch and Blow* method described in the previous chapter if you are doing a leeward takedown. If your rounding involves a jibe use the *Jibe Drop* described earlier in this chapter. For any asymmetrical drop you have the option of taking down the pole first.

Conclusion

Asymmetrical spinnakers on conventional boats provide great reaching performance. The handling methods are a hybrid of conventional and sport boat technique. It will take some testing to sort out the best mix for your rig.

10.7 Conclusion

If you've not sailed a sport boat it is hard to fully appreciate their appeal. One word of caution before you take a test sail: Once you try it you may never want to go back to the complexity of conventional rigs. Sprit boats are fast, fun, and easy. We'll cover trimming methods in Chapter 12, to follow.

Fig. 6 - Jibing an asymmetrical spinnaker on a conventionally rigged boat requires jibing the clew around the front, outside the luff of the spinnaker. The old sheet must be eased and the new sheet trimmed to pull the sail around.

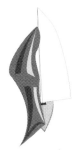

CHAPTER 11 - SPINNAKER TRIM

11.1   INTRODUCTION

11.2   INITIAL TRIM

11.3   REACHING TRIM

11.4   MORE REACHING TRIM

11.5   RUNNING TRIM

11.6   CONCLUSION

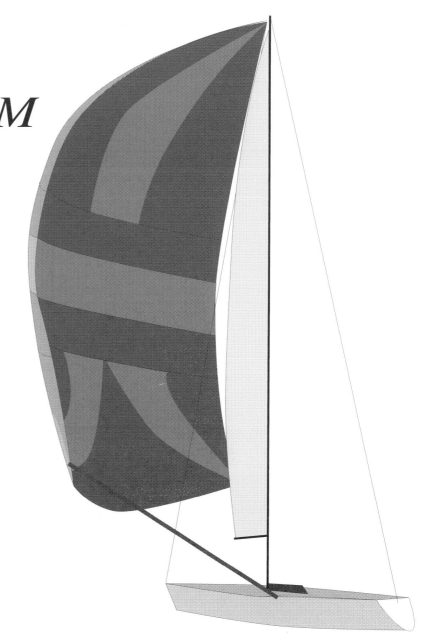

CHAPTER 11 - SPINNAKER TRIM

11.1 Introduction

The racing spinnaker is really two sails in one - a reaching sail and a running sail. Modern materials and design allow us to change the shape of a spinnaker much as we do with any other sail. We can fine tune spinnaker shape for peak performance in a wide variety of conditions and wind angles.

This chapter will start with initial spinnaker trim. From there we will look at refined trim for reaches, runs, and special conditions, such as heavy air and close reaching. Asymmetrical Spinnaker Trim is covered in Chapter 12, next,

11.2 Initial Trim

The are three standard rules of spinnaker trim:

One, trim the guy to set the spinnaker pole perpendicular to the apparent wind. Refer to telltales or the mast head fly to set the pole angle.

Two, set the pole height so the clews even. The clews should be at an equal height above the deck, regardless of heel.

Three, play the spinnaker sheet - ease to a curl and trim - ease and trim.

These initial settings are only the beginning. From here you can refine trim and control shape just as you do with your other sails. Fig. 1.

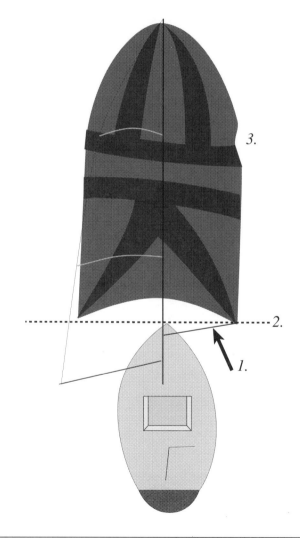

Fig. 1 - There are 3 rules to initial trim:
1. Set the pole perpendicular to the wind.
2. Adjust pole height so the clews are even.
3. Play the sheet - ease to a curl and trim; ease and trim.

11.3 Reaching Trim

Trim on reaches means maximizing straight line speed. Later, we'll look at running trim, where both speed and angle come into play.

On a reach the spinnaker behaves and trims like a genoa. At apparent wind angles of 60° to 135° there is flow across the sail. Since we have flow, spinnaker telltales are a useful trim guide on a reach. Put a set of telltales half way up your sail, about 15" from each luff. The telltales work on a spinnaker much as they do on a genoa. The outside telltale is a particularly valuable guide to prevent over trimming and stalling. Fig. 2.

Spinnakers are designed symmetrically because the luff and leech reverse when we jibe. This shape- with the draft up the middle, and the leech shaped exactly like the luff - is less than ideal. Sails with discreet luffs and leeches are never designed this way. A better shape puts the draft further forward, and opens the leech for easier flow. We will trim to the spinnaker to this preferred shape.

Sail selection

If you have a choice of spinnakers your reaching angle may help you decide which one to use. On a close reach, where the sail is heavily loaded, select the heavier cloth. Spinnaker cloth is stretchy by nature, and the heavier sail will stretch less and hold a better shape. On a broad reach use the lighter spinnaker. It will set up better and sail faster. Lighter weight sails have been proven faster for broad reaching.

Spinnaker controls

We have three controls which affect spinnaker shape: Pole height, guy trim, and lead position. These three are all secondary, of course, to the spinnaker sheet, which must be played constantly. We'll look at each.

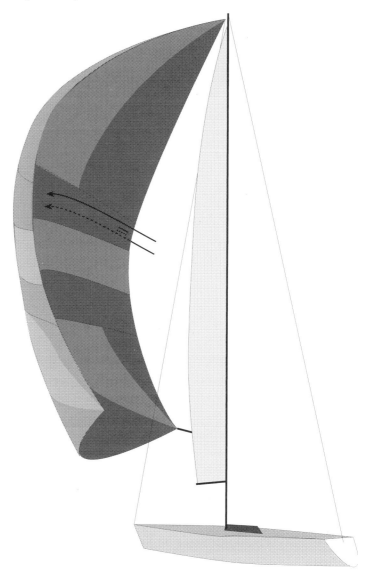

Fig. 2 - On reaches the spinnaker has flow across the sail, from luff to leech. Starting from initial trim settings, our goal is to adjust shape to suit the conditions.

Sheet Trim

Spinnaker trim requires the trimmer's full undivided attention. The sheet should be played constantly. An overtrimmed spinnaker is slow. Ease to a curl and trim, ease and trim. If the trimmer stops playing the sheet the boat speed will suffer; and if the trimmer fails to give the spinnaker his full undivided attention the spinnaker will collapse in a fit of jealous rage. Fig. 3.

The spinnaker telltales can help with sheet trim. The outside telltale is the important one - if it stalls the sail is overtrimmed. On a broad reach the telltales may not fly, but keep playing the sheet.

Pole Height

Pole height is controlled by the topping lift. Starting from our initial position with the clews even we can fine tune to draft position. Lowering the pole will pull the draft forward, just as adding luff tension pulls the draft forward in other sails. It creates a more open leech, and a rounder entry. On a reach the tack will be slightly lower than the clew. Correct pole height is shown in figure 3.

If the pole is too low, the shoulder along the luff will cave in, and the leech will twist open, spilling power. Fig. 4.

If the pole is too high, the luff will fall to leeward, and the leech will close, creating excess heeling force. Fig. 5

Pull the draft just forward of the middle of the sail. On heavy air reaches a low pole will prevent the draft from being blown aft. In light air a high pole position, with the clews even, will provide extra power.

The heel of the pole on the mast should be adjusted to keep the pole level, but don't sweat it if the pole is six inches out of level.

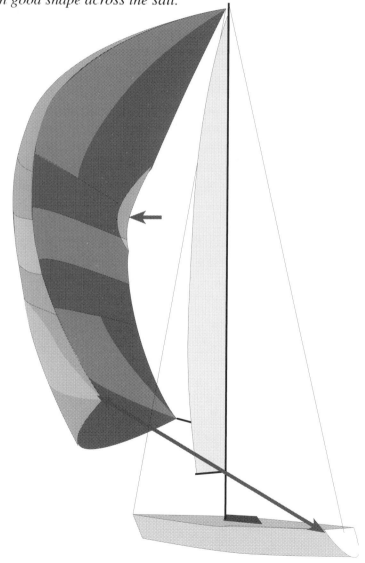

Fig. 3 - Spinnaker Sheet, and pole height.
Play the sheet constantly - ease to a luff and trim, ease and trim. Play the sheet constantly. The pole height here is correct, with good shape across the sail.

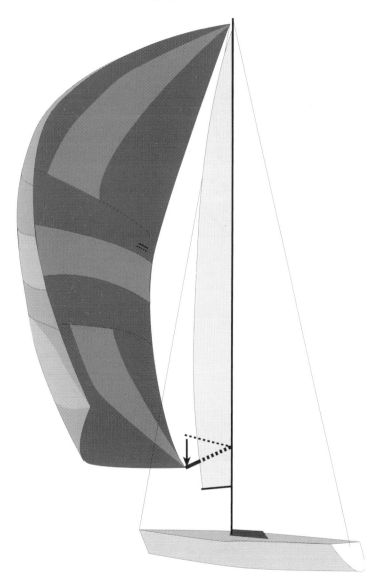

Fig. 4 - Here, the pole is too low. The upper luff is caving in, and the leech is spilling open

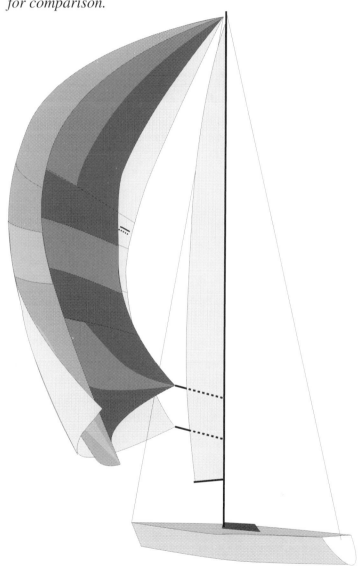

Fig. 5 - Here, the pole is too high. The upper luff is falling away, and the leech is closed. A proper sail shape is silhouetted for comparison.

Guy Trim

Guy trim controls pole position. From the initial trim position with the pole perpendicular to the wind you can trim the pole aft a little further.

Look for a vertical spinnaker luff from the shoulder to the tack. If the pole is too far aft the luff will fade to leeward of the pole. Ease the pole forward. If the pole is too far forward the shoulder of the spinnaker will project out to windward of the pole. In this case pull the pole aft.

The other guide to guy trim is shape across the foot of the spinnaker. Try to match the shape across the foot to the shape across the horizontal panels. If the foot is deep trim the guy and pull the pole aft. If the foot of the spinnaker is flat or the spinnaker is strapped against the forestay ease the guy (and the sheet). Fig. 6.

Sheet Lead

The spinnaker sheet lead is used to control reaching spinnaker shape much the same way the genoa lead controls genoa shape. The first step in shaping is to follow the sail with the lead. This means that on a close reach the lead should be all the way aft, at the quarter.

As the course opens up to a broad reach and the sheet is eased the lead should be moved forward, chasing the clew. If the lead is left aft as the clew moves forward the sail will float too high - sacrificing area, the leech will spill open - spilling power. Fig. 7.

On a broad reach, with the lead in the correct position we can make further adjustments to suit conditions. The lead can be choked down further for extra power and a more stable shape in chop, or it can be eased aft to spill open the leech in heavy air.

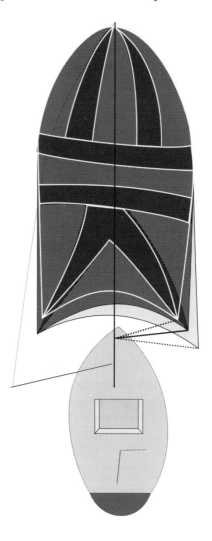

Fig. 6 - There are two guidelines to guy trim:
First we want a vertical spinnaker luff from the shoulder to the tack.
Second, the shape across the foot of the chute should match the shape across the horizontal panels.

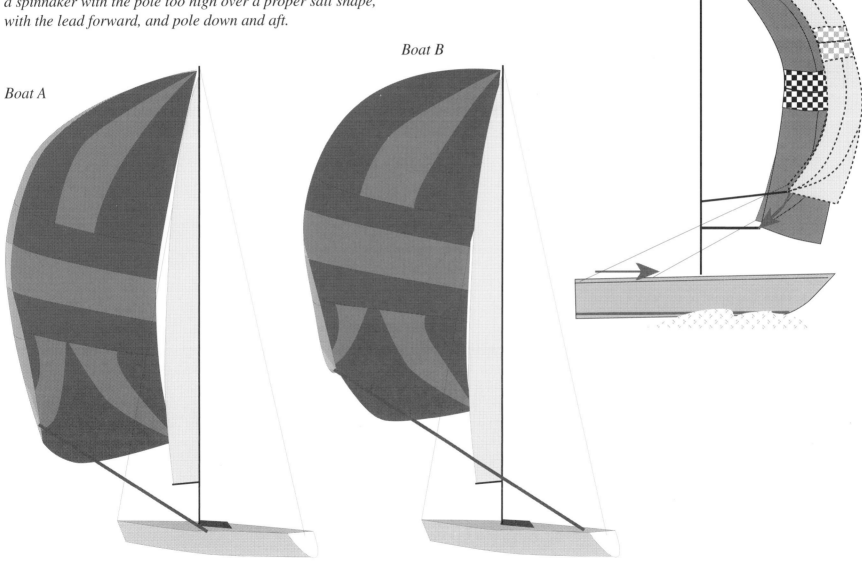

Fig. 7 - As the spinnaker rotates forward on a broad reach the lead should move forward too, as on Boat A. Otherwise the sail will float too high, as on Boat B. Boat C silhouettes a spinnaker with the pole too high over a proper sail shape, with the lead forward, and pole down and aft.

Boat C

Boat B

Boat A

11.4 More Reaching Trim

Close Reaching Trim

It is on a close reach, with the wind forward of the beam, that the spinnaker behaves most like a genoa. It is here that the telltales are most useful. Proper trim can be judged by telltale flow, rather than a curl, with might lead to a collapse.

You can improve close reaching performance by adjusting the spinnaker shape to conditions. For closer pointing in light to moderate air set the pole a little high. This gives the sail a flatter entry, which is a closer winded shape. This high pole position puts the draft aft, creating more heeling forces and drag, so it is slow; but it is better than a collapsed spinnaker and it allows a few extra degrees of pointing.

For heavy air close reaching try a low pole position, and pull the pole a foot off the headstay. This pulls the draft forward, flattens the sail, and opens the leech to spill excess power. This pole position creates less drag and heel, but the round entry does not point as high as a normal shape. Fig. 8.

It is imperative in heavy air conditions that the sheet be eased in puffs or when overpowered; otherwise you round up, out of control. The sheet should be eased as a puff hits, before the boat heels over, so the extra force can be translated into speed rather than heeling. The vang and mainsheet should be in hand, ready to dump in a big puff to prevent a round up.

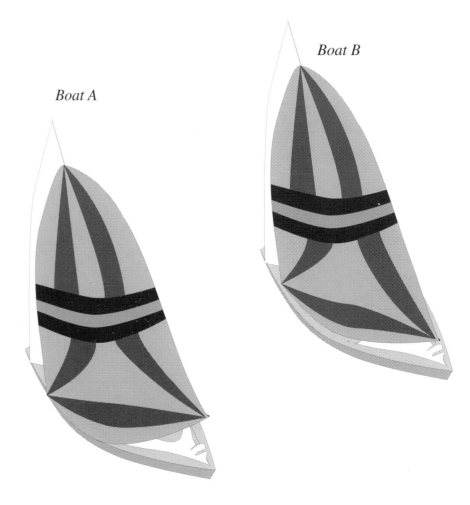

Fig. 8 - Boat A - On a close reach in moderate air adjust the pole to control power and pointing ability. Note the genoa on deck, rigged, and ready to go.
Boat B - In heavy air a low pole position pulls the draft forward and opens the leech, helping to de-power.

Boat B

Boat A

Spinnaker Staysails

Staysails can add valuable tenths to boat speed. They are most effective in ideal conditions - beam reaching in smooth water and moderate breeze. The further conditions are from ideal the less effective the staysail will be.

Set the tack of the staysail half way between the main and the spinnaker, as far to windward as possible. On a beam reach the staysail should be tacked along the center line. As the pole is trimmed aft on a broad reach the staysail tack should follow the pole and move to windward and aft. Set the halyard tight and adjust the luff cloth tension separately for a smooth even shape. Position the lead to keep the staysail between the main and spinnaker, and set the lead so the sail sets a little soft up high. Fig. 9.

Never overtrim a staysail. It will starve the spinnaker and cause a collapse. Trim the staysail a little soft, and dump the sheet if the spinnaker collapses.

The Magic Rule

Use the staysail only if it improves speed. (WOW!) If it slows you down take it down. If it doesn't help speed, or it makes the spinnaker difficult to trim, then douse it. Remember that the spinnaker is the first priority.

Fig. 9 - Staysails can add speed in ideal conditions.
Boat A - On a beam reach tack the staysail on the centerline, and trim the staysail halfway between the mainsail and spinnaker.
Boat B - On a broad reach move the staysail tack outboard and aft, following the spinnaker pole.

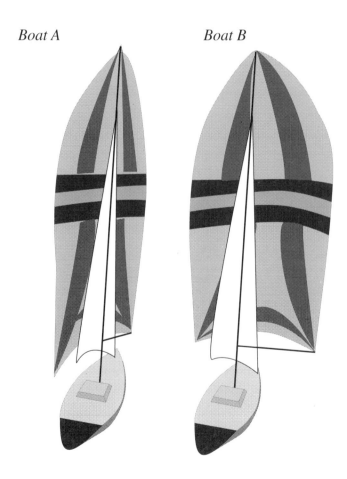

Boat A   *Boat B*

11.5 Running Trim

Sailing a spinnaker run rarely means pointing at the mark and sailing to it. Usually it involves tacking downwind, reaching up for extra speed and sailing extra distance. On reaches we were concerned only with speed. On runs we are concerned with both speed and angle.

Light Air - 3 to 10 knots

In winds from 3 to 10 knots it pays to tack downwind aggressively. The jibing angles nearly match our tacking angles upwind - about 40° above dead downwind, or 140° true wind angle. We more than make up for the extra distance sailed with extra speed. Light air sheets will help the sail fly (as will removing the lazy guy if you normally use one). Fig. 10.

Sheet Trim

Play the sheet, with an emphasis on easing the sail every chance you get. The apparent wind angle will be near the beam (90°), to perhaps 110°. In these conditions the driver maintains a steady true wind angle, working up and down only 5° or so, in response to changes in wind and boat speed. The trimmer should help call the boat up or down as sheet load changes.

Pole Height

From our initial setting, with the clews even, we can adjust pole height to the improve spinnaker shape. In the low end of the wind scale carrying the pole a little high can help lift the entire sail. As the wind speed nears ten knots holding the pole down can pull the spinnaker into a more efficient shape. Play with pole height to find the position which provides the best speed and easiest trim.

Fig. 10 - In light winds of 3 to 10 knots optimum performance is obtained at a consistent true wind angle of 140°-145°. The apparent wind angle shifts aft, from about 95° in the lightest air to 115° in 10 knots. See Boats 1-4.

In moderate winds of 10 to 14 knots, the optimum true wind angle changes dramatically. In 10 knots a rue wind angle of 145° is best. The optimum angle swings aft to 165° in 14 knots of wind. Boats 4, 5, and 6.

In heavy winds, over 15 knots true, a direct course to the mark, or a course which allows surfing, is the fastest. Boat 7.

Guy Trim

In the lightest air the pole will be near the headstay. As the wind builds the pole can be pulled back beyond the initial *perpendicular to the wind* setting. As described earlier, try to match the foot shape to the shape across the middle of the sail. If the foot is too round, pull the pole back. If the foot is stretched flat, then ease the pole forward.

Lead Position

In virtually all light air work the lead should be left aft. The exception would be in …

Chop

Chop can shake the wind out of the spinnaker. Try choking down the lead and pole for a more stable shape. It is easy to mistake a shake for a luff - be careful not to overtrim the spinnaker. And reach up. Get enough speed to crush the chop.

Crew Weight

Keep weight forward and leeward in the lightest winds to lift the stern out of the water and reduce wetted surface. As the breeze builds move weight up and aft to control heel.

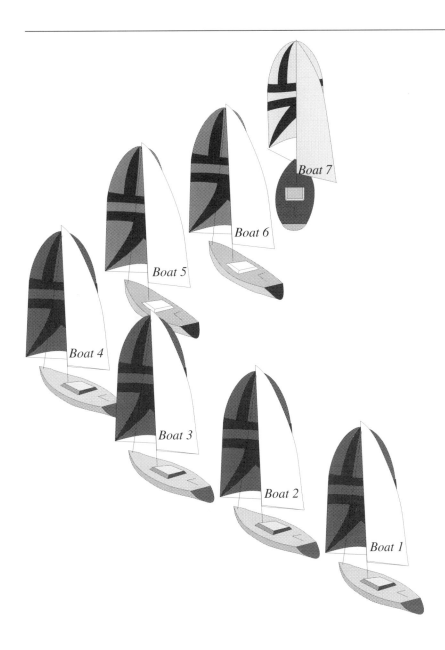

Boat 7

Boat 6

Boat 5

Boat 4

Boat 3

Boat 2

Boat 1

Moderate Air - 10 to 15 knots

Across the moderate wind range performance changes dramatically. From an optimum true wind angle of 140° in 10 knots of wind we can push down to 165° true wind angle in 15 knots of breeze. The apparent wind angle will also swing dramatically, from about 115° to 155°.

Sheet Trim

The trimmer and driver must work together to sail the boat as low as possible while maintaining speed. The best gauge is *not* matching true wind angle to wind speed. Instead, use sheet load as your guide. Anytime the sheet is pulling hard drive the boat down, and whenever the load is light come up. Big changes in course and trim are appropriate in response to changes in wind speed.

Pole Height

As the pole comes aft it should also go up. When the apparent wind is forward we keep the pole lower to hold the draft forward. As the wind and pole move aft a higher pole position opens up the luff at the head for bigger projected area. If the pole is too high then the top of the sail becomes too flat, and area is lost below the pole.

Guy Trim

Play the pole constantly, in unison with the sheet and with the changes in apparent wind angle. Trim to maintain a vertical luff and proper foot shape.

Crew Weight

Sail the boat flat to maintain a neutral helm. Adjust crew weight to help steer the boat, as described in Section 4 of Chapter 13 - *Not Steering Downwind.*

Heavy Air - 15 knots +

When the true wind speed exceeds 15 knots never mind tacking downwind. Point the boat at the mark and sail as fast as you can.

Sheet Trim

The sheet must be eased way out to get the spinnaker out from behind the main. Ease to a curl and trim, ease and trim. Keep the clew of the spinnaker to leeward of the forestay. If the clew rolls out to windward of the forestay, the foot becomes too round, and we lose projected area.

Pole Height

Set the pole to control luff shape and to hold a 50% draft position. If the pole is too high the luff will be open and flat. Also, if the pole is too high it will allow the entire spinnaker to float up, costing projected area. If the pole is too low the luff will be too round, and cave in.

Guy Trim

Trim the guy back as far as possible while keeping a vertical luff. On a very deep broad reach the pole will be trimmed out perpendicular to the boat, maximizing area. If the boat starts to roll out of control let the pole forward to put the center of the spinnaker directly over the bow.

If the spinnaker has a deep shape throughout then flatten the sail by trimming back on the guy as the sheet is trimmed. If the sail is strapped flat then ease both sides. When the spinnaker clew floats out to windward of the forestay the sheet should be trimmed to get the clew back to leeward. Often the guy can be trimmed at the same time, spreading the entire spinnaker into a bigger shape.

Fig. 11 - In heavy air surf the waves. Use smooth driving to carry speed, and aggressive trim to keep up with changing apparent wind angles.

Lead Position

The lead should be forward, to keep the spinnaker from floating too high, and outboard to project more sail area. Leading the sheet under the outboard end of the boom can accomplish this. If the spinnaker sheet sags down and needs the support of the boom then there is not enough wind to sail effectively on a run - reach up for speed.

Crew Weight

Put weight to windward can create windward heel. This will help the spinnaker fall out from behind the mainsail, and it will also help force the boat down to a lower angle while carrying speed. When things get out of control balance crew weight side to side - well separated - and move everybody to the stern.

Surf

Rather than sail straight at the mark, alter course to take advantage of the waves. To catch a wave, trim and head up to build speed. As you start down the wave drive off to stay on the wave, and trim as the apparent wind shifts forward. Be ready to ease as you fall off the wave and the boat slows; and head up to catch the next one. Fig. 11.

Too Much Wind

Running downwind in *very* heavy air can be hair raising, as the boat starts to roll and control becomes marginal. To minimize rolling choke down the sheet lead (perhaps as far forward as max beam) and lower the pole. Also, tighten the vang. Keep the spinnaker in front of the boat. Trim so the center of the sail is over the bow. If the spinnaker gets too far to windward it can roll the boat to windward and cause a jibe broach. Not a pretty picture. Steer the boat under the spinnaker and head up slightly to avoid an accidental jibe.

Fig. 12 - A jibe broach can make a mess. Avoid them by steering up, over trimming, and putting weight to leeward. When you do crash, hold on. Make sure you spinnaker halyard is ready to run, and dump it.

Whoa

WHOA

WHOA

WHOA WHOA

WHOA WHOA WHOA

Wow.
That was cool.
Let's do it again.

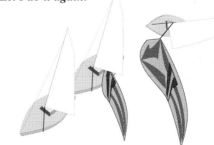

When You Crash...

A jibe broach starts with innocent rolling. Suddenly you find the world has turned on its side. Hold on. Dump the spinnaker halyard and the boat will stand up. (Make sure the halyard is ready to run in heavy air - not in coils, but belayed, or trailing behind the boat. Pull the sail on board, repack it, and try again... Fig. 12 (previous page).

Too Little Wind

You may have noticed that we start light air at 3 knots of wind. When the wind is lighter than that, do anything you can to get the boat moving. Speed is your only friend. Once you are moving then you can try to aim more or less at the mark (or back to the harbor). Good luck.

BLOOPER Trim

If you carry one, well, good luck to ya. For trim, we suggest you select one of the three approaches listed here:

1. Sailing on a run in moderate to heavy air set the blooper on a three foot pennant from the jib tack fitting. Lead the sheet outboard of everything (including the spinnaker sheet) and hoist the blooper to leeward of the spinnaker. Ease the halyard and sheet to get the blooper clear of the main. Play the sheet to keep the sail full. Play the halyard to keep the sail out of the water. When the sail luffs sometimes you have to trim, sometimes you have to ease, and sometimes it is best to just pump the sheet to resuscitate the sail. Fig. 13.

2. Get the guy you bought it from to you to show you how it works.

3. Race in IMS, where bloopers are prohibited.

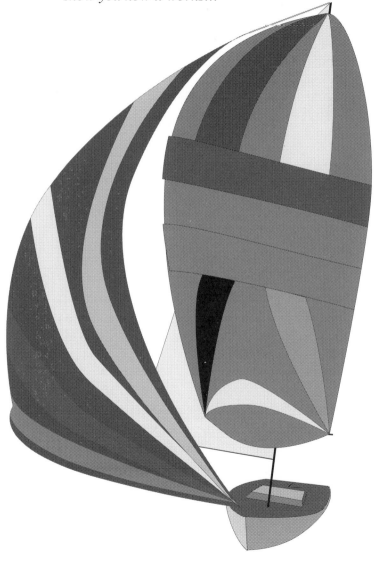

Fig. 13 - If you own a blooper make the guy who sold it to you show you how it works...

11.6 Conclusion

Spinnaker trim starts from an initial setting with the pole perpendicular to the wind and the clews even, but there is much more to it than that. Work with your spinnaker controls to shape your spinnaker to suit conditions. If you get confused in the fine tuning process the go back to the initial settings and try again.

Color Selection

Once critical and under appreciated part of spinnaker trim is the original color selection. A spinnaker which is pleasing to the eye is easier to trim than some garish color sampler. Fig. 14.

From a practical standpoint it is best to have contrasting colors along the edges of the spinnaker. A sharp contrast between the first and second panels makes the curl easier to see, particularly at night.

Range and Care

If properly cared for your spinnakers will give you years of top performance. To help assure their long life use them only in conditions appropriate to the cloth weight. *Appropriate* depends on the weight of the cloth, the weight of your boat, wind strength, sea state, and sailing angle. Your sailmaker can tell you more.

Your sail will perform better if you pack it clean and dry. The colors may run in a wet sail. Also, do not leave your spinnaker in stops for weeks at a time.

For the latest on spinnaker handling, including packing, sets, jibes, douses, and peels, go back to Chapter 9 - Downwind Boat Handling. For a look at Asymmetrical Spinnaker Trim, turn the page to Chapter 12.

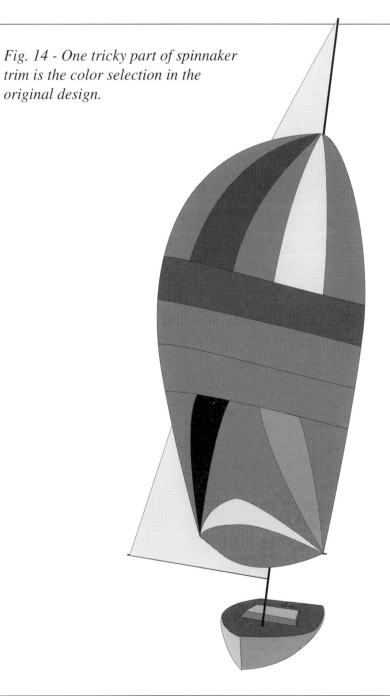

Fig. 14 - One tricky part of spinnaker trim is the color selection in the original design.

CHAPTER 12 - ASYMMETRICAL SPINNAKER TRIM

12.1 REACHING

12.2 BROAD REACHING

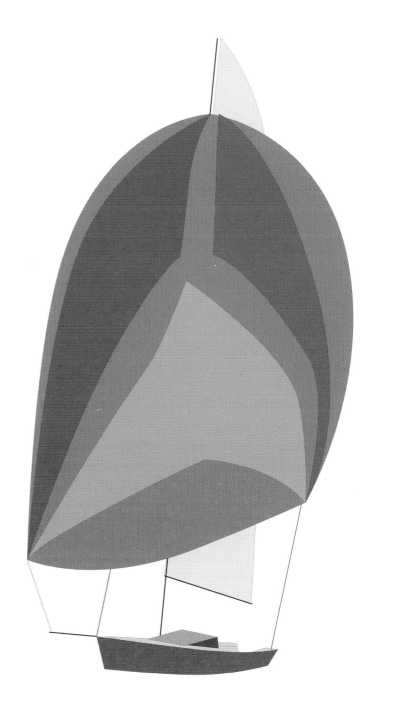

CHAPTER 12 - ASYMMETRICAL SPINNAKER TRIM

12.1 Reaching

The asymmetrical spinnakers on sports boats obviously trim differently than conventional spinnakers. Due to their extended, fixed position bow sprit they differ from the asymmetricals flown on conventionally rigged boats as well.

Aside from the sheet and halyard, the only other controls over spinnaker shape are the spinnaker tack line, which runs from the end of the sprit to the spinnaker tack, and a twing, or choker, for the sheet. Not all boats are rigged with twings.

Ease and trim

Regardless of point of sail the basic principles apply: Ease to a luff and trim. Given the rapid acceleration of these boats the apparent wind angle is changing all the time. Aggressive trimming is required to keep up as the boat builds speed, and an equally aggressive ease is needed to prevent a stall as the boat slows. Overtrimmed is very slow. On a close reach trim to telltales, or a small curl. On a broader reach force the sail out to a bigger curl. You will be surprised how far out it can go.

Tack Line

As the course opens up from a close reach to broad reach the tack line should be eased. On a close reach the tack should be snug to the pole, putting the sail into a gennaker shape. On a broader reach add power and allow rotation out from behind the main by easing the tack line a few feet.

There are a couple of clues to guide how far to ease the tack line: One guideline is sail shape. Easing the tack line adds power, so adjust accordingly. In light air ease the tack line

Fig. 1 - Boat A, on a beam reach, is trimmed with some ease in the tack line, which creates extra shape and power.
Boat B, on a close reach, has snugged the tack line down, for a less powerful, higher pointing shape.

some, even on a beam reach. Broad reaching in a big blow you may not want to ease as far as you would in lighter air.

Another valuable guide is the spinnaker telltales. Put telltales 1.5 to 2 feet from the luff at 1/3 and 2/3 height. When your tackline is set at the proper height the telltales should behave similarly high and low.

Boat A

Boat B

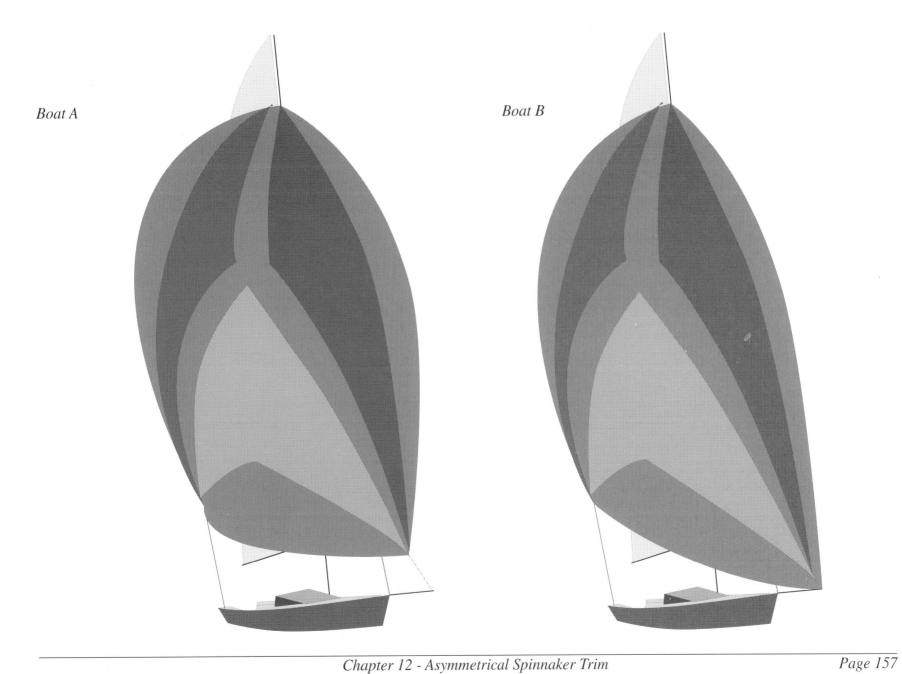

12.2 Broad Reaching

One of the challenges of asymmetricals is squaring down to a broad reach with a fixed pole on center line. With proper technique the boats can sail fairly deep. The first trick is speed. The goal is to keep the apparent wind angle favorable even as the true wind angle is pushed aft. You should always feel the breeze blowing across the boat - not stern to bow. When you lose apparent wind flow across the boat head up to rebuild speed and apparent wind.

For best broad reaching performance the tack line (and sheet) must be eased to allow the sail to roll out to windward. As you work the boat up and down it can be fast to play the tack line and the sheet. As the boat bears off and the sheet is eased ease the tack line. As you head up trim the tack line to keep the sail from blowing off to leeward. Windward heel can also help.

At times on a broad reach it may pay to ease the halyard a foot or two as well. This will allow the entire sail to rotate further out to weather. There are a couple of things to guide you in how far you ease the halyard: Does the sail rotate out to weather? Can you sail lower or faster? If the sail hangs down, instead of rolling out to weather, then you have over-eased the halyard - or you are sailing too low! Likewise, if you lose control with the halyard eased then snug it up. Fig. 2.

Marginal Planing Conditions

As the true wind builds to around 15 knots you may be able to plane. It will pay to reach way up to get on a plane and then carry the plane down. Your planing speed will overwhelm the extra distance sailed worked up to get on a plane - and crush the competition. On the other hand, if you can't plane you can waste plenty of energy going the wrong way...

Fig. 2 - Boat A: On a broad reach ease the sheet and tack line to get the spinnaker out from behind the main.
Boat B is able to sail deeper by easing the halyard a few feet, which allows the entire sail to rotate further out to windward.

Boat A

Boat B

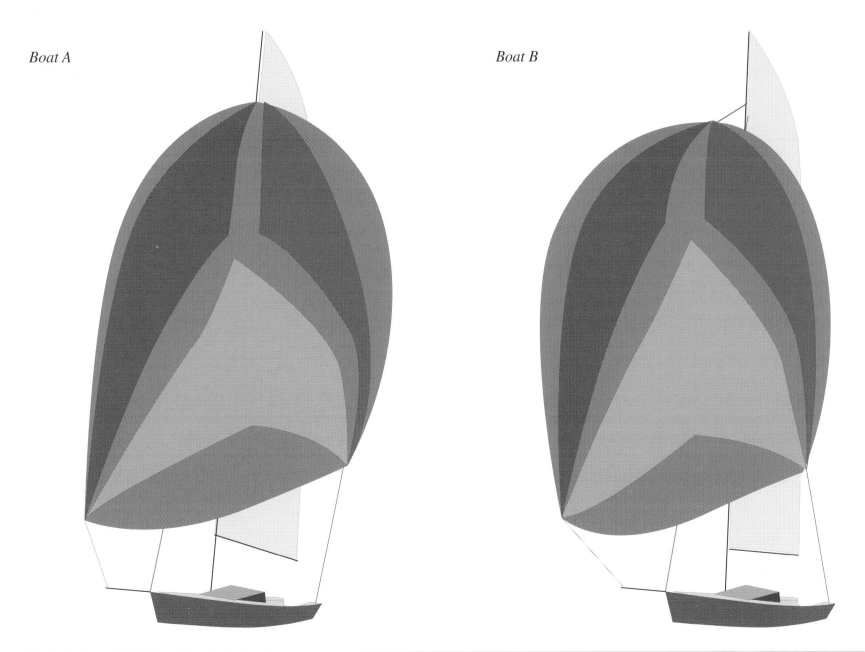

Running By the Lee

Often it is fast - very fast - to run by the lee. With the wind over the starboard quarter the main should be set to starboard, with the spinnaker to port. Ease the tack line and halyard several feet to fly the spinnaker well out to weather. The boat will roll to weather. Let it roll, and hang on! Fig. 3.

BONUS Boat Handling Tips:

Ducking is dangerous!

On a port - starboard crossing when tacking downwind beware the hazard when ducking. As you reach up to take the starboard boats stern you accelerate, and need to head up higher still! You may suddenly you find yourself rail down, with your spinnaker draped over the starboard boat, or you may round up and broach.

So are mark roundings

If you are trying to cut inside a competitor at a leeward mark rounding, make sure you retract your sprit. Otherwise, you may get your bow inside the rival's stern, only to foul him as your sprit sweeps over his stern!

Similarly, when approaching a weather mark on port tack, with starboard tack traffic, it pays to keep your sprit retracted as you maneuver. Conversely, starboard boats should go for full extension, to keep port boats from crossing.

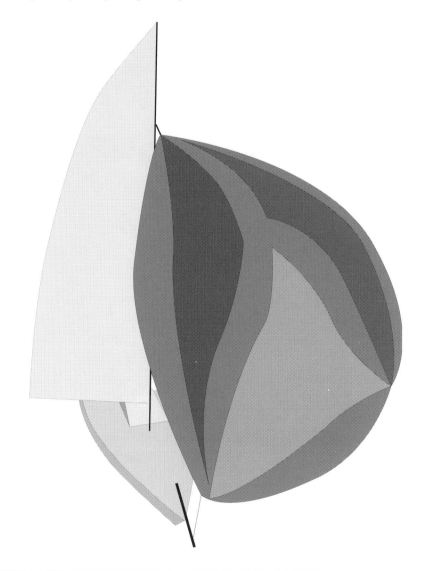

Fig. 3 - In moderate to heavy breeze, sailing slightly by the lee, and carrying the asymmetrical spinnaker wing and wing is a very tricky, but fast, point of sail.

CHAPTER 13 - DRIVING DOWNWIND

13.1   INTRODUCTION

13.2   REACHING

13.3   RUNNING

13.4   NOT STEERING DOWNWIND

13.5   JIBES, & ROUNDINGS

13.6   CONCLUSION

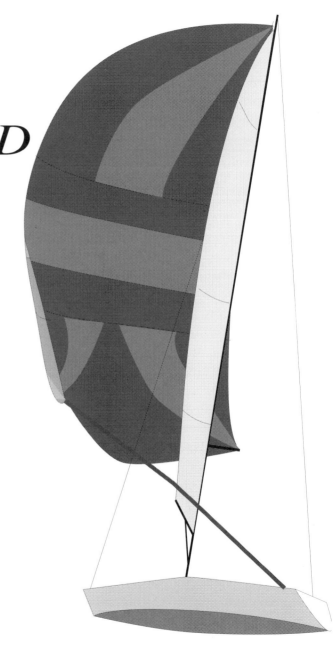

CHAPTER 13 - DRIVING DOWNWIND

13.1 Introduction

Steering off the wind, on reaches and run, requires a coordinated effort between the helmsman and spinnaker trimmer. The spinnaker trimmer often has as good a feel for performance as the driver, and together they can coordinate efforts to take advantage of changes in conditions as they happen.

Of course the driver must respond to other inputs as well. The tactician may suggest one move, and changing sailing conditions may suggest another. At the same time, he is trying to respond to the trimmer's input based on sheet load and boat speed. More often than not there are conflicting suggestions - *Go up. Go down. Be more aggressive. Steer less.*

One effective way to give the driver some peace is to channel all suggestions through the trimmer. Since your tactics won't succeed without good trim, it helps to keep the trimmer in the communications loop. This keeps the trimmer informed. It also makes life easier for the driver, as he must listen and respond to only one voice.

13.2 Steering on Reaches

Light to Moderate Air

The shortest distance between two points is a straight line... at least, on a reach it is. Plan your reaches with this as your basic tenet. From there you will have to make modifications based on tactics and changes in the sailing conditions.

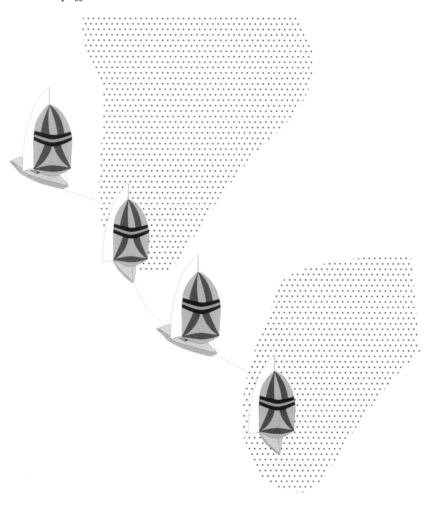

Fig. 1 - On reaches it is best to head up in the lulls and foot off in the puffs.

Performance Racing Trim

In fluctuating wind conditions the helmsman should work up and down as necessary to maintain speed while holding a good average course. *Up in the lulls, off in the puffs*. It is good advice on a reach. Better still is working with the trimmer, heading up when the sheet load is light, and bearing off when the spinnaker sheet is fully loaded. The amount of course change required depends on wind speed. In lighter air a more aggressive luff will be required to load the sail. In more moderate winds it is easier to rebuild speed, and you can be more aggressive working down when fully powered. Fig. 1.

Tactically on a reach there are times when the helmsman must head up abruptly, either in an effort to pass another boat or to defend his position. Alerting the trimmers prior to the move improves the chances of success. An abrupt course change without warning to the trimmers will usually doom the tactic to failure.

Heavy Air

In heavy air the helmsman is at the mercy of his trimmers. The vang, main sheet, and spinnaker sheet must be eased when the boat is overpowered or it will round up and broach. It is fast to carry as much power as you can *as long as you can control it*. Carrying weather helm is OK as long as the rudder doesn't stall, leading to a round up. Don't let an occasional round up discourage you. Regroup and see how long you can go before you round up again.

If you do broach you can speed the recovery by luffing the main and spinnaker. Bear off to a course below your desired sailing angle before you trim. Work up to course only after you trim and regain control at a lower angle. Fig. 2.

Fig. 2 - On a heavy air reach luff the main and dump the vang and spinnaker sheet to prevent a round up.
When you do broach, luff your sails until you can bear off to a course below your earlier angle before you retrim.

Aggressive trim is needed in puffy conditions to relieve helm load and build speed. Easing the sails in puffs translates the force of the puff into speed rather than heeling force.

13.3 Driving on Runs

Goals on a run vary with the wind speed. The driver and trimmers must be clued in to the same goal.

Light Air (4-10 knots true)

In light winds (up to ten knots true) the optimum sailing angle is about 140° true wind angle (40° above dead downwind). The angle changes very little as the wind speed fluctuates. *It is not correct to head up in the lulls and off in the puffs on light air runs*. Tacking downwind, keeping the apparent wind forward, is fast. Play the sheet to the wind, while steering a steady course. Fig. 3, Boats 1-4.

Moderate Air (10-15 knots true)

In moderate winds the optimum speed and sailing angle changes dramatically with every change in wind speed. For every knot of wind the optimum course shifts five degrees. In ten knots of wind the optimum angle is 140° true wind angle. In fifteen knots of wind a 165° true wind angle is optimum.

With every change in wind speed the driver should respond aggressively, driving off with the puffs, and heading up in the lulls. This is in distinct contrast to the correct practice in light air. As the driver steers to course the trimmers must also respond aggressively, working not only the sheet, but the guy and topping lift as well. Fig. 3, Boats 4, 5, 6.

Of course, every movement of the helm slows the boat. To minimize steering refer to the technique described in the next section entitled, *Not Steering Downwind*.

Heavy Air (15 knots and up!)

When the wind exceeds fifteen knots you no longer need concern yourself with changing sailing angles. Aim for the mark. Sail fast. Keep control. Surf if you can. Fig. 3, Boat 7.

Use crew weight to balance the helm, or try some windward heel to push the boat down - as long as you have control. In over powering wind - say twenty plus - control becomes a bigger issue, and windward heel is not such a good idea.

A heavy air run can lead to *death rolls* and broaches. To control rolling avoid sailing dead downwind, trim the spinnaker directly in front of the boat - don't let it float out to windward, and choke down the sheet and pole. Also, move crew weight aft. In big breeze everyone should be in the back of the boat. Fig. 4.

A word of caution on boom preventers. In a heavy air broach they tend to break after providing a false sense of security (or the boom breaks). The preventer can also cause a broach if the boom hits the water on a roll to leeward. And once you do broach, if the preventer holds it can keep you pinned until someone finds a way to release it.

Helmsmanship in heavy air conditions must be forceful to keep control of the boat. But remember, every jerk of the helm slows the boat. Smooth is fast.

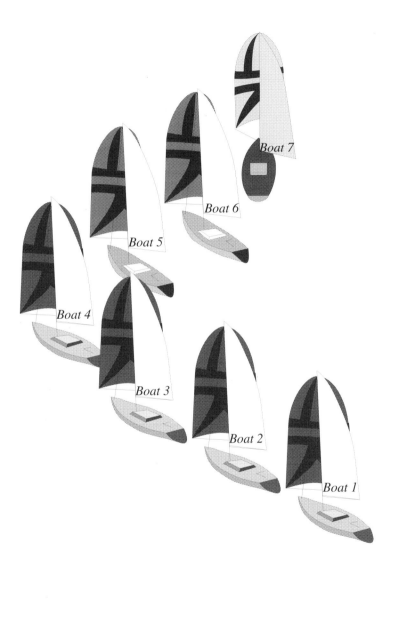

Fig. 3 - Boats 1-4: Running in light winds, of up to 10 knots, emphasizes boat speed with little change in optimum sailing angle.
Boats 4, 5, 6: In moderate winds of 10 to 14 knots the optimum angle changes dramatically.
Boat 7: In winds of 15 knots or more a direct route is fastest.

Fig. 4 - Boat A is rolling in very heavy air, making control difficult. Boat B has regained control by choking down the spinnaker sheet and moving the pole down and forward. It also helps to tighten the vang, head up and put crew weight to leeward.

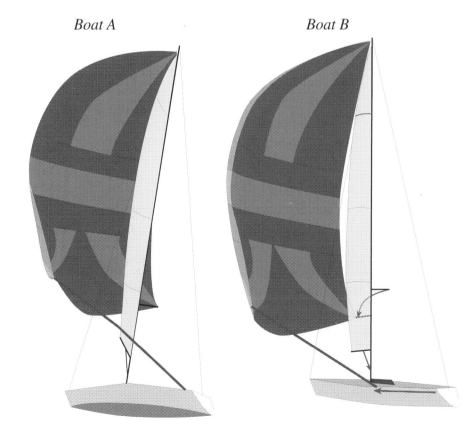

Boat A   Boat B

13.4 Not Steering Downwind

It happens almost without words. As the puff hits Jim and Ron move off the cabin top to the rail. Rob trims back on the guy and Tom eases the spinnaker sheet. Russ raises the topping lift a few inches. Melanie eases the main. The boat bears off slightly and accelerates.

As the puff fades Jim and Ron slide inboard, the pole goes forward and down, and the spinnaker sheet is trimmed. The main comes in. The boat heads up and carries speed.

Dave, at the helm, sits nearly motionless, the tiller extension moving in his hand as the crew steer the boat with weight and trim.

Gradually we pull away from the other 37 footers, lower and faster down the run.

You can use crew weight and sail trim to steer any boat downwind. Steering with weight and sails is not just for dinghy sailors. It is fast in big boats too. The less you use the rudder to steer the faster you will be. Here's how it works:

To Bear Off

We want to bear off with puffs. As the puff hits and we build speed we can sail lower and still keep target speeds. Bearing off will also help us stay in the puff longer.

To bear off move crew weight to windward and rotate the spinnaker to windward. Ease the spinnaker sheet in any puff. A puff will shift the apparent wind angle aft, and the sheet should be eased. Trim back on the guy as the sheet is eased to keep proper spinnaker shape and to rotate the spinnaker to windward. Raise the spinnaker pole slightly to help the spinnaker shape properly for the new breeze. Also ease the main for less weather helm. Fig. 5.

You will need to move some crew weight to windward just to counter the heeling forces of the puff. It will take an additional increment of crew weight to actually help the boat bear off.

To Head Up

As the puff fades you want to head up to keep apparent wind speed. As the boat slows you will no longer be able to sail as low as you could in the puff.

To head up reverse the process of bearing off. Trim the spinnaker sheet and ease the guy. Lower the pole slightly. Trim the main and move crew weight forward and to leeward. Fig. 6.

Not Steering Downwind

The next time you are steering downwind in light to moderate air use your crew weight and trim to help steer the boat. Better yet, let your crew do all the work and try *not steering downwind.*

Fig. 5 - To Bear Off ease the sails, trim back on the guy, and move crew weight to windward.

Fig. 6 - To Head Up reverse the process: Sails in, pole forward, weight to leeward.

13.5 Jibes and Roundings

Jibing

Turn at the pace of the crew work. Keep the spinnaker on the downwind side of the boat. As you turn the boat, the spinnaker should be trimmed around the boat. Hold the boat on a very broad reach, and jibe to a broad reach, without hesitating dead down wind. It is hazardous to hold the boat dead downwind in mid jibe. When the boat is dead downwind, it rolls, making steering and trimming difficult. Furthermore, on a dead downwind course air circulates from both sides of the spinnaker, with can cause a collapse or wrap. Fig. 7.

On reach to reach jibes start your turn early and coach the crew to rotate the spinnaker as fast as possible. It can help to drive off sharply from a beam reach to a very broad reach, and then hesitate for a moment to give the trimmers a chance to catch up, before finishing the turn.

Jibing is covered in great detail in the Chapter 9 - Downwind Boat Handling.

Mark Roundings

Use a smooth turn to carry momentum. Learn the character of your boat and give yourself plenty of room to come in wide and finish close; without having to jam the helm over and kill speed.

At jibe marks try to set up high and jibe early, so your jibe is completed as you pass the mark. This is particularly helpful is the next leg is a beam reach.

At a leeward mark rounding find a reference to help you come to close hauled amidst the fury of the spinnaker take down. Pace your turn to the natural turning radius of your boat and the speed of the trimmers. Fig. 8.

Fig. 7

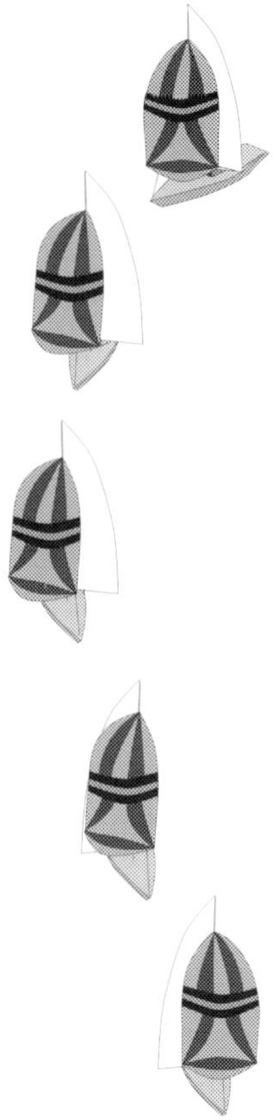

Fig. 8

Fig. 7 - Use a smooth turn from broad reach to broad reach. Match the pace of your turn to the sail trim, and do not hold the boat dead down wind.

Fig. 8 - At mark roundings come in wide and finish close. To carry momentum use the natural turning of you boat.

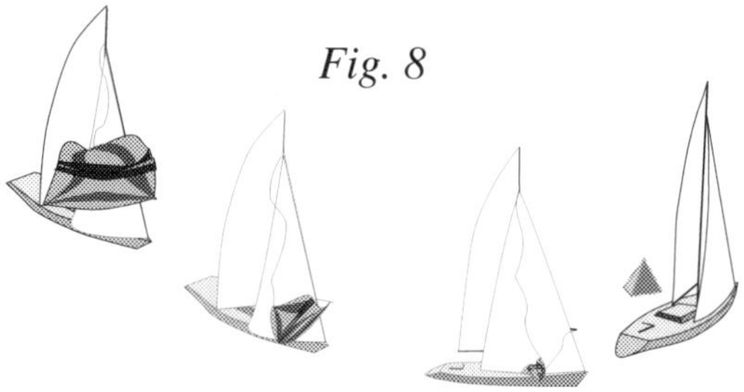

13.6 Conclusion

There are many downwind drivers - one of whom is at the helm. It takes coordinated effort on the part of the entire crew steer fast downwind. Goals change depending on course and conditions, and the techniques required to succeed vary. In the end the fast boats are those with great trim, a balanced helm, and a smooth driver.

CHAPTER 14 - BOAT PREPARATION

14.1   INTRODUCTION
14.2   BOTTOM PREPARATION
14.3   BELOW DECK
14.4   ON DECK
14.5   CONCLUSION

Tactics

Boat Speed

Boat Handling

Boat Preparation

CHAPTER 14 - BOAT PREPARATION

14.1 Introduction

Boat preparation is the hidden foundation of our performance pyramid. A well prepared and well organized boat is the first ingredient to success. If you are not as well prepared as the competition, you will have to out sail them just to come out even!

Boat preparation pays dividends directly in proportion to effort. The trick is to get your preparation done early, so you can get your boat in the water early, and have plenty of time to practice before the season starts. It is a shame to lose practice time to preparation.

Preparation centers on three areas: Hull preparation below the water line, below decks, and deck gear. Rig tuning is covered in the next chapter.

14.2 Bottom Preparation

Your pre-season effort below the water line in shaping, fairing, and smoothing your keel and hull will pay dividends all season long. Your keel and hull underbody are as important to upwind performance as your sails. Once things are put right below the waterline you never have to worry about it again, short of cleaning the bottom (weekly) and not running aground.

There is little you can do for the overall bottom configuration of you boat (except trade it in); but there is plenty you can do to improve the performance of the existing shape. Modern keels are designed to very precise shapes. For starters, make sure yours matches its design! From there you can fair and smooth it. Fig. 1.

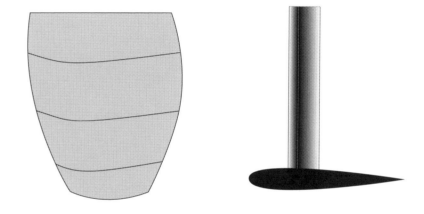

Fig. 1 - You may not be able to change the overall profile of your keel, but you can make sure it is fair and smooth. Remember, your keel shape is as important to upwind performance as sail trim. Make sure it is right.

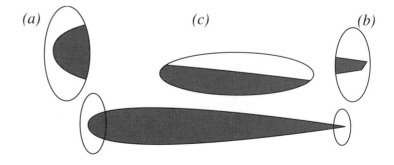

Fig. 2 - The leading edge (a) of your keel should be round, while the trailing edge (b) should be cut off at an angle. The keel should have a flat run aft, with no hollows (c).

The leading edge should be a section of a circle, opening into a parabolic shape which runs back to the point of maximum thickness. From this point, about one third of the way aft, the shape should run straight and flat back to the trailing edge. The run aft can be slightly convex. It should not be at all concave. The trailing edge should be cut off sharply. Ideally it would be a knife edge - but that would break off. More realistic is a sharp cut off, perhaps a $1/4$" thick. Cut off the trailing edge of the keel and ruddder at an angle to minimize speed robbing hum. (Yea, it sounds great, but it is drag.) Fig. 2.

A "typical" fin keel might have a thickness of 10% at 33%. This means the maximum thickness is 10% of the chord length, and the thickest point is one third of the way aft. Some designers use slightly thicker shapes, some use thinner. Designers are also working with elliptical shapes, and there is plenty of confusion over winged keels. The intent is to match the keel to the potential of the hull and rig. To get the details of your boats keel design consult your boat's designer.

Once you know the desired shape you want to match your keel to it. Sand down high spots and fill in low spots with epoxy putty. When you have a good shape, sand it smooth using a sanding batten. Work your way down from coarse paper to 400 or 600 grit wet and dry paper. Spend about half your effort on the keel, and the other half on the hull; and put in an extra 10% for the rudder. After sanding have bottom paint sprayed on and sand again to achieve a mirror smooth finish. Total effort: 110%!

Two final points:

First: Misery loves company. Plan a work party and get the entire crew to join in sanding the bottom. A great loyalty test. Be sure to have plenty of sand paper and beer. Bring out the sandpaper first.

Fig. 3 - There are two preferred locations for weight. Off the boat, or on top of the keel. Get all weight out of the ends. Anything you can't take off should be concentrated low & amidhsips. Get your sails out of the bow and pile them up on the cabin sole. Get the tool chest off the boat - bring only the essentials along for the race.

Second: Be sure to wear eye protection and a face mask. All this stuff is toxic. It will irritate your eyes and lungs, and poison your blood. You might even consider paying an exorbitant price to have it done professionally. Once you try to do it yourself, you'll see how reasonable that exorbitant quote really was.

14.3 Below Deck

There are only two acceptable places for weight. Off the boat, or low enough in the boat to improve stability. Except as required by the rules all weight should be concentrated low and amidships, or eliminated. Weight in the ends - bow, stern, or rig, is slow. Periodically, and especially after a long race or cruise, take everything off the boat, (clean it,) and put back only what is necessary. Boats have an extraordinary ability to take on clutter. Fight it. Fig. 3 - Previous page.

Crew weight, as opposed to equipment weight, is moveable and useful. Extra crew does not add much to overall weight and contributes significantly to righting moment (stability). The trick is to keep the weight in the right place. Your deck layout should encourage this.

14.4 On Deck

Your deck layout should encourage proper weight placement and allow crew members to do their jobs without interference. For example, some boats have all halyards lead aft, while others have halyard winches clustered around the mast. Make sure your layout encourages proper weight placement on your boat.

Make sure all your equipment is suited to its function, and look around to find new ideas. Above all make sure all your equipment works. After all you've put into your boat don't skimp on the details.

Try some of the following:
• Color code your lines so they are easy to recognize.
• Mark your headfoil about 6 feet off the deck. Place corresponding marks on your jib luffs when set with proper halyard tension. (This works much better than number strips on deck and marks on the halyards.)
• Mark your main halyard for each reef position so you know how far to lower it when you reef.
• Add a ball bearing traveler so you can play the traveler.
• Install a cascading mainsheet for extra power and control, or try a double ended cascading mainsheet for ease of use. Fig. 4.
• Add adjustable jib leads for better control of genoa shape.
• Double end your foreguy/spinnaker downhaul so it can always be adjusted from windward.
• Lead your backstay adjuster forward to keep (crew) weight out of the stern, and to make the backstay more accessible.
• Add footblocks for the helmsman so it is comfortable to steer when heeled.
• Get rid of equipment you can do without - reduce weight and clutter.
• Get a strong block and tackle system with shackles at each end - known as a hobble. It has plenty of uses. For example, use it as a temporary genoa sheet during sail changes or while you clear over rides, or as a barber hauler, or as a boom stabilizer, or … Fig. 5.
• Replace your topping lift with a very long topping lift (the next time you switch out a halyard) so you can leave the topping lift hooked up when you tack after a take down.

14.5 Conclusion

Don't let the brevity of this chapter fool you. Many boats are out of the running before the race even starts.

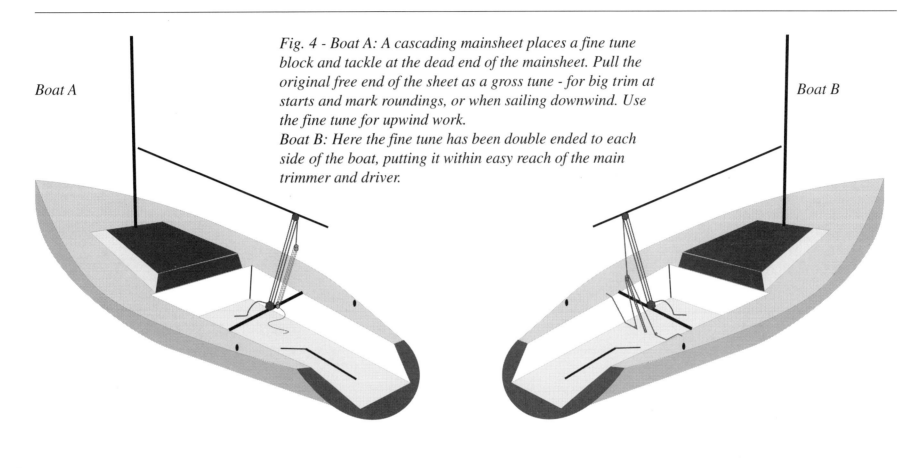

Boat A

Boat B

Fig. 4 - Boat A: A cascading mainsheet places a fine tune block and tackle at the dead end of the mainsheet. Pull the original free end of the sheet as a gross tune - for big trim at starts and mark roundings, or when sailing downwind. Use the fine tune for upwind work.

Boat B: Here the fine tune has been double ended to each side of the boat, putting it within easy reach of the main trimmer and driver.

Fig. 5 - A hobble is a block and tackle with shackles at each end - like a boom vang. It has a number of uses, including as a temporary genoa sheet during a sail change, as shown here.

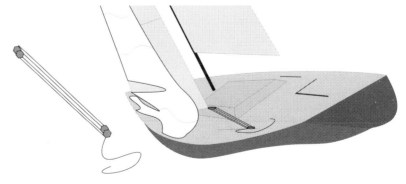

CHAPTER 15 - RIG TUNING

15.1 INTRODUCTION

15.2 MASTHEAD RIGS

15.3 FRACTIONAL RIGS

15.4 CONCLUSION

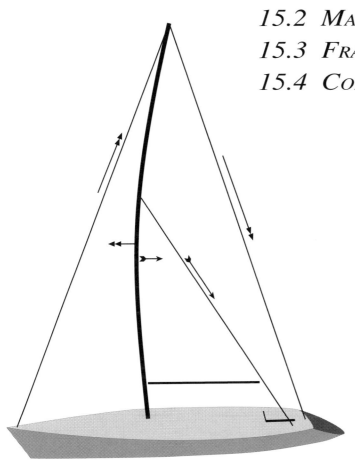

CHAPTER 15 - RIG TUNING

15.1 Introduction

Without a properly tuned rig proper trim and performance are unattainable. Fortunately, rig tuning is a straight forward step by step process.

This chapter will look at the particulars of tuning and controlling both masthead and fractional rigs.

The goals in rig tuning are: Fig. 1.
- Eliminate side bend and lean.
- Set mast rake for proper helm balance.
- Tune pre-bend to match the mainsail design.
- Control mast bend and headstay sag.

15.2 Tuning Masthead Rigs

Side Bend and Lean

1. Check that the mast step is centered in hull and that the mast butt is secured to step.
2. Center and block the mast at partners. (Before stepping the mast run a line from stem to mid stern to check that the partners are centered in deck.)
3. Tighten the upper shrouds evenly, keeping the mast centered. Measure with main halyard and shock cord to make sure the mast is centered. Hand tension is not accurate. Measure to chain plates and other points of symmetry. Fig. 2.
4. Continue to tighten the uppers; counting turns and measuring. Back off if the mast goes out of column. Be careful not to strip the turnbuckle threads - do not overtighten.

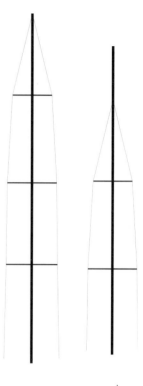

Fig. 1 - Regardless of the type of rig, the goals in rig tuning are to: control side bend, lean, rake, pre-bend, mast bend, and headstay sag.

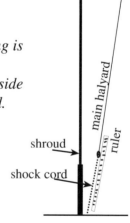

Fig. 2 - The first step in rig tuning is to center the mast in the boat. Measure to fixed points on each side to make sure the mast is centered.

5. Proceed down to the intermediates and lowers, tightening the shrouds evenly on each side and keeping the mast straight.

6. This is the initial setting, with mast centered, straight side to side, and all shrouds firm.

7. Go sailing in 10-12 knot breeze. Sail a series of tacks, counting turns as you tighten the leeward shrouds. Start with the uppers to eliminate lean; then tension the lowers to eliminate side bend. Fig. 3

8. Sight up the mast to check for side bend. If the middle bends to leeward, tighten lowers. If the top appears to fall off to leeward, it may be the middle popping to windward. Either loosen the lowers or the tighten uppers. Over-tight lowers or loose uppers allow tip fall off and a narrow angle of intersection between the uppers and the mast. Beware - this can overload the shroud fittings and cause rig failure. Fig. 4.

9. Proper tension will leave the leeward shrouds taut with 15 degrees of heel and a full crew on the rail. The uppers will have to be tighter than the lowers to allow for stretch over longer distance.

10. Check the rig periodically, particularly after sailing in heavy air. Beware stretch of uppers or over-tensioned lowers which can overload the upper spreaders.

Fig. 3 - After preliminary tuning at the dock, it is time to go sailing. Sail a series of tacks, tuning as you go.

Fig. 4 - Beware over-tight lowers or loose uppers which allow side bend & a dangerously narrow angle of intersection of the mast and uppers.

Rake

Rake is the lean of the mast forward and aft. Changes in rake change the balance of the helm. Raking the mast aft creates weather helm. Standing the mast up straighter reduces weather helm. Changing the rake may be as simple as easing the forestay and tightening the backstay, or it may require moving the mast step. Fig. 5.

The goal is to find a setting which provides some weather helm upwind in light air without becoming unbearable in a blow. Most boats are designed for some rake; but the amount depends on sail design, predominant conditions, and even the size of the crew. To find an optimum rake experiment with several settings in a variety of conditions. You want 3-4 degrees of weather helm in moderate conditions.

Pre-Bend

Pre-bend is bend permanently tuned into your rig. It differs from *Rake,* which is leaning the mast aft. Pre-bend is achieved by a combination of compression (tight rig tension), and mast blocks at the deck partners. Your mast will need some pre-bend - from an inch to a few inches - depending on the luff curve of your main. Fig. 6.

Proper pre-bend will give you the correct range of adjustment in your main, from full to flat. If your main tends to be too deep, then add more pre-bend. If you cannot get enough power from your main then straighten the mast by putting blocks in front of the mast at the partners. As your main ages you may find you need more prebend. This will help take out some to the extra depth - but it will exacerbate the other problem of age - the draft creeping aft. Tapered full length battens can alleviate that problem.

Fig. 5 - Set the rake to get proper weather helm in all conditions. Raking the mast back adds more weather helm.

Fig. 6 - Pre-bend is bend which is tuned into the rig to match the design of the mainsail.

Mast Bend and Headstay Sag

Working with the backstay and a combination of running backstay, baby stay, and/or vang, it is possible to control mast bend and headstay sag separately.

Backstay tension will bend the mast through compression as well as tighten the headstay. The mix depends on running backstay tension. If the runners are tight, they restrict mast bend, and the backstay impacts headstay sag. Looser runners allow more mast bend. Fig. 7.

With a stiff mast, backstay tension translates primarily into headstay tension, controlling sag. A baby stay is then used to add bend. The backstay contributes to bend as well, particularly once bend has been initiated by the baby stay. Fig. 8.

Fig. 7 - Running backstays allow us to control mast bend independent of headstay sag. A tight backstay will tighten the headstay and bend the mast. Tensioning the runners will straighten the mast.

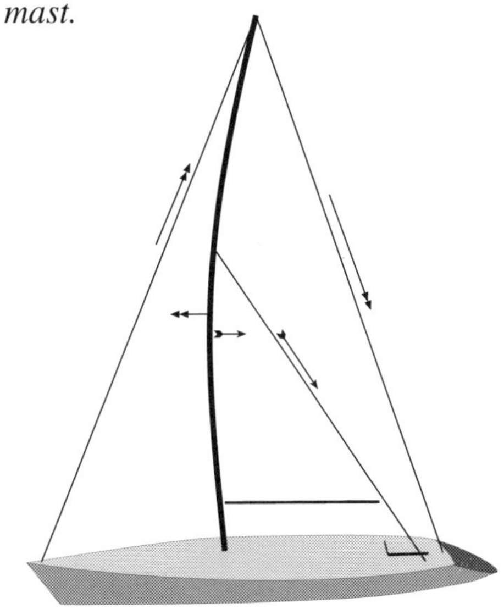

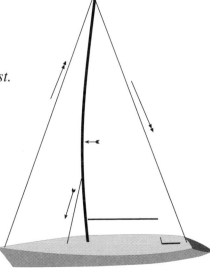

Fig. 8 - The backstay bends the mast and tightens the headstay. A babystay can help bend a stiff mast.

15.3 Tuning Fractional Rigs

The goals are the same, but the procedures for tuning a fractional rig differ slightly from those for a masthead rig. The varied configurations of fractional rigs (swept spreaders versus straight with runners, etc.) make it difficult to generalize. The procedure describer here is for swept spreaders. Straight spreader procedure is a mix of this and the masthead procedure described above.

With swept back spreaders shroud adjustment affects lean, side bend, rake, sag, and mast bend. Fig. 9.

1. Spreader deflection angle should be fixed; spreaders should not swing. Use pins &/or epoxy to secure swinging spreaders.
2. Center mast at step and partners.
3. With lowers loose pull the backstay to max. Tighten the upper shrouds, keeping the rig centered and mast straight side to side. If the mast tends to bend sideways, you may have to ease backstay slightly.
4. Release the backstay. The mast will still have bend. Tighten the lowers to remove bend as necessary to fit the main.
5. The rig is now tuned for maximum headstay tension, which is often difficult to achieve. Backstay tension will bend the mast and add some headstay tension.
6. To get bend more easily, ease the lowers. To translate backstay to headstay tension, tighten the lowers. There is a limit to the headstay tension which can be achieved without running backstays. If your mast tends to bend too much try less spreader sweep. To encourage bend add more sweep, and ease the lowers.

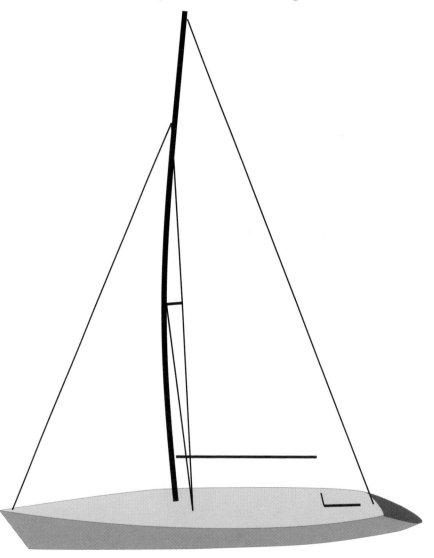

Fig. 9 - Fractional rigs with swept back spreaders require a different tuning technique than mast head rigs.

7. Upwind in a breeze the top of the mast will fall off to leeward; and the middle will bow out to weather. This side bend de-powers the rig to a greater degree than fore and aft bend. Easing the lowers may reduce sidebend but it will allow more headstay sag and fore and aft mast bend. The other solution is longer spreaders, which will push in harder on the middle of the mast. This can reduce, but will not eliminate, side bend, and may interfere with genoa trim.

8. Changing rake requires a complete retuning of the shrouds. Rake should be set for a balanced helm.

9. Shrouds must be adjusted day by day to achieve proper mast bend and headstay sag characteristics for varied conditions. Upper and lower shrouds should be eased in light air for less bend and less headstay tension; and tightened for best performance in a breeze.

10. Running backstays are required if sag is to be properly and independently controlled with a fractional rig. Fig. 10.

15.4 Conclusion

The tune of the rig must match the designed luff curve of the main and luff hollow of the jibs. It is often necessary to retune the rig for new sails. If performance is not all you hope for perhaps your rig tuning is at fault. Small changes in rig tune can have a surprising impact on your boats performance.

If you decide to fiddle with your rig, carefully mark and note your current settings. That way, you can revert if you are unhappy with the changes you make

Fig. 10 - Boat A: On a fractional rig the backstay controls mast bend. Without running backstays headstay sag is not directly controlled.
Boat B: Running backstays allow separate control of headstay sag and mast bend. On a fractional rig the runners control headstay sag, while the backstay controls mast bend.

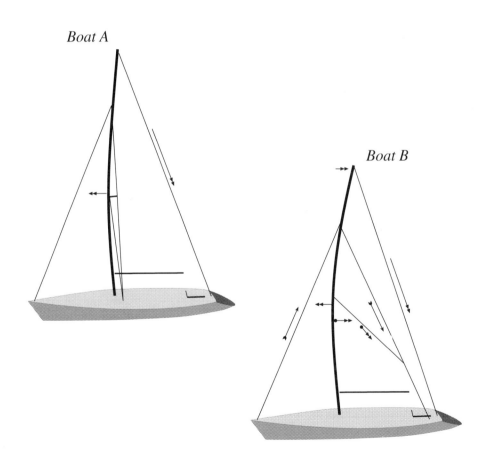

Boat A

Boat B

CHAPTER 16 - PERFORMANCE INSTRUMENTS

16.1   INTRODUCTION

16.2   THE NEW INFORMATION

16.3   PERFORMANCE PREDICTIONS

16.4   VPP'S

16.5   TARGETS

16.6   UPWIND TARGETS

16.7   DOWNWIND TARGETS

16.8   WORKING WITH LEVEL 1 INSTRUMENTS

16.9   INSTRUMENTS AND TACTICS

16.10   CONCLUSION

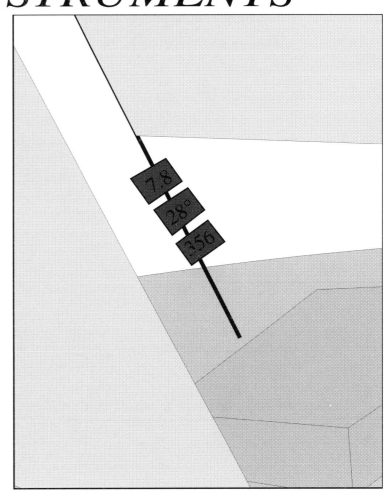

Chapter 10 - Performance Instruments

16.1 Introduction

Electronics are changing the way we race. Increasingly sophisticated equipment and functions are giving us information never before available. This new information allows us to understand performance in new ways, and when combined with performance prediction functions, allows us to evaluate and optimize performance for all wind directions and wind speeds.

Instruments can provide information to confirm and quantify (but not replace) our seat of the pants feelings. Sophisticated instruments have also given us insights into details of performance which we might otherwise never have considered.

There are two broad areas where instruments can help our racing. The primary use is performance related. Instruments can help us sail our boat to its potential, particularly upwind and downwind. When properly used, instruments can provide a dramatic improvement in performance. As you read about instrument and performance consider that a 2% improvement in speed is almost imperceptible (from 5 knots to 5.1 knots for ex.) yet adds up to the margin of victory in most races (about 14 seconds per mile).

The other area where instruments are valuable is strategic - helping us keep track of wind and current strength, direction, and trends. The information can help us race better both around the buoys and point to point.

This chapter will take a look at instruments - both the information they provide and how to use it. We will start with a brief look at instruments and the information they give. Next, we will look at *Velocity Prediction Programs* which are used to model and predict performance. Then we will explore new concepts in instrument use and apply those to performance in various conditions. We will also look at ways to use the new concepts with less sophisticated instruments.

16.2 The New Information

Modern instruments give more accurate information than in the past, and they give new information not before available. When combined with Velocity Prediction Programs (VPP's) we have powerful new tools and techniques for optimizing performance. VPP's are predictions of a boat's performance for a given wind speed and wind angle. Simply put, they tell how fast you should be able to sail in a given set of conditions.

Before we put our instruments to work lets take a brief look at the information they provide. We can consider instruments in levels of sophistication, starting with the basics:

Level 0 - Seat of the pants. Still fundamental. One of the most reliable and affordable sources of information. Occasionally misleading, as we shall see.

Level 1 - Provide direct readings of Boat Speed, Apparent Wind Speed, and Apparent Wind Angle. Your compass is also a level 1 source.

Level 2 - Processes Level 1 data to provide True Wind Speed and True Wind Angle. Also capable of giving Velocity Made Good upwind and downwind.

Level 3 - Adds an electronic Flux Gate Compass and gives compass course and True Wind Direction.

Level 4 & … - The addition of a GPS interface and a computer are the next phase of sophistication. The GPS can provide Course and Speed Over Ground (correcting for current), and Velocity Made Good to a waypoint. The computer can compare actual performance to predicted performance; and it can also record performance and help us refine our predictions.

Along with more accurate, integrated instruments the microprocessor revolution has also brought us increasingly accurate performance prediction capabilities. Computer programs can predict how fast you should be able to sail your boat in every wind speed and wind angle. You can then race against the predictions.

For one-design racers there are always other boats to race against. You know (sometimes all too well) how you are doing. In a mixed fleet having predictions to race against can provide a big boost in performance. When you are one-of-a-kind boat, VPP's tell you if you are sailing your boat to its potential.

US Sailing's IMS Velocity Prediction Program and *Design Systems Velocity* program are two sources of VPP information. This information can be programmed into the instruments, or it can be used independently, as we shall see. Regardless of how the information is displayed the key is that VPP's tell us how fast we should be going.

16.3 Performance Predictions

Modern design systems and computers can predict the performance of conventional boats as accurately as our instruments can measure it. For a given wind speed the data show how fast we should be able to sail at every wind angle. The performance predictions used here are a fictitious example for my mythical boat - a Fantasy 47 IMS racer named Bill's Big Boat (why not fantasize in the big leagues?). Although the boat in our examples is a Fantasy 47 the concepts apply for virtually all keel boats. Though the boat speeds differ the wind speeds and angles are remarkably consistent with virtually all PHRF, IMS, IOR, & MORC boats.

We are presented with two forms of the same information. One form is simply columns of numbers, showing performance for each wind speed and a variety of wind angles. The other form is a graphic representation of the same information in a Polar Diagram.

Polar Diagrams are graphic plots of the predicted performance data for a particular boat. The curves are created from performance prediction data and simply show the information in a different form. Each curve shows performance for a given true wind speed. In the figure we can see the data for 7 knots of true wind. Each data point is plotted, and the points are connected by a curve.

To understand the information on the Polar Diagram imagine our boat sailing from the origin point. At each true wind angle the distance to the curve shows the speed we should be able to sail.

Fig. 1 - VPP's and Polars
The adjacent numbers show the predicted performance for Bill's Big Boat in 7 knots of true wind. On the far page is a graphic representation of the same information in a polar diagram. The numbers around the perimeter of the polar correspond to the numbers in the last column in the VPP. Optimum upwind and downwind performance is shown in bold.

Fantasy 47 **VPP's for 7 Knots True Wind Speed**

	Tr>	Boat Spd	AppSpd	App>	VMG	See Polar
	36	4.7	11.8	26	3.8	1
	40	5.1	12.0	28	3.9	2
	44	5.6	12.3	30	4.0	3
Upwind	**44**	**5.6**	**12.3**	**30**	**4.0**	**3**
	50	6.2	12.4	33	3.9	4
	60	6.8	12.4	37	3.4	5
Genoa/87°/	75	7.2	11.7	44	1.8	6
Spinnaker	90	7.3	10.5	52	0.0	7
	105	7.1	8.9	61	-1.8	8
	120	6.4	7.1	74	-3.2	9
	135	5.5	5.4	93	-3.9	10
Downwind	**144**	**4.9**	**4.7**	**108**	**-4.0**	**11**
	150	4.5	4.3	120	-3.9	12
	160	4.1	4.1	139	-3.8	13
	170	3.8	4.0	161	-3.7	14
	180	3.6	4.0	180	-3.6	15

16.4 Sample VPP's

Let's look at the predicted performance for Bill's Big Boat in 7 knots of wind. On a True Wind Beam Reach (90°) our speed should be 7.3 knots. With a true wind angle of 75° boat speed should be 7.2 knots. Speeds for other wind angles are also shown. Thus on any reach we can determine if we are sailing up to predicted speed. If we are slow we know we have a problem with trim. The predictions can also help us with sail selection at the genoa/spinnaker split.

One thing to note on the polar plot is the dimple at the cross over between a genoa and a spinnaker. You should never sail in the dimple. Reach up, and sail with your genoa, or drive off and set the chute. The depth and position of the dimple depends on the sails you carry. If you sail with only regular genoas and conventional spinnakers the dimple is most pronounced. If you have a reaching jib and an asymmetrical spinnaker the dimple will be smoothed over - as long as you set the appropriate sail.

More interesting than the reaching data is the information for upwind and downwind performance. The data show the optimum speeds and angles for achieving best performance (VMG) upwind and downwind. The Velocity Made Good shows the speed towards an objective upwind or downwind. Pointing straight at an upwind mark is not the fastest way to get there - we know that. The same is true downwind. The question is, how wide an angle should we sail? If we sail too high we

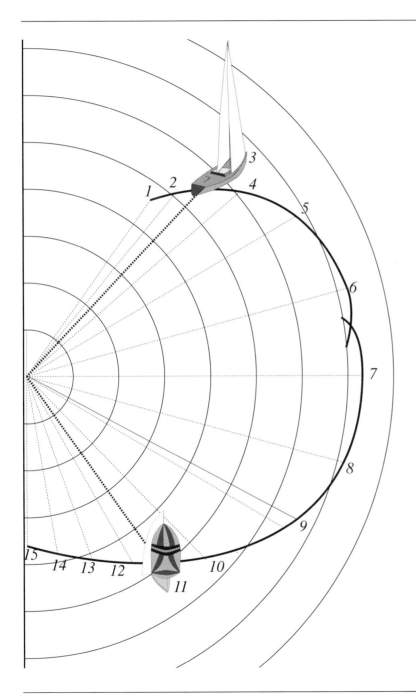

are pinching and going too slow; footing low gives us extra speed, but not enough to overcome the wider angle. The performance prediction information tells us what the correct angles are. On the Polar Curve the optimums are the highest (for upwind) and lowest (for downwind) points on the curve. These optimums are marked by a box on the curves.

In this example, in 7 knots of true wind, the optimum upwind angle is 44 Degrees True Wind Angle (TWA), 30 Degrees Apparent, with a VMG of 4.0 knots. Pinching higher brings too great a sacrifice in boat speed, hurting VMG; and footing lower increases boat speed, but not enough to overcome the angle, and VMG again goes down. Fig. 1.

Downwind in 7 knots true wind the optimum angle is 144 degrees true wind angle, with a boat speed of 4.9 knots, and a VMG of 4.0 knots. At 150 degrees we sail a closer angle, but lose too much speed, and VMG is only 3.9. This is the equivalent of pinching upwind. At 135 degrees boat speed is faster, but VMG is only 3.9 knots. This is equivalent to footing upwind. Fig. 1.

What have we learned? First, we stand to gain or lose about .1 knots VMG by sailing the high or low. Big Deal. Well, it is: ***That equates to 23 seconds per mile!*** And you were fighting your PHRF Committee for 3 lousy seconds! The trick is that the proper angle would be difficult to pick by seat of the pants.

The second thing we see here is that the proper angle is far from straight downwind. A True wind angle of 144° means sailing 36° above dead down wind. The apparent wind angle would be about 108° (pretty near the beam). Would you arrive at that seat of the pants? If not you'd be over a minute behind at the end of a three mile leg.

16.5 Target Boat Speeds

How do we use the performance data?

When sailing upwind and downwind we sail to the target (predicted) boat speed, and that should put us on the appropriate angle. The targets give one-of-a-kind boats a benchmark to race against - the equivalent of racing a one design.

Sailing upwind and downwind optimum VMG is our objective. VMG readouts even on the best instruments are by their nature too volatile to trim and steer by. To achieve optimum VMG our primary guide is boat speed, with wind angle as a secondary guide. Upwind we use Apparent Wind Angle, as it is a simple and direct read out. Downwind the Apparent Wind Angle is too volatile, and we use True Wind Angle. For each knot of wind speed we have a Target Boat Speed and Target Angle. Fig. 2.

The performance data do not cover all wind speeds. For performance between the wind speeds given in the data we interpolate. This information is derived from the charts and should be posted next to the instruments, in the form of a target boat speed strip. A sample *Target Boat Speed Strip* is shown. Fig. 3.

Let's take a closer look at the upwind and downwind sailing on our Fantasy 47.

16.6 Upwind Targets

With performance data we try to sail the boat at the predicted boat speed. If our speed is fast then we sail a little higher, if we are slow then we drive off slightly. If our angles (True or Apparent) do not match predicted then we may have to adjust trim to achieve target performance. Fig. 3 - next page.

It is easy to overreact. Try to narrow the range of steering, and only correct by a degree or two. Steering by chasing the numbers tends to be erratic because the information from the instruments is history. The numbers should not be the focus of the helmsman's attention; steer by sight and feel, giving attention to the sails, seas, heel, and helm. The trimmers can report performance data. The helmsman should sense how the boat feels when the numbers are right, and then steer by feel.

In steady conditions we should be able to settle into a narrow steering groove, fine tuning trim and helm to slight fluctuations in wind and seas. In puffy conditions a more aggressive technique is appropriate.

Fig 2. - This polar diagram shows the complete polar curves for 7 knots and 10 knots of true wind plus the optimum upwind and downwind performance points for 3, 5, 7, 10, and 14 knots of true wind. The VPP for 10 knots is shown below.

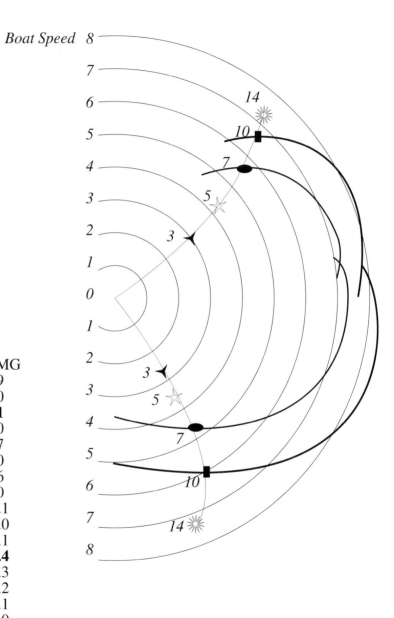

Fantasy 47 VPP - True Wind Spd 10 Knots

	True Angle	Boat Speed	App WSpd	App Angle	VMG
	36	6.0	16.0	26	4.9
	40	6.4	16.2	27	5.0
Upwind	**42**	**6.9**	**16.4**	**29**	**5.1**
	44	7.0	16.4	30	5.0
	50	7.5	16.4	33	4.7
	60	7.9	16.0	39	4.0
Genoa/87°/	75	8.1	14.9	48	2.6
Spinnaker	90	8.3	13.5	57	0.0
	105	8.3	11.8	68	-2.1
	120	7.9	9.7	80	-4.0
	135	7.3	7.7	97	-5.1
Downwind	**144**	**6.7**	**6.7**	**111**	**-5.4**
	150	6.2	6.3	122	-5.3
	160	5.8	6.0	141	-5.2
	170	5.2	5.9	162	-5.1
	180	5.0	5.8	180	-5.0

Puffs, Lulls and Windshifts Upwind

In variable conditions our target speed changes with each puff and luff. If the wind puffs from 7 to 10 knots our target speed jumps from 5.6 to 6.9. The tendency when a puff hits is for the boat to heel over and the helmsman to feather up. The puff brings an apparent wind lift, and the helmsman is inclined to follow it up, but this is wrong. The correct response is to ease sheets slightly as the puff hits, and hold the boat down to course in order to accelerate quickly to the new target. As the boat accelerates the sails are re-trimmed. To achieve this technique the crew must have sheets in hand, and be ready to ease at the first sign of the puff. Waiting for the boat to heel up, or for the puff to register on the instruments, is to wait too long, and waste performance.

In a lull the boat will seem headed. (Imagine the wind dieing completely - you would suddenly appear to be in irons.) When a lull hits (to 7 knots from 10 for example) our target speed drops. Rather than drive off with the apparent (false) header, hold course. Overtrim for a moment to keep the sails from backing, and ease to normal trim as speed drops to the target for the lower wind speed.

One key to playing the puffs and lulls is recognizing the difference between a genuine lift and a puff lift; and between a genuine header and a lull header. You must observe the wind speed and wind angle recognize the difference. In reality, puffs and lulls are usually accompanied by shifts. Your observations of conditions on a particular day will help you anticipate what will happen next. Your instruments only tell you what has already happened.

Without going into the details, allow me to mention that instrument analysis confirm the value of *footing to a header, and pinching to a lift*.

Fig. 3 - An upwind target boat speed strip such as the one shown gives the helmsman and trimmers targets to sail to when sailing upwind. The target speeds and angles are derived from the VPP's for each wind speed.

Fantasy 47 Upwind Targets

True Wind	Boat Speed	App Angle
3	2.8	30
4	3.6	30
5	4.4	30
6	5.0	30
7	5.6	30
8	6.1	30
9	6.5	29
10	6.9	29
11	7.0	28
12	7.1	28
13	7.1	27
14	7.2	26
15	7.3	26
16	7.3	26
17	7.4	26
18	7.4	26
19	7.5	26
20	7.5	26

16.7 Downwind Targets

There are 3 segments in the downwind speed curve. Up to 10 knots is light air, 10 to 14 is moderate, and over 14 is heavy air. Each segment requires a different approach to optimize performance. Fig. 4.

Light Air - up to 10 knots true

In light air conditions **boat speed is the big variable**, while sailing angle remains nearly fixed

In winds of 10 knots or less we achieve our target speed at a True Wind Angle of 140 -145°s. Once we achieve target speed we work up and down *slightly* to stay on target. If we find we are too fast we sail low and burn off our the extra speed while pointing closer to the mark. When we are slow we sail a little high to accelerate back to speed. The changes are subtle, and the angle is narrow.

Puffs and lulls

A look at the polars shows graphically how the proper angle remains nearly fixed for winds up to ten knots. Target boat speed, on the other hand, changes markedly with wind speed. In light air the traditional practice of *up in the lulls and off in the puffs* is wrong. In a puff your target angle does not change. In fact, you are below target speed, and might want to head up to build speed! (On a reach the concept remains valid. Only when our objective is downwind is the truism flawed.)

Fig. 4 - Downwind Targets
For each wind speed there is a target speed and optimum angle. The angle remains nearly constant for winds up to 10 knots, while boat speeds build dramatically. In winds of 10 to 14 knots the wind angle changes dramatically.

Fantasy 47 Downwind Targets

True Wind	Boat Speed	True Angle	
3	2.4	139	
4	3.1	140	
5	3.8	142	
6	4.4	143	Light
7	4.9	144	
8	5.5	144	
9	6.1	144	
10	6.7	144	
11	6.9	148	
12	7.1	153	Moderate
13	7.2	158	
14	7.3	164	
15	7.5	166	
16	7.7	168	
17	7.9	169	Heavy
18	8.1	170	
19	8.4	171	
20	8.7	172	

Moderate Winds - 10 to 14 knots true

In moderate winds the target *angle is the big variable*, while our target speeds are relatively stable.

In winds of 10 to 14 knots the VPP's show our optimum True Wind Angle changes dramatically, from 144° to 164°. In this range our boat speed does not change dramatically with changes in wind speed, as it did in light air. What changes is our ability to carry speed at lower angles. With each knot of increase in wind speed we can sail 5° lower (with a slight increase in speed).

Puffs & Lulls

In winds over 10 knots our technique changes. In these conditions the target *speeds* don't change substantially with wind speed, but *angles* do. In these moderate conditions we sail aggressively to the old adage, *off in the puffs and up in the lulls*. As a puff hits we can sail lower while keeping target speed. In a lull we must come up to keep boat speed at target.

Heavy air - 15 knots true and above

When the wind speed exceeds 15 knots we have a choice of angles between 160° and 180° (dead downwind). A look at the Polar Curves shows that the curves are fairly flat across a wide band in this wind range. What this means is that we can sail to the same VMG by sailing high and fast (at 160°) or low and slow (at 180°) . We can choose our course for a favorable wave angle, for control, or for strategic or tactical reasons.

Puffs & Lulls

Control is the key to speed in heavy air. Move crew weight aft, and be sure to ease the sheets in a puff to keep from overloading the sail plan and rudder. Trim aggressively in lulls to keep the chute from collapsing as the apparent wind angle swings forward.

16.8 Racing with Level 1 Instruments

Sailing without the most sophisticated instruments does not prevent us from taking advantage of some of the lessons they have taught us.

The most useful concept is target boat speed downwind. In winds of 10 knots or less we want to sail at 140° - 145° True Wind Angle. This means we'll jibe through 70 - 80°. As we turn downwind to a run we should know the wind direction (as an average of our close-hauled compass courses) and we can figure the compass courses 145° off the wind. (A few degrees below the reciprocal of your closehauled course is a great first guess.) By sailing one of these compass courses we can get a target speed and try to maintain it. When we can no longer keep good speed on the course we must determine if we are in a lull or lift. In a lull we work for the best speed at the proper angle; if we are in a lift then it is time to jibe to the headed tack. We will jibe through 75° to the proper angle on the other tack, and work for target speed there. Admittedly, it's not the same as working with true wind instruments, but it is the best we can do.

16.9 Instruments and Tactics

Round the Buoys

True wind instruments can simplify a tacticians work. The wind shifts are easy to find when you have the True Wind Direction displayed on deck. Instrument systems which record data over time and display it graphically can also show trends in wind speed and direction which might otherwise be missed.

Distance Racing

Over a long reaching leg Polar Diagrams can help select a proper reaching angle. Normally, on a short leg, when wind conditions will not change, the fastest course on a reach is a straight line. During a distance race, when conditions will change the proper course may not be directly at the mark. A better course might be one slightly off the mark which at higher speed. (For more, see *Distance Racing Strategy* in *Performance Racing Tactics*.)

16.10 Conclusion

Three final points

1. Using your instruments to advantage requires that your instruments be properly calibrated. As computer critics have said for years, "Garbage in, garbage out."

2. Don't become a slave to your instruments. If you turn off the seat of your pants when you turn on your instruments, you will be a net loser.

3. Although the boat we used in our example was a Fantasy 47, the concepts apply for virtually all keel boats. Though the boat speeds differ, the wind speeds and angles are remarkably consistent with virtually all PHRF, IMS, IOR, & MORC boats.

CHAPTER 17 - CONCLUSION

17.1   CLIMB THE PYRMAMID

17.2   A TACTICAL WIZARD

17.3   ONLY THE BEGINNING

17.4   THANKS

CHAPTER 17 - CONCLUSION

17.1 Climb the Pyramid

Sailboat racing is a complex endeavour, drawing on all our abilities. To race successfully requires strong fundamentals - sound boat handling and competitive boat speed. It also requires a well prepared boat. Finally, when all these pieces are in place, it requires sound tactics.

17.2 A Tactical Wizard

If you feel your racing has suffered from flawed tactics, look again. If you went to battle without good boat handling and competitive boat speed, your tactics never had a chance.

The best tactic is boat speed. You will find that when you are fast, tactics are not nearly as complicated as when you are slow.

When you hit the starting line with boat handling which is second nature, and boat speed second to none, you may find that all of a sudden you are a tactical wizard!

17.3 About this Book

The theory and ideas presented here are only the beginning. Use this book as a starting point. Don't ever let something you read stand in the way of what works.

17.4 Thanks

Thanks for reading *Performance Racing Trim*. I hope you have enjoyed it. Good luck in your racing. Sail Fast.

North U Books and CDs

PERFORMANCE RACING TACTICS
The most complete book on modern racing tactics

Written by Bill Gladstone, *Performance Racing Tactics* takes you all the way around the course. The fifth edition covers tactics, rules, weather, and strategy in 200 information-packed pages. The fast moving, easy to follow format is accessible to all readers. The content offers complete information for neophytes and insights which grab the attention of the saltiest dog. Quizzes and skill building sections show how to develop a race winning approach.

Included in this edition are chapters by Peter Isler on Match Racing and from *Ockam U* on Performance Tactics. The book also includes complete, up to date coverage of the Racing Rules.

TACTICS SEMINAR–ON–CD
Now the Boats Move!

Our new Tactics CD puts *Performance Racing Tactics* in motion. The CD covers starting, upwind, and downwind topics, including strategy, tactics, and rules. In addition to the animation of the book illustrations, the CD includes over 100 photographs of tactical sequences which are not included in the book. A Pittman Award Nominee for new product innovation.

The CD also includes a voice over by the author, Bill Gladstone.

PERFORMANCE RACING TRIM
The most complete book on modern sailing performance

To win races you have to sail your boat well and sail it fast. *Performance Racing Trim* shows you how. *Performance Racing Trim* treats boat speed and boat handling topics in the same accessible style as **Performance Racing Tactics.** The *TRIM book* gives complete coverage to upwind and downwind sail trim and boat handling. Topics include helming, mainsail and genoa trim, and the trim and handling of both conventional and asymmetrical spinnakers. With hundreds of illustrations, and a unique *Trim Solutions* seciton,, *Performance Racing Trim* solves the most baffling performance questions.

TRIM SEMINAR–ON–CD
See Trim in Action!

The *TRIM CD* is a companion to *TRIM book*. The CD puts performance in motion, and shows how changes in trim change the sailing characteristics of a boat. In addition, coverage of boathandling topics shows the most up to date techniques for spinnaker sets, jibes and douses, for both conventional and asymmetrical spinnakers. In addition to animated graphics and 100's of photographs, the *TRIM CD* includes a voice over by the author, Bill Gladstone.

CRUISING WORKBOOK
Concise Coverage of North U. Cruising Course Topics

The North U *Sailing, Cruising and Seamanship Workbook* is the text for our classes. The workbook covers a broad range of cruising topics, from upwind and downwind sail trim, to docking under power, short-handed sail handling, anchoring, navigation tricks, and safety. The format is graphically driven, with illustrations and captions covering the essentials of successful cruising and sailing technique.

CRUISING SEMINAR–ON–CD
Cruising Technique Brought to Life

The *Cruising CD* is a companion to *Crusing Workbook*. The CD puts words into motion. Now you can see why anchors need scope, visualize how spring lines work, watch the effects of current, understand the impact of wind shifts. You'll also see how changes in sail trim change sail shape, and impact your boat's speed and performance.

THE ANNAPOLIS BOOK OF SEAMANSHIP
by John Rousmaniere - 3rd Ed

The revised, expanded, and updated third edition of the definitive book on sailing and cruising technique covers the full spectrum of sailing and seamanship topics. Richly illustrated by Mark Smith, this is the single best book on sailing. Boat selection, sail trim, maintenance, navigation, safety, weather, rules of the road, anchoring, storm sailing, emergencies - it is all here. Buy it if you don't own it, upgrade if you own a previous edition, and read it. A magnificent book, a wealth of information, superbly presented.

NORTH U.

Order from the Web at: www.Northu.com

CD AND BOOK ORDER FORM

Name _____

Address _____

Address _____

City _____ ST ____ Zip _____

Country _____

Phone_____-_____-_____ Fax (_____-_____-_____)

e.mail _____

Paid by: Check # _____ MC   Visa

_ _ _ _ _ _ • _ _ _ _ • _ _ _ _ • _ _ _ _ _

Expiration Date: _____/_____

Signature _____

Item	Qty	Price	Total
Performance Racing **Tactics** book	___	$25	$_____
Performance Racing **Tactics CD**	___	$50	$_____
Performance Racing TRIM book	___	$25	$_____
Performance Racing TRIM CD	___	$50	$_____
Race Pack (All four above)	___	$135	$_____
Cruising Workbook	___	$20	$_____
Cruising CD	___	$50	$_____
Annapolis Book of Seamanship	___	$40	$_____
Cruise Pack (All three above)	___	$100	$_____
Postage and Handling*			$_____
Total US$			[_____]

* Postage per order:	Books	CDs only
US	$5	$2
Canada/Mexico	$7	$5
Rest of World	$10*	$6

*$15 to areas not accepting Global Priority Airmail.

Prices subject to change

North U.

MAIL: 29 High Field Lane • Madison CT 06443-2516 USA
PHONE: 203 245-0727 FAX: 203 245 -0472
bill@northu.northsails.com

Private lessons, on your boat...

... because there is no boat like your own

RACE AND WIN

We can show you how, working with you and your crew, on your boat.

STOP GUESSING

Rig tuning, spinnaker handling, mainsail shape, helming. We will answer all your questions.

FOR YOUR CREW

After all you have put into your boat and equipment, get North U. Performance Sailing Services for your crew.

ON YOUR BOAT

Can you think of a better place?

WITHIN YOUR BUDGET

Our regional staffing puts expert instruction within your reach. Let us design a program to match your needs and interests.

LEARN MORE

Our training covers every facet of racing trim, tactics, and boat handling. *Call to learn more.*

NORTH U

Performance Sailing Services

800 34-SAILS

Turning sailors into racers and racers into winners since 1980